Advance Praise for

The Better World Handbook

Wow! What an incredible resource! It reminds me that what people really want out of life is to make a difference and have some fun — and this book tells you how to do both at the same time.
We in the Simplicity movement encourage people to buy less stuff, but books are exempt — particularly books like this!
— Cecile Andrews, author,
The Circle of Simplicity: Return to the Good Life

Cynicism is the social disease of our age. Cynicism is what passes for insight when courage and vision are lacking.
If there is such a thing as a single cure for cynicism, this book is it.
The Better World Handbook gives us a step-by-step "blueprint" for creating conscious global citizens. It's a manual for better living that you will find yourself using over and over again.
— Kevin Danaher, Cofounder, Global Exchange; author of
Ten Reasons for Abolishing the World Bank and the IMF

This handbook helps you answer that age-old question,
"What can I do?" — With the help of the handbook, it turns out you can easily do a lot. Buy it, share it or get it from the library.
But, most of all, use it to change our world for the better.
This is an impressive resource for people who want their everyday actions to reflect caring and compassion for the environment and others.
— Betsy Taylor, Executive Director, Center for a New American Dream

An excellent look at issues we face and concrete actions — small and large — that we can take to address them.
The book also includes a large collection of useful resources.
— Paul Loeb, author of *Soul of a Citizen: Living with Conviction in a Cynical Time*

More Praise for
_____

The Better World Handbook

People everywhere are hungry for meaning and purpose,
wanting to make a difference, and be of service to something larger than
themselves. *The Better World Handbook* provides valuable information
and resources to manifest these intentions into practical reality.
Keep a copy on your desk or reference shelf, and use it!
— Michael Toms, CEO, New Dimensions Radio, and co-author of
True Work: Doing What You Love and Loving What You Do

We can make the world a better place and this book shows you
how easy it is to really make a difference. I highly recommend that you
buy it, use it and enjoy what you can do to help create positive change.
— Jeffrey Hollender, President, Seventh Generation, and author of
How to Make the World a Better Place.

This is exactly the resource consumers need to help create
a sustainable world. The extensive background information and
action steps are great tools for anyone looking for ways
to make change happen now!
— Alisa Gravitz, Executive Director, Co-op America

The Better World Handbook provides a wealth of practical ideas
for transforming our everyday activities of shopping, living, and working
into an artful way of life that is more sustainable, just, and meaningful.
— Duane Elgin, author of *Voluntary Simplicity and Promise Ahead*

The Revolution is not just around the corner, it's around every corner.
I love this old saying because it captures the important truth highlighted in
this inspiring book: The world can be changed through action in our
everyday lives — where we spend our money, how we help out in our
community, the ways we travel. This practical, enjoyable handbook shows
how small improvements can add up to a big difference in the world.
— Jay Walljasper, editor *Utne Reader* and
co-author *Visionaries: People and Ideas to Change Your Life* .

The BETTER WORLD HANDBOOK

FROM GOOD INTENTIONS TO EVERYDAY ACTIONS

ELLIS JONES, ROSS HAENFLER, and BRETT JOHNSON
with BRIAN KLOCKE

NEW SOCIETY PUBLISHERS

Cataloguing in Publication Data:
A catalog record for this publication is available from the National Library of Canada.

The authors will divide 50% of their royalties from the sale of this book among organizations working for a more just and sustainable world, and a fund to help start a nonprofit organization to carry on the work of this book.
Contact the authors at:
The Better World Network, P.O. Box 7457, Boulder, CO 80306-7457, U.S.A
<www.betterworldhandbook.com>.

Cover design by Diane McIntosh with Ellis Jones. Cover image: Photodisc

Printed in Canada on 100% post-consumer waste recycled, acid-free paper using soy-based inks by Friesens.

New Society Publishers acknowledges the support of the Government of Canada through the Book Publishing Industry Development Program (BPIDP) for our publishing activities, and the assistance of the Province of British Columbia through the British Columbia Arts Council.

BRITISH COLUMBIA ARTS COUNCIL
Supported by the Province of British Columbia

Paperback ISBN: 0-86571-442-8

Inquiries regarding requests to reprint all or part of *The Better World Handbook* should be addressed to New Society Publishers at the address below.

To order directly from the publishers, please add $4.50 shipping to the price of the first copy, and $1.00 for each additional copy (plus GST in Canada). Send check or money order to:
New Society Publishers
P.O. Box 189, Gabriola Island,
BC V0R 1X0, Canada

New Society Publishers' mission is to publish books that contribute in fundamental ways to building an ecologically sustainable and just society, and to do so with the least possible impact on the environment, in a manner that models this vision. We are committed to doing this not just through education, but through action. We are acting on our commitment to the world's remaining ancient forests by phasing out our paper supply from ancient forests worldwide. This book is one step towards ending global deforestation and climate change. **It is printed on acid-free paper that is 100% old growth forest-free (100% post-consumer recycled), processed chlorine free**, and printed with vegetable based, low VOC inks.

For further information, or to browse our full list of books and purchase securely, visit our website at: www.newsociety.com

NEW SOCIETY PUBLISHERS   www.newsociety.com

TABLE OF CONTENTS

PREFACE

IN 1990, at the height of the environmental movement, bookstores were packing their shelves with practical, action-oriented books on how to live a more Earth-friendly existence. It was right around this time that Ellis had a flash of inspiration: Why limit practical actions to environmental issues? The world's problems were certainly not limited to just this one area. What was needed was a book that would cover all of the challenges that face us as human beings on this planet: violence, poverty, social injustice, and inequality. Instead of leaving social change up to academics, politicians, or even activists, everyone needed to have access to being part of the solution. But the book never showed up on the shelves, and despite his inspiration, Ellis found the task of writing it impossible for one person.

It wasn't until almost seven years after the original idea was formed that four idealistic friends came together around a common desire to make a difference. Thus was born a gang of dedicated, passionate, hopeful authors determined to write a book that would help people make the world better. Ellis brought vision; Brett supplied rigor; Ross provided momentum; and Brian came with resources. An amazing, transcendent chemistry occurred within the group, and we were able to accomplish far more collectively than we ever could have as individuals. We came together as a team and supported each other whenever one of us faltered. The book finally began to take shape.

We came into the process with many complicated questions, put in thousands of hours of research, and compiled our results into what we believe is the best book available on informed and effective actions to build a better world. In the end, the book turned out to be different and better than any one of us could have imagined. And it passed our ultimate test: *The Better World Handbook* is the book we had always wanted to find in the bookstores.

Our book answers three basic questions. First: What stops people from getting involved in making a difference in the world? Second: What are the major challenges facing our world? And third: What can the average person do in his or her everyday life to make the world better?

Although most people may not participate in traditional activism, many of us want to have a positive impact on the world. We've written this book to help you recognize the profound impacts you have on your local and global communities and to inspire you to turn your good intentions into everyday actions that will make a difference across the entire spectrum of the world's problems.

ACKNOWLEDGMENTS

We would all like to thank: Steve Graham, Jim Downton, and Seana Lowe for their invaluable support. Chris Plant, Judith Plant, Justine Johnson, Audrey Keating, Lisa Garbutt, and everyone at New Society. David Pellow, Ruth Ollila, Jennifer Johnson, and McCrystie Adams for giving valuable feedback on several chapters.

Ellis: Ara Francis, my fiancée. Paul Todisco, my best friend. Joel Federman, my longtime mentor. Carl McKinney, my greatest teacher. Erik and Garda Persson, my Swedish grandparents. Harold and Opal Jones, my American grandparents. The Puengprasith's, my Thai family. The Ramirez's, my Panamanian family. My AFS and Peace Corps friends. All of the students in my Nonviolence classes who wrote their own books to build a better world. Brett, Ross, and my parents, especially my mother Anita.

Ross: My wonderful soul mate Sarah; Mom; and Brad, my amazing brother. Dad and Carolyn; Grandpa and Grandma Burfeindt; Grandpa and Grandma Haenfler; and the rest of my family. Nate Miller for a lifetime of friendship. Boulder/Denver XStraightEdgeX and hardcore kids. Boulder Mennonite Church (and small groups!); all of my students; Brett and Ellis; and God.

Brett: My partner Jen for her love, support, and book feedback; Grover and Sam for their playfulness; my parents for their unconditional love and support; and my wacky comrades Ross and Ellis for their humor, passion, and the thousands of ways they made this book project one of the most amazing experiences I will ever have.

INTRODUCTION

Our Mission for This Book

Our mission is to have a positive impact on the world
by encouraging you to:

- *rediscover your relationship with the world*
- *understand your power to make the world better*
- *turn your values into effective actions*

MANY PEOPLE CARE about making the world a better place but feel they don't have the time or the energy to really make a difference. If you fit into this category, then this book is perfect for you. *The Better World Handbook* is the definitive guide for people who care about creating a better world but are not sure where to begin. It will help you to recognize the profound impacts that you have upon your local and global communities and will inspire you to put your values into action.

The Better World Handbook **has three major sections.**

BUILDING A BETTER WORLD begins with an explanation of what stops people from actively contributing to a better world and a discussion of how we can move beyond these obstacles. This section takes you through a simple process that will allow you to turn good intentions into actions.

THE SEVEN FOUNDATIONS OF A BETTER WORLD explores how we can build this better world. This section summarizes the main challenges that humanity faces in the 21st century, provides viable alternative solutions that we can implement, and shares examples of what thousands of people around the globe are already doing.

ACTIONS FOR A BETTER WORLD makes up the bulk of the book and is divided into 13 chapters. In this section, we've sifted through an overwhelming amount of information and focused on the most practical, effective actions that you can take to create a better world. Read the action chapters in whatever order best suits your curiosity and desire to act. We hope that you find actions applicable to every area of your life — actions that you can take to make a positive difference in the world.

You may begin reading this book and become so inspired that you want to change everything in your life all at once. Or you may find yourself so overwhelmed by all of the changes mentioned that you shut down completely. Avoid both of these pitfalls — find a balance within yourself. No one changes his or her life overnight. Take on more than you can handle, and you'll almost certainly burn yourself out very quickly. A few changes that last for the rest of your life are far more powerful in their impact than dozens of changes that you can only sustain for six months or a year. The trick to changing your daily actions permanently lies in your finding a way of living that integrates your desire to make the world better with your desire to pursue your own personal dreams.

While reading, you will undoubtedly come across values, issues, and actions that you don't agree with. Don't let that stop you from making a difference. The beauty of this book is that it includes a vast array of actions based upon many different values. Some will interest you more than others. Identify those actions that you truly do believe in and that you can commit to integrating into your life right now. Act on those issues that inspire you, and find out how you can act on the values that we don't cover here. You must decide for yourself how you can contribute to making the world a better place.

We encourage you to make this book your own. As actions excite you, dog-ear the page or scribble notes in the margin. And be sure to check off actions as you implement them in your life. We want this book to be an essential resource that will inspire you for years to come.

HOW YOU CAN HELP

If the ideas and actions presented in this book encourage you, please visit our website at: <www.betterworldhandbook.com>, where you can find updated information on all kinds of ways to make a difference. If you have any suggestions to improve the next edition of the book, please don't hesitate to email us at:<suggestions@betterworldhandbook.com>, or write to us at The Better World Network, P.O. Box 7457, Boulder, CO 80306-7457, U.S.A. We'd love to hear from you!

For those of you who would like to learn more, we are available for lectures and workshops worldwide. For speaking engagements, email us at: <speaking@betterworldhandbook.com>.

If this book truly inspires you, you can help build the non-profit organization we're creating to carry on what we've begun with this book. You can make a donation on our website at: <www.betterworldhandbook.com>.

BUILDING A
BETTER WORLD

The Cycle of Cynicism

The Cycle of Hope

Traps

You must be the change you wish to see in the world.
— M.K. Gandhi

WE HAVE BECOME A NATION of sleepwalkers. We look around at the
world's problems and wish they would go away, but they stub-
bornly persist despite our most heartfelt desires. So we end up living in a kind of ethical haze. It's not that people are bad or that evil is winning some kind of eternal battle. The vast majority of us have good intentions
when we go about our daily lives. It's that we have been lulled into a sense of
complacency about the world's problems, as if they are less-than-real occur-
rences. We react similarly to how we might normalize the strange events that
occur while we're in the middle of a dream. People starve, communities fall
apart, violence thrives, families fade, and nature disappears, and we continue
on with our lives as if nothing is wrong. We are stuck in our daily patterns,
living on auto-pilot when it comes to the rest of the world.

But like a whisper in the back of our minds that stays with us always, we
have the feeling that something has gone awry. We have lost our faith in each
other. Politicians are corrupt, corporations seek to make a profit at any cost,
and lawyers win cases without justice being served! It seems that everything

1

and everyone is for sale. Nothing remains sacred. We feel that perhaps we can only truly rely on ourselves. When these negative beliefs become widespread, we disengage from the outer world, recoiling into our own personal lives. As we withdraw, we see our society rushing aimlessly toward an unknown future, without any sense of morality or conscious purpose to direct it. Awash in a sea of knowledge, we lack the wisdom to guide our own destiny.

How did we end up here? Many people point the finger at a culture that breeds apathy. In fact, beneath apathy there lies an even bigger culprit: cynicism. Cynicism is the deeply ingrained belief that human beings are, and have always been, inherently selfish. Cynicism in this form is not just a long-term emotional state or an adopted intellectual philosophy, it is a way of relating to the world.

Cynicism fundamentally destroys hope. We begin to see the world as a place that will always be filled with social problems, because we are convinced that people look out for their own best interests above all else. The pursuit of happiness becomes little more than an attempt to accumulate material wealth, increase your social status, and indulge any desire. Helping others, giving something back, and making a difference in the world no longer show up in popular culture. Indeed, people who decide to seriously pursue such goals are often labeled as odd, naïve, overly sentimental, unrealistic, or simply irrational. The most you can strive for under this worldview is to come out somewhere nearer the top than the bottom.

In a world of constantly increasing complexity, cynicism becomes the safest, most strategic position to adopt. It involves no action and thus no risk. Cynics can portray their inaction as more rational, objective, and even more scientifically founded than people who are trying to change the world. Apathy becomes an acceptable state of being.

So what happened? How did we become this cynical? Simply put, our modern society manufactures cynicism. Every day we are bombarded with media reports of crime, disaster, conflict, and scandal, both locally focused and from around the globe. The stories are usually too brief for us to gain any meaningful understanding of the problems and lack any options for us to contribute significantly to their resolution. Waves of negative imagery wash over us relentlessly as we try to keep up with what's happening in the world around us. Like sponges, we absorb the negativity; it spills over into how we look at the world and affects how we act or fail to act.

The Cycle of Cynicism begins when we first find out about society's problems. When we recognize that others are suffering, we want the suffering to stop. We even wonder if there is anything we could do to help. When no viable avenues for action are presented, and we fail to generate any ourselves, we do nothing. We end up feeling powerless and sad. We may become angry and blame people in positions of power for not doing anything to stop it, either. We feel that we are good people, we see an injustice, but we don't do anything about it. In the end we reconcile this dissonance by accepting that perhaps nothing can be done. And we initiate a process of slowly numbing ourselves to the suffering. We subtly begin to avoid finding out about the suffering in the first place, since knowing only makes us feel bad. Over time we shut out our awareness of most social problems and retreat further and further into our insular, personal lives. We become apathetic.

THE CYCLE OF CYNICISM

1. Finding out about a problem
2. Wanting to do something to help
3. Not seeing how you can help
4. Not doing anything about it
5. Feeling sad, powerless, angry
6. Deciding that nothing can be done
7. Beginning to shut down
8. Wanting to know less about problems

Repeat until apathy results.

How do we break out of the cycle of cynicism? We must stop blaming others for not doing anything and begin to take personal responsibility for being good people in the world. We need to seek out information that provides us with a basic understanding of our world's problems and a variety of options for action. We have to generate a form of practical idealism based on well-informed actions that actually make a difference in the world. Each of us must decide what we want our life to stand for and how we can uniquely contribute

THE CYCLE OF HOPE

1. Taking personal responsibility for being a good person
2. Creating a vision of a better world based on your values
3. Seeking out quality information about the world's problems
4. Discovering practical options for action
5. Acting in line with your values
6. Recognizing you can't do everything

Repeat until better world results.

to a better world. By thinking about what we can provide for the next generations rather than about what we can take for ourselves in this lifetime, we can choose to create our own destiny, instead of leaving our children's future up for grabs. Finally, throughout it all, we need to recognize that we can't do everything.

We must reconnect with a set of core values that every one of us can embrace despite our many differences — values like compassion, freedom, equality, justice, sustainability, democracy, community, and tolerance. (No society — especially one as powerful and rapidly changing as ours —survives for very long without a moral compass to guide its evolution and progress.) We have to deliberately build our society to increasingly reflect and nurture the growth of these values in the world.

Think about the world that you would like to live in. Let yourself imagine the a world that you could be proud to leave for your children — a world where peace, justice, compassion, and tolerance prevail and where each person has more than enough food, shelter, meaningful work, and close friends. What would a more loving, accepting, patient, understanding, and egalitarian world look like? Your vision of a better future will provide you with an inspiring goal to work toward and will keep your passion alive for the journey ahead. As we start out, we must be aware of the many traps that can stop us from making a difference in the world.

TRAPS

Trap #1: "That's just the way the world is"

If you look back through history, you'll discover that the world has always faced seemingly insurmountable challenges: slavery, hunger, warfare, and intolerance. But can you imagine how the world would be different if all people throughout history had resigned themselves to just accepting the troubles of their time? Can you imagine the cynics of the day saying that:

- America will always be an British colony
- slavery will always exist
- women will never be allowed to vote
- whites and Blacks will never share the same classrooms
- people in wheelchairs will never have access to public buildings
- free public schooling won't work because the poor don't want to be educated...so there's no point trying to change anything.

For every social problem that has existed there have been people dedicated to solving it and creating positive social change. Every situation that has been created by humans can be changed by humans. A better world is *always* a possibility. Although current problems may seem overwhelming, to surrender hope only ensures that nothing will change. Embrace your vision for a better world and you'll find all the hope you will ever need.

Once you let yourself envision a better world, you can then consider where you fit into this whole picture. Our culture teaches us that we are each completely responsible for our own well-being — that we are independent creatures who should make our own way in life without depending on others. But really we all rely on each other for our daily existence. We eat food that grows in soil nurtured by microscopic organisms. We drink water that has vaporized from the oceans. We breathe oxygen respired by the trees and wear clothing made by people across the planet whom we will never meet. We rely on our friends and family for support and create a sense of belonging and meaning within our communities. Our personal well-being is inextricably linked to the well-being of our families, our friends, our communities, and our planet. And the well-being of others, in turn, is shaped by our own well-being.

When you truly understand the interconnected nature of the world, you realize that you are both very powerful and yet very small — you influence everything around you, yet there is so much more to life than just you. When you validate the clear connections that bind us all together, you gain awareness of how each of your actions affects other people and the planet around you.

Trap #2: "It's not my responsibility"

You may be saying, I didn't cause the world's problems so why should I be responsible for fixing them? That may seem true on the surface, until you realize that the problems that our world faces are created by the daily actions of millions and millions of people. The CEO of a company may be the person who should be held most responsible for the pollution created by her/his company. But don't the shareholders bear some responsibility, and the people who purchase its products, and the local television station that covers car crashes and celebrity weddings instead of investigating local water quality?

All of us hold some measure of responsibility for the challenges that our society faces, even if it's only because we have not taken the time to become informed about our world and about the well-being of others. We don't like to take responsibility for other people's messes, and we like to think that our own messes are very small. But our impact on the world is much larger than we think. For example, try to answer the following questions:

- Whose car causes smog?
- Whose use of energy causes global warming and climate change?
- Whose apathy leads to the lowest voter turnout in history?
- Whose frown makes people think that your city is not a friendly place?
- Whose purchases keep an unethical company in business?
- Whose lack of support for a community group causes it to close its doors?

The answer to these questions is, *All of us together*. The responsibility lies with the group as a whole and with each individual. How you spend and invest your money, the career you choose, the car you drive, your participation or non-participation in our democracy, and countless other decisions all have an impact on our planet and its people. This book offers many concrete suggestions on how you can take responsibility for your part by creating forward-looking solutions to today's problems.

Trap #3: "One person can't make a difference"

Even if you are willing to take responsibility and do your part to make the world a better place, you may be thinking, But I'm only one person on a planet of six billion people. I can't possibly make a difference!

Problems such as racism, hunger, and inequality seem so big that it's easy to feel small and powerless. How much of a difference can you actually make anyway? In truth, you can make one person's difference — no more, no less. On a daily basis, you not only have the power to perpetuate the world's problems, you have the opportunity to stand up for the creation of a world based on your own deeply held values.

✓ Your money invested in the right bank could help create more wealth for poor communities.

✓ Your letter can be the one that changes the behavior of an entire corporation.

✓ Your vote can elect government officials that really make a difference.

✓ Your timely call to a friend can change their outlook for the day.

✓ Your donation can help a social change organization meet its lofty goals.

✓ Your purchase can allow a locally owned business to thrive in your community.

✓ Your participation can transform a small group of people into the beginnings of a social movement.

Not only does each of your actions have a direct impact on the world, but also every choice you make sends a message to those around you. Your choice to use your bicycle instead of your car, set up recycling bins at work, or volunteer for an organization you care about can inspire others to do their part. We create momentum for each other. At the same time, we support each other to live in a manner that creates possibilities for a better future.

Don't ever let anyone convince you that you have no power — together we have the power to change the world. All significant changes in the world start slowly, at a single time and place, with a single action. One man, one woman, one child stands up and commits to creating a better world. Their courage inspires others, who begin to stand up themselves. You can be that person.

Once you become aware of how your actions affect others and accept responsibility for your role in creating a better world, your values will come to the forefront of your life. In what ways do you want to change the world? What do you value most in life? What would the world be like if everyone was taking responsibility for how their life creates and shapes the world?

Trap #4: "Building a better world seems totally overwhelming"

Wanting the world to be a better place is one thing, but being willing to personally take on bringing that world into being is another. As you more fully integrate your values with your actions, you are bound to become frustrated. The first thing you may notice is that we all live in contradiction with many of our values.

- You wish people were friendlier, but you realize that you are often too busy to smile and say Hello to the cashier at the place where you go every day for lunch.
- You detest the thought of children slaving away in a sweatshop, yet you find out that the new pair of shoes you just bought (at a bargain price) were made by workers paid only a fraction of their living expenses.

Your realizations may leave you feeling frustrated, guilty, or even hypocritical. But remember we don't have to be perfect people, have perfect knowledge, wait until the perfect time, or know the perfect action to take before we begin making the world better. (Those are all just ways that we keep ourselves from making a difference.)

Keep in mind that the goal is a better world and not a perfect world. It is not an all-or-nothing commitment. That's why it's called *The Better World Handbook* not *The Perfect World Handbook*. You take those actions that are sustainable for your unique life. Once you start, you'll gain better knowledge, better timing, and better actions and ultimately become a better person for it.

Learn to live with your imperfections; embrace them — they are what make us human. And consider this: If you were somehow able to manage to be perfect, who would be able to live up to your standards? Who would want to join you in making a difference? Who would be able to do what you do? No one.

With each conscious choice you make to create a better world, you take responsibility for your existence. You increasingly become the director of your life as you more fully integrate your values with your actions. You create a stronger and healthier society and planet. Now is the time to commit to transforming your good intentions into action.

Trap #5: "I don't have the time or the energy"

The last thing most of us want is to add even more responsibilities to our already busy schedules. Not only do we not have the physical energy for more activities, we don't have the psychic energy to worry about the world's problems. We fill our daily schedules with bill paying, message returning, meal making, appointment keeping, note writing, house cleaning and appearance fixing. We surround ourselves with more and more technology to save ourselves time and then often find ourselves at the mercy of it. In the end, it seems that we have even less time and more to get done.

When you take the time to reschedule your life, based on your most deeply held values, you will find all of the time necessary to live a fulfilling life that contributes to others. Upon examining your priorities, you may discover that although you value spending time with your family, you actually spend most of your free time watching TV. Why not shift your energies?

Many of the actions in this book take very little time to complete yet make a real contribution to the world. Some, such as installing a low-flow showerhead or setting up an account at a socially responsible bank, you only have to do once. Others, such as buying less stuff, will actually save you time that you would otherwise spend in traffic, in lines, and in working to pay for the stuff you bought. In fact, we expect you to find that living out your values and engaging in meaningful daily action actually gives you energy! And there's no better feeling than the feeling that you're making a positive difference in the lives of others.

Trap #6: "I'm not a saint"

You don't have to be a saint to make a difference in the world. Many people stereotype individuals committed to social change as people who have put aside families, convenience, and pleasure for a cause they deem to be of greater importance. Images of Mother Teresa, Cesar Chavez, Martin Luther King, Jr., and Mahatma Gandhi come to mind. We see these individuals living in poverty, fasting, or protesting and we label them as self-proclaimed martyrs. We can't imagine doing the things they do, and we think, I'm not someone who can change the world, I don't want to sacrifice everything, or I'm not that good.

This book is not about giving up your whole life for a cause, nor is it about good deeds that you do twice a year when you finally get all of your chores done. It is about living a life full of passion and power — one that will enrich you and the world around you. The point is to balance your personal needs, your family's needs, and your community's needs. The goal is not to live the perfect life but to make improvements in your life so that your actions are increasingly in line with your values. (And be sure to forgive yourself when you don't live up to your own expectations.)

Committing yourself to making a difference can be fulfilling, meaningful, and fun. You don't have to move to a cabin in the woods, read dense political theory all day, live in poverty, or walk around with a frown because of the heaviness of the world's problems. Rather than being a sacrifice, working for a better world can help you create a deep happiness beyond your imagination.

Once you have committed to living out your values, the next step is to learn about and take the most practical, effective actions available to bring about the better world you envision. Without adequate information, it's difficult to take effective actions and easy to take actions that unintentionally work against what you're trying to accomplish.

Trap #7: "I don't know enough about the issues"

None of us wants to feel like we're leaping into action uninformed. Because the world's problems are so complex, it's easy to think we will never know enough to act in ways that will really help solve these problems. Make an effort to get quality information about the world so that your actions will actually be effective (see the Media chapter for tips). At times you will just know in your heart which actions you should take.

In our ever-changing world there will always be more to know, but taking action can actually help inform you about the issues you care about. When you become involved, it connects you with others who care about the same issues and creates numerous opportunities for learning. Don't worry, you don't have to start from scratch. This book provides you with plenty of information to get started, and you can seek out further information as you get inspired.

Trap #8: "I don't know where to begin"

In fact, you have already begun. You already act in ways that take others' well-being into account, whether you lend your mower to a neighbor, jump-start a co-worker's car, or let a car change lanes in front of you on the freeway. You have probably already taken some of the actions in this book. Go ahead and check them off.

Just start where you feel the most comfortable. Maybe pick an area in your life where you are already taking some actions. Then work up to actions that will be more challenging. Or start with the action that would be the most fun, the one you could do with a friend, or one that will give you the most fulfillment.

Throughout the book, we suggest that you focus your energies. Identify actions that are important to you and that are realistic for you to take on. Be open to challenging yourself, but don't overwhelm yourself with unrealistic expectations. If making the world better isn't fulfilling for you, you won't keep it up very long.

Trap #9: "I'm not an activist"

When many of us think of social change, we imagine environmentalists in tie-dyed shirts blocking logging trucks or gas-masked rebels facing off with lines of riot police. Not wanting to get involved in such intense actions or to be associated with what the media portray as irrational or radical protesters, we don't get involved. In reality, people of all professions, backgrounds, interests, and lifestyles are involved in social change. Lawyers, teachers, autoworkers, computer programmers, cashiers, and clerical workers are among the many people making a difference in the streets, in the office, in their communities, and at home.

You can be yourself and fulfill your commitment to a better world. You don't have to follow some pre-designed path for making the world better. You don't have to change who you are in order to live out your values. In fact, with your values at the forefront of your life, you're actually being more true to yourself. This book provides you a range of actions with which to carve out your own niche. Be creative, forge your own unique path, and translate commitment into action in your own way.

People all over the world are living out their vision for a better world. Many people are simplifying their lives, buying less stuff, working less, and giving back more to their community. Concern and knowledge about the environment has been spreading for the last 30 years, and recycling has become a widespread habit. People are taking time to learn about other cultures and appreciate diversity. No matter where you turn, you see individuals doing their part. You are not alone in building a better world.

A WORD OF CAUTION

Beware! When you start living your life more in line with your values, some conflicts may arise. Your actions will sometimes threaten others who haven't put as much thought into how they want to live their lives. They may even try to stop you from making changes in your life because they do not want to examine their own existence in the world. Accept this — it comes with the territory.

It is also common to take on a self-righteous attitude when you have strongly held values. This attitude is destructive to the goal of a better world. People do not want to be around someone who lives life to show others how wrong they are.

If you have an understanding of the beauty and the complexity of life, then you will always attract people who are yearning for peace and fulfillment. Understand that you are no better than anyone else; you are just someone trying to live life the best way you know how.

The Seven Foundations of a Better World

Economic Fairness

Comprehensive Peace

Ecological Sustainability

Deep Democracy

Social Justice

Culture of Simplicity

Revitalized Community

The arc of the universe is long
but it bends towards justice.
— Martin Luther King, Jr.

MAKING THE WORLD a better place is a lifelong journey. If we plan and prepare for this journey as we would for any other, it will make the trip less frustrating and more gratifying. When we learn a bit about where we have been and consider where are we going, it helps us to understand our current place in the voyage. An understanding of the scope of the world's

11

problems and their potential solutions will help you realize the importance of your everyday actions and will inspire you to create meaningful change.

This section outlines seven essential foundations upon which we can begin to build a better world. We begin our exploration of each foundation by describing the challenges that face us at home and around the world. Then we launch into concrete goals — viable alternatives that can confront the challenges and help us construct the foundation. We also give inspiring examples of dedicated people around the world who are already making a positive difference. We end with some of the best, most accessible resources from which you can learn more about each issue.

CHALLENGES	GOALS
Economic Inequality	Socially Responsible Governments
Third World Debt	and Corporations
Corporate Sweatshops	Workers Rights
	Alternative Economic Institutions
War	Ethical Foreign Policy
Militarization	Reasonable Gun Laws
Gun Violence	Death Penalty Moratorium
The Death Penalty	Constructive Children's Television
Media Violence	Conflict Resolution Education
Overconsumption of Resources	Cleaner Energy Sources
Air Pollution and Climate Change	Efficient Resource Use
Ecosystem Destruction	Sustainable Population Growth
Overpopulation	
Lack of Democracy	Open and Honest Politics
Money in Politics	Democratic Media
Media Control	Civic Participation
Inequality of Women	Equal Rights
Racism	Empowerment of Disadvantaged
Heterosexism	Communities
Inadequate Health Care	Universal Health Care and
Prisons	Education
Advertising Overload	Rejection of Materialism
Commercialization of Childhood	Culture of Simplicity
Materialism and Overconsumption	
Fragmented Communities	Revolution of Caring
Loss of Humanity	Thriving Communities
	Strengthened Community
	Institutions

FOUNDATION #1: ECONOMIC FAIRNESS

A world dedicated to economic fairness would strive to meet every person's basic needs so that no one would lack food, shelter, clothing, or meaningful work. People's strength of character and passion should determine their opportunities rather than the economic circumstances they were born into. Everyone would benefit from economic prosperity.

CHALLENGES

Economic Inequality – Third World Debt – Corporate Sweatshops

Economic Inequality

Every year the gap between the world's richest and poorest citizens continues to grow. In 1960, the wealthiest 20% of the world's population made 30 times as much income as the poorest 20%. By 1999, they made 74 times as much and received 86% of the profits from the world's economic activity; the poorest 20% received just over 1%.[1] This cycle does not bode well for the 1.3 billion people — over one-fifth of the world's population — who lack access to clean water and the 24,000 people who die from hunger-related causes every day.[2] As global economic inequality increases, the developing world's voice in the global economy decreases — leaving the world's poor in even a more powerless position.

Here in the U.S., huge corporate mergers concentrate the world's wealth by generating millions of dollars in profits for wealthy stockholders and executives, often while laying off (downsizing) tens of thousands of workers. In 1980, the average American CEO earned 42 times as much as the average worker they employed. By 1999, the gap had grown to almost 475 times as much.[3]

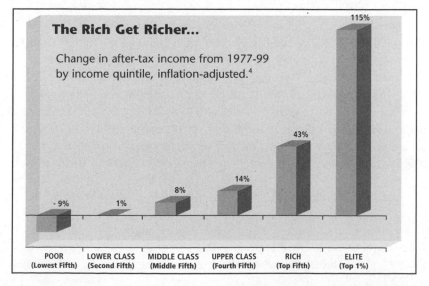

The Rich Get Richer...

Change in after-tax income from 1977-99 by income quintile, inflation-adjusted.[4]

POOR (Lowest Fifth)	LOWER CLASS (Second Fifth)	MIDDLE CLASS (Middle Fifth)	UPPER CLASS (Fourth Fifth)	RICH (Top Fifth)	ELITE (Top 1%)
-9%	1%	8%	14%	43%	115%

Since the 1970s, the U.S. economy has increasingly become top heavy —
with the privileged gaining huge amounts of wealth and the middle and lower
classes often struggling to survive, let alone move ahead. Currently, the richest 1% of Americans own almost as much wealth as the entire bottom 95% of
the U.S. population combined![5] Media coverage of the booming stock market has often neglected to mention who really wins when the stock market
goes up. Almost half of all wealth in the stock market is held by the top 1% of
stockowners. Meanwhile, the bottom 80% own just 4% of total stock hold-
ings.[6] Half of all families in the U.S. own no stock at all.[7]

During the 1990s, the U.S. economy experienced the longest peacetime
economic expansion in its history. The stock market boomed and the GNP
continued to rise. While many are benefiting from the 'new economy,' many
others are stuck working harder than before, often in low-paying, part-time
jobs with little job security. The vast majority of Americans does not have six-
figure salaries or stock options to cash in when the going gets tough.
Contrary to daily anecdotes of IPOs and 20-something millionaires, the average American household brings in about $40,000 a year and almost 20% of
children under six live in poverty.[8]

Third World Debt

Most developing countries owe staggering amounts of money to wealthier
nations and global financial institutions. Interest payments on these debts further exacerbate the hardships poor people suffer. International aid often does-
n't work or doesn't make it to the people who need it most. Despite their
claims to the contrary, the world's major international lending institutions,
the International Monetary Fund (IMF) and the World Bank, have consistently favored First World corporations and are widely acknowledged to have
increased poverty among the world's most desperate peoples. Sub-Saharan
African countries, for example, owe more than $220 billion dollars to sources
such as the IMF and the World Bank.[9]

Once poor countries acquire so much debt that they have no hope of paying it back, the IMF bails them out on the condition they accept 'structural
adjustment programs' (SAPs; also called austerity programs). SAPs require
government budget cuts in all kinds of social programs (which do not increase
the countries' ability to pay off their debts) in favor of programs that focus on
quickly transforming the countries' assets into cash that can be paid directly
to lending institutions. Not surprisingly, the rich government officials who
accepted this debt in the first place don't personally suffer when it comes time
to pay it back. Food subsidies, education, health care, and other services
that the poor depend on are often the first programs to go.[10] Mozambique's
debt payments on its IMF loans are $1.4 million per week, more than four
times what the country spends weekly on basic health care.[11] The Nicaraguan

government spends almost twice as much on debt repayment as on education and health care combined.[12] Worldwide, the United Nations estimates that the lives of seven million children a year could be saved if nations diverted funds from debt repayment to essential health and education services.[13]

Corporate Sweatshops

When companies create jobs in poor countries, they often force workers to endure sweatshop conditions — unsafe work environments, forced overtime, and pitiful wages. Profit-hungry businesses and corrupt governments keep wages low by suppressing unions and failing to enforce labor laws. In 1999, for example, while Disney made millions in profits, their Haitian subcontractor paid its workers $2.15 for an 8-hour day ($0.27 per hour). This translated to barely over one-third of the average daily living expenses of the workers.[14] In Bangladesh, workers producing shirts sold at Wal-Mart make $0.09 to $0.20 each hour.[15] In 1993, a fire in a Thailand toy factory killed 188 workers because all of the doors were chained shut.[16] Forced overtime, 16-hour work days, beatings, child labor, toxic fumes, and mandatory pregnancy tests for women are commonplace.[17] A study of 360 corporations that use international labor uncovered that only one in five had a code of conduct to help insure workers' basic rights in the factories.[18]

Sweatshop labor is a major reason we North Americans can walk into gargantuan department stores and find aisle after aisle of inexpensive goods. In effect, cheap goods may come at the expense of other people's suffering. Sweatshop workers make athletic shoes, electronic components, clothes, toys, trinkets, and more. Sweatshops are not just problems in faraway lands, either. The U.S. has its share of sweatshops, particularly in large cities like Los Angeles and New York. In addition, large fruit and vegetable growers across the nation have hired Latino migrant farm workers as a source of inexpensive labor for decades. Mistreated workers are afraid to speak out due to the threat of deportation.[19]

GOALS
Socially Responsible Governments and Corporations — Workers' Rights — Alternative Economic Institutions

Socially Responsible Governments and Corporations

Citizens around the world are pressuring their local and national governments to create and implement foreign policies that are both practical and ethical. In the late 1990s, the Jubilee 2000 Coalition turned their commitment to the world's poor and disenfranchised into action by lobbying for the cancellation of international debt for the world's 41 poorest countries. Largely because of the over one million Jubilee protesters around the globe, the U.S., Canada, and United Kingdom have already agreed to cancel $100 billion in Third World debt.[20] Conservatives like Pat Robertson and progressives like Ralph Nader have come together with leaders around the world to ask industrialized countries to forgive Third World debt so that developing countries once again have an opportunity to grow and progress along with the rest of the world.[21] On a more local level, Bangor, Maine's city council recently passed an 'ethical purchasing policy' that requires the city to purchase clothing (such as uniforms) made with fair labor practices rather than in sweatshops. The Council also stated that all clothes sold in Bangor should be produced under fair working conditions.

In the corporate world, thousands of investors around the world have let it be known that they don't want the quest for profits to destroy the planet and undermine workers' lives. In 1999, socially concerned investors filed over 220 shareholder resolutions to limit CEO pay, adopt environmental principles, increase racial and gender diversity of boards of directors, phase out use of old-growth wood, stop predatory lending practices aimed at the poor, and implement independent monitoring of factory working conditions.[22] By 1999, U.S. investors controlled over $2 trillion (roughly one of every $8 professionally managed) in 'socially responsible' investments that balance returns with conscience — an increase of 82% from 1997.[23]

Workers' Rights

Throughout our history, ordinary Americans have had to organize, struggle, and fight for safe working conditions and economic security. In 1999, janitors who clean Denver's downtown office buildings, members of the Service Employees International Union (SEIU), won guarantees for 24% wage increases over three years. More than one-half of the part-time workers were also upgraded to full-time with health insurance.[24] Since 1994, over 50 cities and counties in the U.S. have enacted some form of a 'living wage' law to increase the minimum wage up to double the federal level — some ordinances also include health insurance and vacation time.[25]

U.S. workers concerned with losing American jobs to sweatshops in Third World countries have joined forces with human rights activists. The American Federation of Labor — Congress of Industrial Organizations (AFL-CIO), the largest American union, took this cause head-on in 1999, as thousands of members joined others in Seattle to protest the World Trade Organization (WTO) and corporate-driven globalization. College students around the country have picked up the torch and joined the struggle. United Students Against Sweatshops (USAS) has over 200 chapters at colleges and universities across the country. Students have convinced many of their schools to stand for just wages and working conditions in the apparel industry through a number of creative actions, including sit-ins, hunger strikes, and shantytowns.[26]

Alternative Economic Institutions

An economically just future must also include businesses and financial institutions that are committed to community development and a just distribution of the world's wealth. Community development banks, credit unions, loan funds, and land trusts are committed to creating wealth among the economically disadvantaged. These institutions create strong, vibrant local economies that large corporate banks and state governments often leave behind. More than 450 Community Development Financial Institutions (CDFIs) provide capital to the U.S. poor for homeownership and small business growth.[27] In the last 30 years, ShoreBank of Chicago has lent over $600 million to businesses and individuals in its mission to promote community development in the South Side of Chicago.[28]

On an international level, the Fair Trade movement, now 50 years old, supports fair prices and working conditions for cultural goods in the Third World that are produced for First World consumers. Yearly sales of $400 million of fairly traded coffee, art, and clothing create sustainable jobs in countries needing economic development.[29] Also worth noting, Grameen Bank has perfected the art of 'micro-lending' (loans as little as $10) to create wealth among Bangladeshi peasants. Every month, they lend over $30 million to more than 200,000 impoverished villagers.[30]

RESOURCES

📖 Anderson, Sarah, John Cavanagh, and Thea Lee. *Field Guide to the Global Economy*. The New Press, 2000.
This visually appealing and very readable account of corporate-led globalization introduces the reader to progressive economic analysis backed up by high quality statistical research. Includes the forces behind globalization, the ten claims of globalization, and examples of grassroots resistance.

📖 Collins, Chuck and Felice Yeskel. *Economic Apartheid in America*. The New Press, 2000.
Engaging, accessible summary of economic inequality in the United States, including taxes, wealth, income, and political corruption. The second half thoroughly discusses the policies and actions that are necessary to more equitably share our economic gains.

📖 Korten, David. *The Post-Corporate World*. Copublished, Berrett-Koehler and Kumarian Press, 1999.
Korten supplies a well-researched, thorough criticism of a corporate-dominated economy, proposes new ways of structuring our economy and society to support humanity and the environment, and then gives inspiring examples of what's already working in the creation of a post-corporate world.

   📖 Mander, Jerry, and Edward Goldsmith. *The Case Against the Global Economy: and for a turn toward the local.* Sierra Club Books, 1997.
This edited volume uses many accessible essays to criticize corporate power from a number of perspectives and posits alternative ways of structuring an economy. Includes discussion of trade agreements, local currencies, and alternative measures to the GNP for economic health.

   📖 Moore, Michael. *Downsize This! Random Threats From an Unarmed American.* HarperPerrenial, 1997.
Filmmaker/author/activist Michael Moore uncovers corporate power at its worst. He explains how the U.S. government gives more welfare to rich corporations than to its poorest citizens and how corporations lay off thousands of workers while making record profits. Moore's biting humor makes *Downsize This!* a disturbingly funny read.

FOUNDATION #2: COMPREHENSIVE PEACE

A world committed to comprehensive peace would shift its creative energies toward cooperating rather than competing, resolving conflict rather than escalating it, seeking justice rather than enacting revenge, and creating peace rather than preparing for war.

CHALLENGES
War — Militarization — Gun Violence — The Death Penalty — Media Violence

War

We live in the age of total war. War has always been humanity's most destructive invention, and over time we have become increasingly effective at harnessing its power. Scholars estimate that at least 10 million people lost their lives in World War I.[31] Despite cries of "never again," by the time we finished World War II, the number of dead had increased fivefold to over 54 million.[32] Since then, in our 50 years of so-called peacetime, over 20 million people have been killed in 150 wars.[33] In the 1990s alone, wars and internal conflicts forced 50 million people from their homes, while civil wars claimed 5 million lives worldwide.[34]

    In the 20th century, civilian populations became legitimate military targets, nations used atomic and chemical weapons to effectively wipe out their enemies, and we created a military arsenal so powerful that it is finally capable of destroying all life on the planet. For technologically advanced nations, war has become easier and less personal. We can fire missiles or drop bombs without ever having to see the face of our faraway enemy or the horrific consequences of our actions. Perhaps the most disturbing trend, however, is that massive bloodshed and civilian casualties no longer shock us — we've become accustomed to slaughter. After the Gulf War, for example, the United Nations imposed economic sanctions on Iraq, restricting food, medicine, and other vital supplies. Since 1990, more than 500,000 Iraqi children have died, yet the U.N. sanctions committee continues to deny them basic necessities.[35]

Militarization

With approximately $800 billion in military and arms expenditures, war has become one of the most lucrative businesses in the world. Not wanting to be left out of the new global economy, the U.S. has become the world's number one arms dealer, exporting over half of all the arms sold to any country, including corrupt dictatorships and human rights violators.[36] The U.S. also funds and trains leaders to make war on their own people through facilities such as the U.S. Army School of the Americas. Every dollar the government spends on the military is one less dollar available for education, health care, and environmental protection.

The U.S. not only spends more on the military than any other country in the world but it spends almost three times as much as all its 'potential enemies' combined, and that's not considering any of its allies' budgets.[37] When you include all related military expenditures, such as paying off debt accumulated during the arms race, the U.S. spends close to 50% of its entire federal budget on military-related expenditures every year.[38] U.S. taxpayers even subsidize weapons sales to foreign countries to the tune of $7 billion per year.[39] The Congressional Budget Office projects that the U.S. will spend over $60 billion on a national missile defense system by 2015 — with huge profits to aerospace companies.[40] Scientists agree that the system is fundamentally flawed and has already ignited international tensions with both allies and foes.

Gun Violence

Though gun violence has historically been a serious social problem in the U.S., it is increasingly affecting people in many other industrialized countries. In 1996, for example, people used handguns to murder 2 people in New Zealand, 15 in Japan, 30 in Great Britain, 106 in Canada, 213 in Germany and 9,390 in the U.S.[41] Americans often justify the need for access to guns as a way of protecting themselves and their families from crime. A study published in the New England Journal of Medicine, however, estimates that for every time someone used a gun at home in self-defense or a legally justifiable shooting, there were 4 unintentional shootings, 7 criminal assaults or homicides, and 11 attempted or completed suicides.[42]

As the rate of gun violence has dramatically increased over the last 15 years, our young people have paid the highest price. Incredibly, they often have easy access to guns, and they are very likely to use them. The Journal of the American Medical Association concluded that between one-third and one-half of all Grade 11 boys believe that they could easily get a gun if they wanted one.[43] Every day, 14 American children are killed with guns.[44] Every six hours in the U.S. a young person aged 10 to 19, commits suicide with a gun.[45] The U.S. still leads all other countries in childhood deaths from firearms. The Center for Disease Control estimates that the rate of firearm death for American children is 12 times higher than that for the children of 25 other industrialized nations combined.[46]

The Death Penalty

Despite the lack of scientific evidence that the death penalty deters people from committing crime and the disturbing evidence raised concerning the innocence of a number of death row inmates, here in the U.S. we are breaking records with the number of people we're putting to death.[47] We began the new century with 3,652 people on death row — over 50% of them being people of color.[48] States executed more people in 1999 than in any other year since 1951.[49] Despite an appeals process (one that falls well below international standards), 85 people sentenced to death since 1973 have later been proven not guilty and released.[50]

Our international reputation on this issue is appalling. Iran, Iraq, Saudi Arabia, China, Congo, and the U.S. currently lead the world in the execution of their own people.[51] Only six countries since 1990 are known to have executed people who were under 18 at the time they committed their crime — Iran, Nigeria, Pakistan, Saudi Arabia, Yemen, and the U.S. Out of that group, the U.S. has killed the most child offenders.[52]

Media Violence

We shouldn't be too surprised that our children lash out in violent ways. Dr. Victor Strasburger, chief of The American Academy of Pediatrics section on adolescents, recently announced, "The controversy is over....There is clearly a relationship between media violence and violence in society."[53] In fact, more than 1000 studies, including a Surgeon General's report as far back as 1972 and a National Institute of Mental Health report a decade later, show a cause-and-effect relationship between media violence and aggressive behavior in some children.[54] The American Psychological Association has concluded that, besides just behaving more violently, many children may become desensitized to the pain and suffering of others and become more fearful of the world around them.[55]

American children watch three to four hours of television a day.[56] According to the American Psychological Association, that means the average American child watches 8,000 murders and 100,000 other assorted acts of violence before finishing elementary school.[57] What are the real impacts of all media violence? Well, one demographic study of a number of diverse countries showed that homicide rates doubled within 15 years after the introduction of television, despite the fact that television was introduced into each country at different times.[58]

GOALS

Ethical Foreign Policy — Reasonable Gun Laws — Death Penalty Moratorium — Constructive Children's Television — Conflict Resolution Education

Ethical Foreign Policy

The foreign policies of all nations around the world need to better reflect the peaceful values of the majority of their citizens. The U.S. must take a leadership role in reducing and eliminating weapons of mass destruction. At the very least, this includes signing the international treaties that we have not signed, including bans on chemical and biological weapons, the production and sale of landmines, and the reduction of nuclear weapons stockpiles. The U.S. should not sell arms to non-democratic governments or ones that persistently violate human rights.

Our international aid should include more resources to help stop conflict before it starts and fewer tools for perpetuating it. We need to fund non-military conflict resolution and channel more of our defense spending into conflict prevention efforts and the advancement of practical, nonviolent resolutions. If we paid off our debt to the United Nations, it would help the U.N. effectively use its resources to resolve conflicts, and if we took a more active role in the U.N.'s workings (outside of just the Security Council), we would strengthen its accountability.

Ordinary people have been challenging the status quo and facilitating the transition to a more enlightened, cooperative approach to foreign policy. For almost 20 years, Witness For Peace has sent over 7,000 U.S. citizens to troubled parts of Latin America and the Caribbean to document the destructive impacts of misguided U.S. foreign policy and to support efforts for nonviolent social change. In 1999, 12,000 people stood up to protest the School of the Americas (SOA), a U.S. government military training facility that has produced some of Latin America's most brutal dictators and generals. Thousands risked arrest and jail, committing civil disobedience and speaking out on behalf of Latin American citizens. Six months later, the U.S. House of Representatives voted to close the SOA. A conference committee later killed the bill, so the fight continues.

Reasonable Gun Laws

The three legitimate uses for guns in our society are hunting, recreational target shooting, and self-defense. Guns designed specifically for any of these purposes should be available to any qualified adult. There is no reason to allow the manufacture, sale, or importation of any other types of guns (assault weapons, semi-automatics, submachine guns), period.

We need background checks and waiting periods on all gun sales, both new and used, as well as regular enforcement and stiff penalties for violating gun sale laws. Manufacturers should build reliable safety mechanisms into every gun they sell, and there should be at least as much education and testing required for a gun permit as there is for a driver's license.

Many Americans have decided to begin to do something about gun violence. On Mother's Day 2000, for example, an estimated 750,000 people marched on Washington. The 'Million Mom March' demanded that legislators pass more sensible gun laws that limit access to and increase the safety of guns.

Death Penalty Moratorium

The federal government, non-governmental organizations (NGOs), and academics must convene a national conference to reevaluate the death penalty's effectiveness and the legitimacy of the process by which states mete it out. Currently, people of color disproportionately fill the ranks of death row inmates, a situation primarily reflective of the racism found throughout the criminal justice system. We must take into consideration the latest scientific studies and data from other countries that have discontinued its use. The states should provide DNA testing for every case in which the results may help prove the innocence of the person involved. In the meantime, there needs to be a nationwide moratorium until we can be certain that we are not killing innocent people along with the guilty.

A number of groups and recognized leaders have begun to demand that we step back and reconsider our use of the death penalty. In 1997, the American Bar Association called for a nationwide moratorium on executions. Religious leaders like Pat Robertson and the Dalai Lama have both spoken out in favor of the halt. In January 2000, Illinois became the first state to agree to stop executing people until more research can conclusively prove that the system works. The U.S. is the last industrialized country to enforce the death penalty. Eventually, we may be able to abolish the death penalty completely.

Constructive Children's Television

We own the airwaves — TV stations don't. Reasserting some control over what kinds of media influence our children's lives is not about censorship. Rather, it is about giving our own values and voices a place to be seen and heard. For example, networks ought to move violent programming out of those time slots when our youngest children are most likely to watch TV. We should give incentives to those shows appropriate for a younger audience that have little or no violence and promote nonviolent methods to resolve conflict. We need to consider bringing back public service messages, similar to the cartoons created by the Children's Television Workshop in the 70s, that educate children on issues around violence and the media.

Opposition to violence on children's television has garnered so much support that the U.S. government itself has begun to get involved. In September 2000, the Federal Trade Commission (FTC) produced a scathing report. It found that the entertainment industry has been specifically marketing violent (clearly labeled appropriate only for adults) to children. The FTC stated that the government would take action if the industry does not change its behavior.

Conflict Resolution Education

The U.S. often solves its foreign policy problems with the barrel of a gun and takes care of crime by executing people. The vast majority of heroic TV and movie characters punch, shoot, and kill their enemies, so it's no surprise that kids learn violence is an effective solution to conflict. Each of us needs to make a commitment to teach nonviolent conflict resolution skills to the children in our lives — especially to young boys. (Society teaches boys that being tough and violent is the way to show you are a 'real man.')

It is essential that we integrate conflict resolution into our schools' curriculum. Our children need to grow up with a wide range of skills and tools they can draw on to solve problems when they become adults.

A number of organizations have cropped up to make conflict resolution education a reality for every child. In the U.S., Educators for Social Responsibility have been extremely successful with getting their Resolving Conflict Creatively Program (RCCP) adopted at K-12 schools across the nation. In 2000, 6,000 teachers and 175,000 young people participated in their program, learning a comprehensive strategy for nonviolent conflict resolution and how to build caring, peaceful communities.

RESOURCES

📖 Ackerman, Peter, and Jack Du Vall. *A Force More Powerful: A Century Of Nonviolent Conflict*. St. Martin's Press, 2000.
Details a number of important victories for nonviolence where the force of organized nonviolent resistance defeated oppression.

📖 Easwaran, Eknath. *Gandhi, the Man: The Story of His Transformation*. Nilgiri Press. 1997.
A very readable biography about Gandhi. Explains Gandhi's nonviolent philosophy, using pictures and quotes. For a deeper exploration, check out Gandhi's autobiography, *My Experiments With Truth*.

📖 Grossman, Lt. Col. Dave. *On Killing : The Psychological Cost of Learning to Kill in War and Society.* Little Brown & Co., 1996.

Dave Grossman takes us through a history of wars to explain the socio-psychological techniques used to make it possible for soldiers to kill other human beings. He then shows how this same dehumanization process is taking place in our society through television, movies, and video games, with terrible consequences.

📖 King, Jr., Martin Luther. *Strength to Love.* Fortress Press. 1986.

A fantastic collection of Martin Luther King's sermons on peace, nonviolence, love, and hope. Check out Dr. King's other books as well: *Trumpet of Conscience* and *Why We Can't Wait* are outstanding.

📖 Nelson-Pallmeyer, Jack. *School of Assassins: The Case for Closing the School of the Americas and for Fundamentally Changing U.S. Foreign Policy.* Orbis Books, 1997.

Makes a strong case for closing the U.S. Army's School of the Americas, a military school for Latin American soldiers in Georgia that provides training in counterinsurgency, torture, psychological warfare, and interrogation. A concise, informative look inside U.S. foreign policy.

📖 Prejean, Helen. *Dead Man Walking: An Eyewitness Account of the Death Penalty in the United States.* Vintage Books, 1996.

This bestseller offers an informative and moving account of Sister Helen Prejean's work with death row inmates. The powerful story profoundly questions the morality of capital punishment.

FOUNDATION #3: ECOLOGICAL SUSTAINABILITY

A world committed to ecological sustainability would create a new vision of progress that recognizes the future of humanity depends upon our ability to live in harmony and balance with our natural world.

CHALLENGES
Overconsumption of Resources — Air Pollution and Climate Change — Ecosystem Destruction — Overpopulation

Overconsumption of Resources

Our demand for bigger, better, and more convenient goods has taken its toll on our planet. David Korten, a former Harvard business professor and current president of the People Centered Development Forum, likens unrestrained economic growth to a cancer spreading across the planet.[59] Like a cancer cell, our current system of economic growth leads to growth in overall size while quality of life often declines; progress moves forward regardless of the impacts upon our families, cultures, communities, and eco-systems. The insatiable jaws of development, for example, swiftly gobble up what remains of our open space.

This growth ideology is penetrating into every corner of the globe. A 2000 report by the World Resources Institute found that increasing demands for natural resources are causing a rapid decline in many of the world's ecosystems. If this trend continues, they argue it will have severe implications for human development and the welfare of all species.[60]

The vast majority of the demand for natural resources comes from the rich industrialized nations of the world — especially the United States. This is no surprise, since the U.S. uses 120 pounds (54 kilograms) of natural resources per person per day.[61] The average American consumes as much energy as:

2	Germans
6	Mexicans
12	Chinese
29	Indians
or 117	Bangladeshi[62]

Since 1940, Americans alone have used up as large a share of the Earth's mineral resources as all previous humans put together.[63] In fact, it would require three additional Earths to support the human race if all people on the planet lived the extremely wasteful lifestyles of North Americans.[64]

Air Pollution and Climate Change

Have you ever noticed a brown cloud hanging over big cities? Or inhaled the crisp, clean air when you camp in a remote wilderness area? Acid rain and air pollution, once problems only in Europe and parts of North America, are now becoming apparent in the Asia-Pacific region, as well as in parts of Latin America.[65] Unfortunately, air pollution is more than just a smelly annoyance; it kills about 70,000 Americans each year (more people than die from breast and prostate cancers combined).[66] And despite coordinated global action to try and limit air pollution, damage to the ozone layer continues faster than expected, with the next ten years predicted to be the most vulnerable.[67]

According to the October 2000 report by the Intergovernmental Panel on Climate Change, human-caused emissions of greenhouse gases have substantially contributed to global warming.[68] Again the U.S. is the biggest culprit — emitting more than twice as much carbon dioxide (the primary global warming gas) per capita as the average rich industrialized nation (U.K., Japan, Germany).[69] Contributing to the problem, U.S. automobile fuel efficiency standards have not changed in 14 years (while the light truck standard, including SUVs, has stagnated for 19 years.)[70] Even as the oil and automobile industries are admitting that precautionary action is warranted to halt global warming, disputes between the U.S. and the European Union over carbon dioxide emissions led to the failure of November 2000 negotiations to curb global warming.[71]

Ecosystem Destruction

According to the World Resources Institute, we have cut or otherwise destroyed nearly 80% of the world's ancient forests. The results are increased global warming, species extinction, and loss of potential medicines. Although rainforests only cover about 2% of the Earth's surface, they contain approximately 50% of all life forms.[72] Development drives an average of 137 species to extinction each day; that's 50,000 each year.[73]

Pollution and overfishing threaten the health of our oceans and their myriad species of life. Despite numerous prohibitions on dumping toxic waste in the ocean, both the U.K. and France continue to unload reprocessed nuclear waste into the sea.[74] The U.S. Justice Department also found a fleet-wide conspiracy within Royal Caribbean cruise lines to save millions of dollars in disposal fees by covering up the dumping of oily waste into the ocean off of Puerto Rico.[75] Over-exploitation of marine fisheries and declining stocks of commercial fish species have created widespread alarm around the world. Globally, more than 60% of marine fisheries are over-exploited.[76] The quest for hefty profits rather than sustainable fishing has created a shortage that now threatens the entire industry and may lead to rampant species extinction.

Overpopulation

In October of 1999, the world's population surpassed 6 billion people, doubling its size since 1960. In 2000, the human population grew by over 212,000 people per day.[77] We might like to think that overpopulation is India's and Africa's problem, not ours, but when population strains lead to deforestation, global warming, war, malnutrition, starvation, and epidemics the problem becomes a global one.

Overpopulation is a complex issue with a multitude of causes. The majority of women in the developing world want to control their fertility but currently don't have access to birth control options. Amazingly, in 1998, the U.S. Congress canceled all funding to the United Nations Population Fund, the primary international family planning resource.[78] Poverty, limited educational and occupational opportunities for women, and the lack of social safety nets further exacerbate this problem. As the developing world increasingly adopts a consumer lifestyle, the potential for ecological damage greatly multiplies.

GOALS

Cleaner Energy Sources — Efficient Resource Use — Sustainable
Population Growth

Cleaner Energy Sources

One of the most important changes we can make is to shift from fossil fuels
to our most powerful and abundant natural resources: sun, wind, and hydrogen. We already have environmentally sound, energy-efficient technologies to
harness these renewable energy sources — we just need to use them. In 1997,
the United Nations sponsored a global climate conference in Kyoto, Japan
emphasizing the seriousness of global warming. The meetings produced a
commitment from 159 countries to significantly reduce greenhouse emissions
by 2012 (the U.S. was not among them). As a consequence, the demand for
non-polluting energy sources is increasing worldwide, and the costs of using
these technologies is steadily declining.

A number of countries are accepting the challenge of moving to a cleaner energy economy. Global production of wind energy doubled from 1995-
1998 (led by Germany).[79] Sales of photovoltaic solar cells grew an average of
16% per year from 1990-1998.[80] Iceland has launched pioneering efforts to
harness geothermal and hydropower to produce hydrogen for use in cars and
boats.[81] Here in the U.S., the California Air Resources Board (CARB) uses
sales mandates to stimulate technological innovation in the automobile industry for cleaner vehicles. By 2003, 4% of car and truck sales by the big six
automakers must emit zero pollutants; another 6% must have extremely low
emissions (for example, hybrid electric cars).[82] Other states have followed
California's lead, and now the CARB standards at least partly cover 30% of the
U.S. market.[83] Also to California's credit, in the Spring of 1999, Santa Monica
became the first major city to meet its municipal energy needs entirely with
green energy (geothermal).[84]

Efficient Resource Use

If we are to live in balance with our surrounding environment we must
learn from the principles of nature. The concept of waste, for example,
does not exist in the forest. A fallen tree becomes a home for animals and
insects, and helps to fertilize the soil for surrounding plant life. We must
also learn to 'close the loop' and use resources wisely. In order to combat
pollution, Denmark, Sweden, Spain, the U.K., and other countries are
adopting Green taxes — they lower income taxes and tax energy use, thereby encouraging energy efficiency and investments in wind and solar
power.[85] Many activists, consumers, and governments around the world are
also holding industry to a higher standard of resource efficiency. In

essence, they are holding the corporation responsible for the waste it creates before it gets to the consumer.

Encouraging examples of this kind of reuse ethic are happening all over the world. For instance, the European Union has drafted legislation stating that by the year 2005, European car producers must take back all cars they make free of charge and reuse or recycle 80% of the vehicle.[86] The world's largest producer of commercial floor coverings (Interface, Inc.) is on the cutting edge of environmentally sustainable businesses. They have implemented the principle of producer responsibility by using fewer materials, creating 100% recyclable carpets, and implementing customer leases that make Interface responsible for reclaiming the floor covering.[87]

The creation of an economy where goods are produced, used, and remade into new products in the most environmentally responsible manner is a challenge that must involve every sector of our society — businesses, all levels of government, and citizens from around the world. Making people pay for throwing away garbage will serve as an incentive to reuse and recycle. Governments must stop subsidizing environmentally destructive industries, such as logging and oil, with corporate tax breaks. Finally, switching from a pesticide- and fertilizer-based agricultural system to sustainable, organic farming will maintain soil integrity and preserve our health.

Fortunately, some people are already stepping up to the challenge. Twenty-six communities in New Zealand are pioneering a national Zero Waste pilot program to significantly reduce the amount of materials headed for the landfill.[88] Canberra, Australia and Toronto, Canada have even aimed to eliminate waste completely by 2010.[89] In 2000, Iceland PLC, a 760-store U.K. supermarket chain, announced they were moving their own-label frozen vegetables to 100% organic.[90]

Sustainable Population Growth

The annual world population increase hit its peak in 1989 at 87 million people. Since then, many industrialized countries have stabilized their populations, while developing countries still struggle with massive population growth. Wealthier nations must provide developing nations with the resources they need to curb their population explosion. These efforts need to be focused on improving the status of women, increasing access to family planning services, and bringing economic opportunity to poverty-stricken agricultural areas.

There have already been some amazing successes around the globe. Bangladesh, the most densely populated country in the world, has actually decreased its annual population growth from approximately 6.4 to 3.4 children per woman. Much of the decline is attributed to the regular use of contraceptives by 45% of Bangladeshis in 1996, up from less than 8% in 1975.[91]

RESOURCES

📖 Brower, Michael, and The Union of Concerned Scientists. *Consumer's Guide to Effective Environmental Choices.* Three Rivers Press, 1999.
Brower has produced one of the few books that separates the wheat of environmental actions from the chaff, with well-researched evidence to back him up. He focuses readers on a handful of the most effective actions they can take to really make a difference for our global ecological crisis.

📖 Brown, Lester, et al. *State of the World 2001.* W.W. Norton, 2001.
This award-winning book provides an in-depth but readable analysis of the greatest challenges that rapid globalization brings to our world. It details global problems and presents potential solutions. Produced by the World Watch Institute.

📖 Brown, Lester, Michael Renner, and Brian Halweil. *Vital Signs 2000: The Environmental Trends That Are Shaping Our Future.* W.W. Norton, 1999.
This yearly book from the World Watch Institute provides global statistics on a wide range of issue categories to keep you completely up-to-date on the state of the world's most pressing problems. It is one of the most well respected and insightful publications of its kind.

📖 Hawken, Paul, Amory Lovins, and R. Hunter Lovins. *Natural Capitalism: Creating the Next Industrial Revolution.* Back Bay Books, 2000.
Paul Hawken strikes an unusual middle ground between capitalism and environmentalism. He uses a number of modern-day examples to illustrate what he sees as a trend toward more eco-friendly, better technologies and more practical, sustainably run businesses.

📖 Rifkin, Jeremy. *Beyond Beef: The Rise and Fall of the Cattle Culture.* Plume. 1993.
Rifkin offers a comprehensive historical analysis of cattle's role in our culture and the environmental impacts of a beef-based diet.

FOUNDATION #4: DEEP DEMOCRACY

A world built on deep democracy would empower citizens to participate in shaping their futures every day, (not just on election day), provide broad access to quality information, and democratize our most powerful institutions.

CHALLENGES

Lack of Democracy — Money in Politics — Media Control

Lack of Democracy

A government is democratic to the extent that average people have the ability to influence decisions that affect their daily lives and the health of their society. Unfortunately, dictatorships of military or wealthy elites rule much of the world without the consent of the people. Government of, by, and for these elites has created tremendous suffering for the average person. For example, it was under non-democratic leadership that Third World countries amassed much of their enormous international debt. Little economic benefit trickled down to the majority of the people, yet they have to pay the bill and suffer the consequences of healthcare and education cuts.

Here in the U.S., we like to think that we're immune to rule by the few, when in fact, despite our historically groundbreaking beginnings, we are slowly moving back to that kind of government. For over the last 100 years, voter turnout has steadily declined. In 1996, for the first time in U.S. history, less than 50% of the voting age population came out to the polls for the presidential election.[92] The 51% turnout in 2000 wasn't much of a gain. In 1998, only 36% showed up to the polls, making it the lowest turnout for a non-presidential congressional election in modern U.S. history.[93] This is a saddening state of affairs for what many people consider to be the greatest democracy in the world. If we measure the health of a democracy by how many of its citizens participate in choosing their government, then the U.S. is one of the worst democracies in the world: we have some of the lowest participation levels of any democratic country. We need to face up to the fact that our democracy is in crisis. Without the participation of average people in government, by definition the government cannot represent the interests of average people.

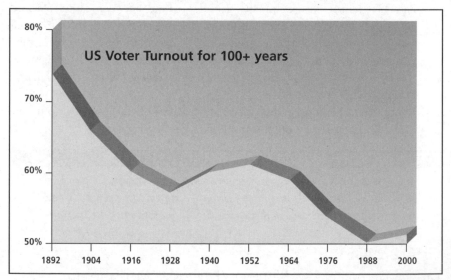

Source: Erik Austin and Jerome Club, *Political Facts of the United States Since 1789* (Columbia University Press, 1986), and U.S. Bureau of the Census, Statistical Abstract of the U.S., 2000.

Money In Politics

It's no wonder that Americans have become cynical about the influence of money on politics when a donation of $100,000 to a national party will get you: (1) access to congressional golf tournaments, (2) admission to retreats with leading party members, and/or (3) photo opportunities with Hollywood legends.[94] This kind of system works well for those who have tens of thousands of dollars to purchase seats at fundraising dinners, but it leaves the rest of us behind. Where does all that money come from?

- One-quarter of 1% of the U.S. population gives 80% of all the private money in our elections.[95]
- In the 2000 election, businesses outspent labor unions 11 to 1 ($368 million to 33 million).[96]
- In the 1998 election, the highest giving communities donated 271 times as much money as the communities with the highest percentage of people of color.[97]
- Resource-extractive industries (mining, oil, timber) outspent environmental groups 59 to 1 ($48.2 million to $814,000).[98]

Such an extreme funding imbalance creates a situation in which the wealthy and powerful gain access, influence, and political clout at the expense of the poor, people of color, workers, and the environment.

Throughout our country's history, many have fought to keep big money out of politics. But now, corporations, labor unions, and wealthy individuals avoid existing campaign finance limits by giving money to political parties instead of to specific candidates. This 'soft money' loophole allows unlimited contributions and is quickly becoming the most corrupting component of campaign financing. The Democrats and Republicans raised an estimated half a billion dollars in soft money for the 2000 election (almost double 1996 figures).[99]

Many people consider the Republican Party to be the party of big business, but the Democrats increasingly provide some stiff competition for that title. For the 2000 election (as of 1 June 2000), more than 110 corporations each contributed over $50,000 in soft money to both the Republicans and the Democrats![100] Some of the top donor corporations, like AT&T, gave roughly $1 million to each of the two major parties in 2000.[101]

Why give money to both parties? This has become a popular form of covering your bets in the corporate world. No matter who wins, the corporations win.

So does money really matter? In the information age, candidates need more and more money for advertising. Politicians have turned to massive TV ad campaigns to gain access to their constituents, because that has proven to be the most effective means of getting voter support. For 2000 federal and state elections, candidates and parties spent $600 million on TV ads — a six-fold increase since 1972 (controlled for inflation).[102] The escalating cost of ads makes candidates even more beholden to their big-money sponsors. Without the millions, they can't run TV ads and they don't get elected. It's not surprising, then, that in 1998 winning candidates in the U.S. Senate spent nearly double, and in the U.S. House triple, what their opponents spent during their campaigns.[103]

Media Control

The integrity of a democracy relies heavily upon the quality of information available to its citizenry. We Americans believe in the First Amendment because our democracy flourishes when we can hear a diversity of voices, and we trust citizens to make up their own minds. The media industry, increasingly under the control of fewer and fewer corporations, is eroding the freedom and diversity that make our democracy great. Mergers and unfriendly takeovers have left fewer than ten corporations in control of the vast majority of the information transmitted in the world.[104] The recent rash of mergers in the past decade has increased the pressure to maximize profits in the media industry.

Devotion to stock prices and advertising revenues often sacrifices quality journalism. Corporate decision makers commonly sweep professional standards aside and fill the news with sensationalized stories and programs that will raise their ratings — the O.J. Simpson trial, Jean Benet Ramsey's murder, and the Monica Lewinsky scandal; or Jerry Springer, COPS, and When Animals Attack. From 1993 to 1996, network news coverage of homicide increased 721% while the national homicide rate decreased by 20%.[105] Viewers did not ask for more detailed coverage of violence. But TV executives know that if they spend more time examining stories about violent crimes, more people will tune in to their news broadcasts. And TV anchors and print journalists often reduce politics to commentary. Instead of providing a vibrant forum for discussing serious social issues, they will comment on how boring a candidate is or cover up-to-date polls projecting who will win.

GOALS
Open and Honest Politics — Democratic Media — Civic Participation

Open and Honest Politics

The creation of a government that is responsive to its citizens and not beholden to powerful interests is one of the most important challenges we face. We need to create and enforce strict limits on political contributions so that large amounts of money do not distort the 'one person, one vote' philosophy of a democracy. Cleaning up politics also requires a ban on soft money contributions, as well as regulating 'issue ads' and any other methods, including lobbying, by which money generates undue influence in the halls of government.

One important way to decrease the need for large political contributions is to ban private purchases of political ads (which usually contain half-truths at best) and give sensible amounts of free TV time to any candidate who is running for office. These changes would substantially lower the costs of campaigns, increase outreach to the public, and raise the overall level of political discourse — the 30-second TV advertisement could give way to a serious consideration of the issues that divide the candidates.

Publicly financing campaigns may seem counter-intuitive at first glance. Why should we want to pay for mudslinging, misleading campaign ads? Well, with public financing, we could lay down guidelines for what are appropriate uses of our money and take back control of how parties run campaigns. Wealthy interest groups would no longer be able to hold millions of dollars over the heads of our government officials, the vast majority of whom plan to run for reelection. It may even be cheaper in the long run for taxpayers, because the representatives that we elect have fewer favors to grant after the election — which mean less corporate tax giveaways and pork barrel projects. Public financing also encourages citizens to run for office — those who are currently scared away by the thought of having to use slimy fundraising tactics or those who wouldn't be able to attract big money-donors.

In fact, some states have already begun taking steps in this direction. Voters in Maine and Vermont, for example, made history by passing laws to provide full public financing for political campaigns. To access public funds, candidates have to get donations from a substantial number of citizens, and the maximum donation allowed is $5 to $50 (that's not a typo!).[106] Consequently, the average person has as much influence as the millionaire across town. Now that's democracy! In the 2000 elections, nearly half of Maine state senators were elected completely free of special interest money.[107]

Another important way to open up politics is to increase the participation of alternative political voices. Smaller political parties, often called third parties, have played a vital role in our country's history. They articulate ideas that the two major parties are not addressing and often influence one or both of them in the process. Minor party candidates who can demonstrate that they represent a significant number of people should have easier access to ballots, participation in debates, and media coverage. These kinds of changes will provide a much more comprehensive discussion of ideas all around.

Lately, under-represented citizens and ideas have shown signs of rallying to provide alternatives to 'politics as usual.' During the 2000 Republican and Democratic conventions, large groups of citizens organized and held shadow conventions to address three important issues that went undiscussed at the major party conventions: campaign finance reform, the failed war on drugs, and poverty and economic inequality.[108] A number of minor parties have also begun advocating for new voting methods that better represent people's preferences. Instant Runoff Voting (IRV) allows voters to rank order all candidates and vote their conscience, since with IRVs, voting for a smaller party will never spoil the election. IRV is currently used to elect the President of Ireland. Alaska will vote in 2002 on the issue of adopting IRV in its elections.[109]

Democratic Media

A well-functioning democracy requires a media system that provides diverse sources of information and encourages civic participation. The government once considered the airwaves such an integral part of our democracy that politicians decided the public should own and control them. It is time for the public to reclaim the responsibility of producing quality media from the large corporate conglomerates that control it. The first step is to break up the concentration of media power. Let's give control to a greater number of smaller companies that could legitimately compete with a broader range of information. Also we must create and maintain a non-commercial public media system (PBS, NPR) as well as independent alternative media that exist outside the control of transnational corporations and advertisers.

Civic Participation

Regardless of the structure of the political system and the media, the overall health of a democracy rests firmly on the backs of its citizens. Civic participation is the soul of a democracy. For a democracy to flourish, average people must choose to educate themselves on the issues of the day, seek solutions to the problems/conflicts that they see, and implement these solutions on a daily basis in their communities. Daily civic participation is essential to creating a just government as well as a just society. Without adequate citizen participation, corporations and special interests tend to get their way — their voices become louder when fewer and fewer of us are speaking up.

Civic involvement includes educating ourselves through a variety of media, joining community groups, participating in boycotts, volunteering for good causes, demonstrating when important social concerns arise, and even just talking with your neighbors about issues you care about.

Our country has a great history of people's movements: the populist movement that fought inequality and the Robber Barons, the Civil Rights movement, the Gay and Lesbian Rights movement, the Women's movements (including the Suffragettes), the Chicano Farmworkers' movement, the Environmental movement, and the anti-Vietnam War movement. Advances in communication technologies, such as the Internet, also open up huge possibilities for worldwide democratic movements for social justice.

Here are two recent examples of participatory democracy working:

✓   More than 270,000 irate citizens blasted the U.S. Department of Agriculture's (USDA) proposed organic standards and helped prohibit the following foods from the organic label: genetically engineered foods, foods fertilized with sewage sludge, and irradiated foods.[110] The response was 20 times greater than for any other USDA standard ever.[111]

✓ On a global level, the protests of the WTO, IMF, and World Bank in Seattle and Prague were just one indication of the growing movement for global justice. In 1997, secret negotiations of the Multilateral Agreement on Investment (MAI), often called the 'corporations' bill of rights, were leaked to the public on the Internet. The outrage from unions and grassroots organizations around the world stopped the negotiations.[112]

RESOURCES

📖 Hazen, Don, and Julie Winokur, eds. *We the Media*. New Press, 1997.
Hazen and Winokur's book uses an engaging format (and excerpts from the most eloquent media critics) to discuss the issues of corporate ownership of the media, media literacy, and the numerous alternative sources of information on TV, radio, and the Web.

📖 Hightower, Jim. *If The Gods Had Meant Us To Vote, They'd Have Given Us Candidates*. HarperPerennial, 2001.
Jim Hightower delivers a common sense, populist message to everyone that is fed up with politics as usual. He explores how the little guy is being squeezed out of a system of democracy that gives us candidates all of whom support big corporate interests and government fat cats.

📖 Loeb, Paul Rogat. *Soul of a Citizen: Living With Conviction in a Cynical Time*. St. Martin's Press, 1999. 🖥 www.soulofacitizen.org
Encourages us to challenge the cynicism of our time by creating sustainable social change in our everyday lives. Read this book — it will make you feel like getting involved in your community.

📖 Robert W. McChesney. *Corporate Media and the Threat to Democracy*. Seven Stories Press, 1997.
Well-known communications scholar McChesney illustrates how corporate control of the media threatens our democratic ideals. When a handful of corporations control the vast majority of the media, they inevitably pursue their own interests over the interests of citizens. Well researched and loaded with data, this book will forever change how you view the media.

📖 Moore Lappe, Frances, and Paul Martin Dubois. *The Quickening of America: Rebuilding Our Nation, Remaking Our Lives*. Jossey-Bass, 1994.
This powerful book illustrates through examples how we can create meaningful communities by living democracy. It challenges our preconceptions about community and offers suggestions on how we might "create the lives we want."

FOUNDATION #5: SOCIAL JUSTICE

A world dedicated to social justice is a place where everyone receives respect and equal access to jobs, education, and health care regardless of race, gender, ethnicity, sexual orientation, age, physical or mental abilities, or economic background.

CHALLENGES

Inequality of Women — Racism — Heterosexism — Inadequate Health Care — Prisons

Inequality of Women

According to a 2000 United Nations Population Fund Report, discrimination and violence against women are still deeply rooted in many cultures around the world. Nations often systematically deny women education, health care, birth control, and equal legal protections.[113] An estimated one in three women is subjected to violence in an intimate relationship.[114] The Taliban in Afghanistan has banned women from most work and forbidden them to leave their homes without being covered from head to toe and escorted by a male relative.[115] In Thailand and other countries, sexual slavery is common, with over 2 million girls aged 5 to15 trapped in the sex trade every year.[116]

Women's health is a low priority worldwide. The International Women's Health Coalition reports that, "One in 13 women in sub-Saharan Africa and 1 in 35 in South Asia die unnecessarily from causes related to pregnancy, unsafe abortion, and childbirth."[117] Hundreds of millions of women still have inadequate access to birth control, leading to 80 million unwanted pregnancies each year and 20 million unsafe abortions, which in turn result in an estimated 78,000 deaths.[118]

Lack of voting rights and women in government positions perpetuate a male-oriented world where women have little power. Worldwide, women only occupy 14% of parliamentary seats.[119]

Despite making tremendous strides, U.S. women still experience numerous injustices. In 2000, only 9 out of 100 U.S. senators were women (and that is the highest number ever), while only 56 women were among the 435 members of the U.S. House of Representatives. Sexual harassment, domestic violence, and sexual violence are still pervasive, with at least 1 in 4 women experiencing sexual assault in their lifetimes. Single women head 55% of all families living in poverty.[120] And, although women have entered the workforce by the millions, they still perform much more housework and childcare than men do.

Racism

Racism has not gone away. Ethnic conflicts in Eastern Europe, Africa, and Indonesia have been among the most brutal in history. Despite over 40 years of struggle, prejudice and discrimination continue to plague the U.S.; racial segregation in housing, a lack of minority representation in government, and racially motivated hate crimes are but a few examples. During 1995-1996, arsonists burned 40 black churches to the ground.[121] The media still subtly portray minorities as criminal, lazy, or unintelligent — whether on the news, 'reality' television shows, sitcoms, or commercials. For example, sports mascots such as the Cleveland Indians' 'Chief Wahoo' perpetuate stereotypical images of Native Americans.

The staggering wealth inequality throughout the world hits people of color especially hard, even here in the US. In 1998, African-Americans (26.1%) and Hispanics (25.6%) were over three times as likely to live in poverty as Whites (8.2%).[122] In 1995, the U.S. median household wealth (how much people own minus what they owe) for African-Americans was $7,400, for Hispanics was $5,000, and for Whites was $61,000.[123] Today, 40% of African-American and Hispanic children live below the poverty line in the U.S.[124] People suffering from poverty also lack access to safe, affordable housing and health care. Millions of families live in substandard housing and pay more than half their income in housing costs.[125] Instead of requiring living wages or training programs to help people escape poverty, state governments have instituted 'welfare reform,' a buzzword for get-tough programs that punish the poor.

Racial inequality does not limit itself to income alone. Education is also often markedly different, depending on a student's race. Schools attended by predominantly African-American and Latino students are poorly maintained, have more unqualified teachers, and few up-to-date textbooks.[126] The problem has become so widespread that the American Civil Liberties Union recently resorted to suing the entire state of California for neglecting its minority children.

People of color around the globe disproportionately bear the brunt of our society's creation of toxic chemicals and pollution. This fact did not seem to phase D.F. Goldsmith when they wanted to ship 118 metric tons of mercury (one of the largest stockpiles of toxic metals in the U.S.) to India.[127] Mexican authorities estimate that less than one-third of the toxic waste created by American companies in Mexico is returned to the United States as mandated by Mexican law.[128] The predominately black residents of 'Cancer Alley,' a stretch of land along the Mississippi in Louisiana, are exposed to 4,517 pounds (2,049 kilograms) of chemical releases each year; the average American is exposed to 10 pounds (4.5 kilograms)[129] These cases are not unusual. Naturally, exposure to such toxins increases rates of illness and mortality.

Heterosexism

Heterosexuals continue to benefit from many privileges that lesbians and gays do not have. Heterosexuals can legally marry, can show affection in public, can be with their partner during severe illness, receive tax benefits, and don't have to worry about discrimination, slurs, or violence. In 1998, FBI statistics indicated a 14% annual increase in hate crimes based on sexual orientation.[130] Eighteen states still legally prohibit lesbians and gays from having sexual relations.[131] Kids continue to torment young lesbians and gays at school, reflecting our society's deeply rooted homophobia. Homosexuals are perhaps the last group that it is still culturally acceptable to slander.

Inadequate Health Care

Billions of poor people have inadequate access to basic health care. The World Health Organization's 2000 report states, "The poor are treated with less respect, given less choice of service providers, and offered lower-quality amenities. In trying to buy health care from their own pockets, they pay and become poorer." Due mostly to the AIDS epidemic, the average life expectancy in Zambia has fallen from 54 in 1991 to 44 in 1999.[132] Before the AIDS epidemic, Zimbabwe's life expectancy was 65 years. By 1998, it fell to 44 years, and by 2010 will likely decline to 39 years. More than 11 million of the 14 million worldwide who have died of AIDS have been Africans.[133] There are enough resources and pharmaceuticals to significantly reduce the AIDS crisis, but the people who need them the most, the poor, can't afford them.

Despite living in the richest country of the world, 16% of Americans (44 million people) have no health insurance.[134] In fact, the World Health Organization ranked the United States health care system 37th in the world because it is enormously expensive and excludes tens of millions of people from quality care.[135]

Prisons

The U.S. is quickly becoming the prison capital of the world. Despite constituting less than 5% of the world's population, the U.S. has 25% of the world's prisoners.[136] In 2000, 2 million people were incarcerated in prisons or jails, the majority for non-violent drug offenses. An astounding increase in imprisonment took place during the 1990s. We had fewer than 200,000 adults behind bars in 1970; 315,974 in 1980; and 739,980 in 1990.[137]

Our incarceration frenzy has hit communities of color the hardest. Human Rights Watch reports that black men are sent to state prisons on drug charges at 13 times the rate of white men.[138] When dealing with the justice system, people of color are more likely than whites to experience police brutality, incompetent defense lawyers, and harsher sentences. The private sector has become increasingly involved in running more and more prisons for a profit.

Consequently, there is an even greater incentive to lock people up rather than address the fundamental causes of crime so that we can work on effective plans for rehabilitation. Companies like AT&T and TWA have prisoners working for much less than the minimum wage taking phone calls from customers (and jobs from workers) on the outside.

GOALS
Equal Rights for All — Empowerment of Disadvantaged Communities — Universal Health Care and Education

Equal Rights for All
We need to ensure that no one faces discrimination due to their personal characteristics, background, or orientation. Specifically, women worldwide should be guaranteed equal pay for equal work, as well as proportional representation in their respective governments and strengthened legislation protecting them from sexual assault. People of color and ethnic minorities deserve non-stereotypical cultural images, equal access to education and jobs, and just treatment in the legal system. Gays and lesbians should have the option to legally marry and openly serve in the military.

Some communities are making positive strides forward. In protests to gain the right to vote and hold elective office, scores of Kuwaiti women have marched into local election offices and registered to vote, arguing that the voting ban violates their constitution's gender non-discrimination clause.[139] Teachers and students all over the U.S. are creating tolerance campaigns in their schools, understanding that no one deserves unfair or cruel treatment based on skin color, sexual orientation, or religion.[140] In 2000, Vermont established 'civil unions' for committed gay and lesbians couples. Civil unions carry all of the rights and responsibilities of marriage within the state of Vermont! This victory would not have been possible without the commitment and hard work of people dedicated to justice.

Empowerment of Disadvantaged Communities
We must reverse the trend of building more and more prisons and instead focus our tax dollars on creating a society that prevents the need for them. Adequate access to education and work that pays a living wage goes a long way toward preventing crime. In 1999, Californian kids, most of them Latino/as, rose up against harsh, racist juvenile crime laws. They joined their elders to protest the building of more prisons and instead asked for more school funding.[141] Their cry of Schools not jails! has mobilized thousands of people. In the 2000 election, California voters easily passed Proposition 36 to provide treatment instead of jail for first-

and second-time drug offenders.[142] The Association of Community Organizations for Reform Now (ACORN) has won living wage campaigns in Chicago, Cook County, Boston, Oakland, Detroit, Minneapolis, and St. Paul. They have also registered over 500,000 voters since 1980, forced companies to clean up toxic dumps, and successfully pressured banks to reinvest in their communities.

Universal Health Care and Education

The world has more than enough resources to provide universal health care and education to everyone. In 2000, for instance, the Human Development Report noted that for just $80 billion a year, the entire world's population could have basic health and nutrition, basic education, reproductive health and family planning services, and water sanitation.[143] That may seem like an overwhelming amount of money. But that figure, equivalent to roughly 15% of the annual Pentagon budget, totals less than one-fifth of one percent of the world's income.[144] According to the United Nations, Americans spent more on cosmetics ($8 billion) in 1998 than it would have cost to provide basic education for all people in the world who did not have it ($6 billion).[145] Extending access to basic health care and nutrition to those who don't have it would cost $13 billion annually — that's 4 billion less than U.S. and European pet owners spend on pet food.[146]

AIDS Coalition to Unleash Power (ACT UP) activists have been instrumental in increasing AIDS awareness and funding for treatment and research. In 1995, the U.N. Fourth World Conference on Women in Beijing called for all nations to improve women's access to health care, political decision-making, education, economic opportunity, and family planning. They called for rape and domestic violence prevention, and for an end to female infanticide and genital mutilation. The Portuguese government now guarantees access to family planning services. Mexico and Peru have passed laws to increase access to reproductive health services.[147]

RESOURCES

📖 Cole, Luke, and Sheila Foster. *From the Ground Up: Environmental Racism and the Rise of the Environmental Justice Movement.* New York University Press, 2000.
Cole and Foster bring us a fascinating history of the environmental justice movement in the United States. Their work documents how thousands of people are now fighting for their children, their health, and their communities.

📖 Hallinan, Joseph T. *Going Up the River: Travels in a Prison Nation.* Random House, 2001.

Portrays the causes and effects of the 'prison boom' that has incarcerated two million people in the U.S. Tells the stories of wardens, inmates, guards, prison planners, townspeople, and others.

Kivel, Paul. *Uprooting Racism: How White People Can Work for Racial Justice*. New Society Publishers, 1995.
Provides an understanding of white privilege and racism and offers concrete suggestions on how to resist oppression.

Kozol, Jonathan. *Savage Inequalities: Children in America's Schools*. HarperPerennial Library, 1992.
Uncovers the extreme disparities in the U.S. educational system, through poignant examples. Compares white, upper middle class schools with inner city schools populated primarily by children of color. Check out Kozol's other books, too: *Rachel and Her Children: Homeless Families in America* (Fawcett Books, 1989) and *Amazing Grace: The Lives of Children and the Conscience of a Nation* (HarperPerennial Library, 1996).

Marcus, Eric. *Is It a Choice?: Answers to 300 of the Most Frequently Asked Questions About Gay and Lesbian People*. Harper San Francisco, 1999.
Answers the questions about homosexuality that most people feel they can't ask. A very readable, helpful book that leaves no topic untouched.

Zinn, Howard. *A People's History of the United States: 1492 to the Present*. HarperCollins, 1999.
This classic presents history from the people's point of view, rather than from the conquerors' and oppressors.' A gripping historical overview that you won't find in conventional history books.

FOUNDATION #6: CULTURE OF SIMPLICITY

A culture of simplicity would encourage each person to find meaning and fulfillment by pursuing their true passions, fostering loving relationships, and living authentic, reflective lives rather than by seeking status and material possessions.

CHALLENGES
Advertising Overload — Commercialization of Childhood — Materialism and Overconsumption

Advertising Overload

Our consciousness is under assault. Advertising saturates every aspect of our lives. Formerly sacred spaces such as schools are succumbing to commercialization. And the assault is working.

North Americans' increasing rate of consumption has closely followed the increase in commercialism. Ever since the advent of modern advertising during the 1920s, many corporations have used carefully chosen, powerful, and emotion-laden images and slogans to forever imprint their brands on our minds. In 2000, corporations spent approximately $233 billion on advertisements.[148]

Why would the most profit-savvy members of our society spend billions of their hard-won dollars to create fleeting images in our minds? Because ads work. Although we hate to admit what market research has shown over and over again for decades, each of us is consciously and unconsciously influenced by the advertisements we see. They change how we behave. Many advertisements encourage us to have self-conscious feelings of inadequacy and dissatisfaction with our overall physical attractiveness, while offering up products that provide us with partial solutions to these so-called problems. The collective impact of the advertising barrage sells our society the idea that satisfying each of our desires is more important than contributing to the welfare of others — a very destructive message that ads convey 24 hours a day, 7 days a week.

We take in more than 3600 commercial impressions every day.[149] Much of this bombardment has come from 'adcreep': commercialism that has moved into previously ad-free parts of our society. Telemarketing, for instance, has recently encroached on our homes and personal time. Some other current examples of adcreep are: TV monitors that show continuous commercials in elevators; ads behind home plate and on outfield walls in professional baseball stadiums; commercials that precede movies in the theaters and on video; unsolicited ads that show up in people's email on a daily basis; and product placement (where companies pay producers to integrate a company's product into the script, props, or scenery) in television shows, movies, and video games. Adcreep is even moving into the halls of government: the Chevrolet Suburban has gained the label 'official vehicle of Texas state parks,' even though environmentalists have rated it the "meanest vehicle for the environment."[150] Excessive commercialism is not only an annoyance but it often undermines many of our deeply held values and sacred institutions that transcend the desire for material possessions.

Commercialization of Childhood

Parents and citizens ought to be especially concerned about the increasing commercial pressures on children. Corporations have recently become excited about the opportunity to 'brand' children with products as early as when the children are 1-1/2 to 2 years old.[151] Currently, corporations target over $2 billion of advertising at children (double the amount spent 10 years ago).[152] Children are also spending 60% more time watching television than they spend in school.[153] They see between 20,000 and 40,000 commercials every year.[154]

One of the most worrisome examples of the commercialization of childhood is the immense increase in advertisements aimed at children while they are at school. For most of our history, we have protected our schools as commercial-free havens for children. Corporations and administrators are now violating this principle. School districts have become strapped for funding, and corporations have come asking for commercial access into the classroom. Corporate advertisements are now pervasive in school hallways, on sides of school buses, on book covers, and within corporate-sponsored educational materials. Some schools even distribute free product samples. Our kids are being seen as 'consumers-in-training.' Consider these examples:

- Kids across the country are learning about the history of the American cowboy as told by the California Beef Council and are winning McDonald's meals as a reward for reading.[155]

- In Evans, Georgia, high school senior Mike Cameron was suspended for wearing a Pepsi T-shirt during a school photo-op that had been arranged to win a contest for promoting Coca-Cola products.[156]

- 'Channel One' is a corporate-sponsored, 12-minute in-class 'news' program that is light on news and big on fluff. Two minutes of commercials bring junk-food ads right into the classroom every day, reaching eight million school kids.[157] Channel One warns advertisers, "If you're not targeting teens, you may be missing out on a relationship that could last a lifetime."[158]

- In order to reach a Coca-Cola contract quota, a Colorado education official encouraged teachers and administrators to increase student use of school vending machines by allowing soft drinks into classes.[159]

Materialism and Overconsumption

You may be wondering So what's the big deal with commercialism? In fact, commercialism is the engine that drives our cultural obsession with material happiness. Our never-ending quest for material possessions to fill the emptiness we feel decreases the value we place on social issues and on playing an active part in creating a better society. The concept of 'good citizen' or even 'good human being' has largely been replaced by the concept of the 'good consumer.'

Consumerism has become a way of life for people. Good consumers attempt to meet every need, solve problems, and enhance their lives by purchasing products ('Exercise in a Bottle' is an actual name of a product). Consumption surpasses other more socially beneficial goals, such as having sound character, contributing to the well-being of others, or becoming a well-educated citizen. Consumerism's exclusive focus on satisfying fleeting individual desires systematically undermines the civic culture necessary for a healthy democracy.

While much of the world suffers from epidemic levels of hunger and poverty, the world's affluent continue unabated in their pursuit of material possessions. On a global level, advertisers encourage people to leave behind their distinctive cultural practices in favor of this new form of materialism. Unfortunately, the global media do not portray to these countries the downside of adopting consumerism (an increase in debt, higher stress levels, environmental destruction, a rise in selfishness, etc.). It seems that the only thing in the world safe from commercialism is religion. Well…maybe not. A group of corporations recently sponsored Pope John Paul's visit to Mexico. As part of the arrangements, select packages of Sabritas potato chips (made by Frito-Lay) contained complimentary pictures of the Pope — a deal approved by the Vatican.[160]

GOALS
Rejection of Materialism — Culture of Simplicity

Rejection of Materialism

We must learn to think, feel, communicate, and experience the world beyond the confines of material possessions. We must learn to value lives fueled by compassion and love rather than by consumption and personal gain. We have begun to realize the seriousness of the problem — more than 80% of the American public are concerned about the pervasiveness of greed and selfishness in our society.[161] If we want to replace materialism as our cultural blueprint, we must start scaling back the march of commercialism. Alaska, Hawaii, Maine, and Vermont have even banned billboards in many public places.[162] As a society, we must demand that our public institutions and values retain their integrity instead of being sold off to the highest bidder.

A great place to start is by reclaiming our shared holidays from Madison Avenue. In recent years, Christmas has become more a celebration of materialism than of the values of generosity, strong families, and spiritual connection. Believe it or not, in 1939 Thanksgiving was specifically moved one week earlier in order to lengthen the Christmas shopping season.[163]

Another important step would be to return to an ad-free school environment. Revenues from advertisements are minor compared to overall school budgets. A school free from corporate slogans and logos would send a strong message to our children that we value their learning environment and independent development. Some countries, such as Norway, have begun to protect their children (even outside the schools) by banning all TV advertisements aimed at children under 12 years old.

Culture of Simplicity

A culture of simplicity is a viable alternative to the culture of excessive consumption. Voluntary simplicity provides people with a more balanced way of living, based on a their most deeply held values. It involves recognizing the trap of consumerism and unplugging (at least partially) from the commercial culture that perpetuates it. Simplicity, in this sense, includes:

- living more frugally

- working less
- slowing down
- spending more time with loved ones
- developing your passions and creativity
- building strong communities
- focusing on inner growth instead of on outward appearances
- engaging in meaningful and satisfying work that contributes to others

Time, energy, and money, currently swallowed by the 'more the better' philosophy, is freed up to pursue more important endeavors. We can return to living as multidimensional human beings.

Currently, just to make ends meet, many two-parent families are compelled to have both parents work full-time while their children are in daycare or school. For a culture of simplicity to flourish, it must be possible for people to have the freedom to work less while still bringing in enough to live on so that their lives can be about more than just 'making a living.'

Many of our grandparents fought for the 40-hour work week, and we've all benefited from their struggles. But in our current economy, the issue has arisen once again. Some nations are experimenting with shortening the work week, so that people can spend more time with families, volunteer, and pursue personal passions. France recently adopted the 35-hour work week, increasing employment and workplace satisfaction.[164] Sixty-five percent of Americans think that a movement to shorten the work week is a good idea.[165] It's time to consider the benefits of a shorter and more flexible work week: an improved quality of life, higher worker morale, less traffic congestion, and more jobs for people.

A culture based on simplicity may seem out of reach for our country of die-hard consumers, but simple living is becoming one of the fastest-growing trends around the world.[166] One in five Americans has already taken important steps toward a simpler life and has reported very worthwhile results.[167] Simplicity study groups are also popping up all over the country, providing an opportunity for individuals to transform their lives while finding support and sharing results. As we limit commercialism and create a culture of simplicity, we will create stronger families and communities, help nurture our natural environment, and foster more meaningful lives.

RESOURCES

📖 Andrews, Cecile. *The Circle of Simplicity*. HarperCollins, 1997.
    Andrews uses a critique of consumer culture to offer a more creative, community-oriented, spiritually full alternative to consumerism. Individual strategies for simple living complement suggestions for society-wide changes that promote a culture of simplicity.

📖 Burch, Mark A. *Stepping Lightly: Simplicity For People And The Planet.*
New Society Publishers, 2000.
Burch looks at simple living not just as a lifestyle that is rich with personal benefits for the practitioner but also as a practical solution for many of
our social and environmental problems as a society.

📖 Klein, Naomi. *No Logo: Taking Aim at the Brand Bullies.*
Knopf Canada, 2000.
Written by a journalist, this book examines the pervasiveness of corporate images in our culture and its effect upon our children and our
identities.

📖 Lasn, Kalle. *Culture Jam: How to Reverse America's Suicidal Consumer
Binge And — Why We Must.* Quill Publishers, 1999.
The founder of *Adbusters Magazine* provides a scathing look at how corporations brand us and, through the media, set the agenda for our
culture. Luckily, Lasn also gives us suggestions for strategies we can use
to put control back in the hands of common folk.

📖 Ray, Paul H., and Sherry Ruth Anderson. *The Cultural Creatives: How 50
Million People Are Changing the World.* Harmony Books, 2000.
Ray and Anderson propose that there are tens of millions of people who
hold a similar set of values around women's rights, the environment,
relationships, and social justice but who don't know that they are linked
by these common beliefs. This book brings a powerful message of hope
and change for the next millennium.

📖 Schor, Juliet. *The Overspent American.* Basic Books, 1998.
Schor is an engaging economist who analyzes the immensity of
American consumer debt, its historical causes, and solutions for escaping
consumerism.

FOUNDATION #7: REVITALIZED COMMUNITY

*A revitalized community would create a healthy and loving environment for
people to celebrate their many shared values while embracing individual differences, and would provide support for each person's physical, emotional, and
spiritual needs.*

CHALLENGES
Fragmented Communities — Loss of Humanity

Fragmented Communities
Many of us are losing our sense of community. We feel increasingly alienated
from each other, so we've chosen to retreat into insular lives that revolve
around our families and friends. We've closed ourselves off to the larger outside world and, in the process, have eroded our own ability to create positive

social change. This trend has led us to abandon our sense of responsibility for the well-being of our communities, our country, and our fellow human beings around the world.

Americans have become much more mobile than they were even 50 years ago. Being able to move to a different city or state provides us with the opportunity to go where our best job prospects may lie. But our sense of connection to any one area or group of people withers away. When we move frequently, there is little reason to invest in making our temporary community more beautiful, more livable, or safer. There may not be enough time, or you may not have the energy to develop deep, meaningful friendships. As a society, we have lost our incentive to plant roots.

In addition, many communities are no longer the vibrant, nurturing places that they used to be. Housing developers have designed spaces that maximize building efficiency while unintentionally creating communities that lack character, uniqueness, and heart. Community after community becomes McDonaldized, duplicating generic versions of themselves all over the country. Warehouse-sized retailers, fast food outlets, and other corporate chains move in to replace small, community-rooted businesses, and soon you have created a place called Anywhere, U.S.A.

Equally alarming, urban planners and developers increasingly design communities for our automobiles at the expense of walking, bicycling, and safe areas for children to play in. We spend more and more time in our cars (often in gridlock) —commuting back and forth to work, driving to the store, taking the kids to school, and running errands. We spend thousands of hours working just to pay for our cars and millions of dollars of our taxes to pay for new roads. We build extra-wide streets to accommodate cars instead of people, and we increase speed limits so that we can work further away from home without losing more time. Current urban planning models leave us with no pedestrian-friendly public spaces or businesses within five miles of our houses. It's no wonder we are in our cars all the time. We shop in one community, work in another, and sleep in another. Many of us spend so much time at work and in our cars that our home is little more than a bedroom oasis between hour-long commutes.

Loss of Humanity

From an early age in America, society teaches us to look out for number one. The U.S., perhaps more than any other country in the world, values the individual. Taking personal responsibility for one's life has become an essential part of what it is to be American. Unfortunately, understanding and taking seriously one's social responsibility has mostly become a question of personal preference. As a society, we generally accept selfishness as both natural and, to a certain extent, desirable. Our exclusive self-interest has left many of us lonely, isolated, and empty. And we cannot survive on selfishness alone. Selfishness lacks the one thing we desire more than anything else — meaning.

Material objects have gained meaning and value at the expense of human relationships. We have stopped valuing such desirable human qualities as nurturing and caring and replaced them with an emphasis on the ability to acquire marketable skills and achieve material success. Our culture's glorification of material progress also teaches each subsequent generation that success is about what you have acquired rather than who you have become. When doing what you want trumps spending time with others, it's not surprising that our kids grow up short on love and human contact, and long on television and video games.

Many of us have also become quite callous to the suffering of others. The media and politicians represent the poor as lazy and irresponsible rather than as lacking the same opportunity we may enjoy, as needing a transitional helping hand, or as a symptom of a possible flaw in how our system is working. Crime reports on television stimulate our instincts of fear and self-preservation, instead of motivating us to make our communities safer. Wars or disasters in foreign countries that take the lives of tens of thousands no longer faze us for more than a few hours as we numb ourselves so that we can carry out the rest of our day. As we neglect the value of our fellow human beings in times of need, we slowly chip away at our own sense of being valued by others.

GOALS

Revolution of Caring — Thriving Communities —Strengthened Community Institutions

Revolution of Caring

We need a revolution of the heart in this country — a revolution that would throw out selfishness and empower compassion. Our challenge is to create a society that encourages loving relationships and strong communities where people can count on each other for support and mutual well-being. To do that, we need people who are willing to act in ways that reflect caring for others' well-being.

We must look into the eyes of the homeless, the poor, the elderly, children, and the disenfranchised and see their humanness as our shared bond. We must embrace those that live beyond our borders and consider everyone as equal members of the human family — a family that values all people regardless of their social or economic status.

We must recognize that our own well-being is inextricably linked to the well-being of our community and that it is valuable to be a part of a healthy and loving community that cherishes shared values and embraces individual differences. We must reassert that contributing to the common good is a worthy calling for every one of us and not just the lifelong vocation of saints and dreamers.

Thriving Communities

To create communities worth living in, we must work together to intentionally plan them. We must bring back the town squares, parks, pedestrian-only streets and other gathering places that bring a community to life. We must intentionally plan our housing and business developments to encourage community building by creating safe, open areas where we can walk, bike, talk to each other, and play with our children. As we begin to reclaim our own sense of community, we will rediscover the value of developing a deep relationship with the place and people around us.

People around the globe have already begun taking back their communities. On 22 September 2000, residents in 800 European cities and towns from 27 countries participated in the European Union's annual 'Car-free Day,' where they banned automobiles from the city centers.[168] Fifty-seven percent of the population of Groningen, a city in the Netherlands of almost 200,000 people, travel around their city by bicycle![169] In Curitoba, Brazil, a local government focused on supporting public transit has come up with a number of creative strategies to encourage usage, resulting in 75% of commuters riding the local buses rather than taking their cars to work — that's more than 800,000 people every day.[170] Public transit has a proven track record — all we need is a commitment from our government to fund it and from ourselves to consistently use it.

Strengthened Community Institutions

We must work together to create a society where justice and harmony prevail. When we revitalize our community institutions, including religious groups, locally owned businesses, parent-involved schools, community centers, homeless shelters, and other social and political groups, it will strengthen our commitment to one another. To make this happen, we must be personally willing to integrate ourselves in our communities. This could involve volunteering for a local organization, keeping up on local events, getting involved in local schools, supporting local businesses, or just getting to know our neighbors by their first names.

As we strengthen community institutions, we can also reevaluate their purposes and how they work. For instance, you could add community service to your local school's curriculum. Community service would more fully integrate the next generation into your community and help instill an ethic of service that will carry on for years to come. Your community could start a locally owned business alliance to help maintain your area's distinct character. Locally owned businesses help create and perpetuate your community's economic wealth, because your dollars stay within the community instead of being siphoned off to distant corporate headquarters. A locally owned business in a locally owned building reinvests 85% of its profits in the local economy, as compared to a typical fast food franchise that invests only 20% of its profits in the local economy.[171]

Citizens have started using their own community institutions to support the common good for their neighborhood or town. In Greenfield, Massachusetts, citizens convinced Wal-Mart to pay for a study that would examine the economic impacts of building a superstore in their community. When they found out that 60% of local businesses would be negatively affected, they rejected Wal-Mart's building proposal.[172]

RESOURCES

Etzioni, Amitai. *The Spirit Of Community: Rights, Responsibilities, and The Communitarian Agenda*. Crown Publishers, 1993.
A very engaging discussion regarding the balance between individual freedom and social responsibility. Proposes solutions to individualism that will strengthen our sense of community while preserving each person's unique character.

Fodor, Eben V. *Better Not Bigger: How to Take Control of Urban Growth and Improve Your Community*. New Society Publishers, 1999.
A practical guide to smart growth, Fodor gives a well-thought-out argument for an alternative to the typical growth pattern of modern communities and then provides the reader with tools to make it happen in his/her own community.

Kunstler, James Howard. *The Geography of Nowhere: The Rise and Decline of America's Man-Made Landscape*. Touchstone Books, 1994.
Kunstler's book is a rousing polemic aimed at getting the reader to rise up and fight the multi-headed beast that creates heartless, sprawling communities that are designed for the automobile and that destroy our social fabric.

Lerner, Michael. *The Politics of Meaning: Restoring Hope and Possibility in an Age of Cynicism*. Perseus Publishing, 1996.
Michael Lerner puts out a powerful call for us to bring meaning back into our lives by rebuilding our communities in such a way that people once again become more important than material things. His work is a tribute of hope to the American spirit that is all but forgotten.

McKibben, Bill. *Hope, Human, and Wild: True Stories of Living Lightly On The Earth*. Ruminator Books, 1997.
McKibben lays out three examples of large communities around the globe that have become beacons of hope for the rest of us. They show how practical idealism can result in thriving cities, where the population has a very high quality of life at the same time as it lives lightly on the Earth.

Ritzer, George. *McDonaldization of Society*. Pine Forge Press, 2000.
An enlightening look into how many aspects of our lives, including education, relationships, family, and entertainment, increasingly take on aspects of the fast-food industry. Explains how society is becoming more rationalistic and focused on efficiency, predictability, and quantity rather than on quality, authenticity, and meaning. Also offers suggestions on how we might resist the 'McDonaldization' trend.

CREATING A BETTER WORLD

You're now ready to take action! We've equipped you with information about the world's problems and a vision of what a better world might look like. If you ever doubt the need for action or find your commitment wavering, reread this chapter.

The rest of the book consists purely of actions. We offer you a broad range of actions to choose from — based on a balance between effectiveness and accessibility. Match your actions to the type of better world you would like to see so that your unique contribution adds to the canvas we all share. Every action — big or small— is important if it makes for a better world. The world we want, we must create.

> *Each time a person stands for an ideal, or acts to improve the lot of others, or strikes out against injustice, he or she sends forth a tiny ripple of hope. And crossing each other from a million different centers of energy and daring, those ripples build a current that can sweep down the mightiest walls of oppression and resistance.* — Robert F. Kennedy

ACTIONS
FOR A BETTER
WORLD

MONEY • SHOPPING • FOOD

PERSONAL • FRIENDS AND FAMILY

COMMUNITY • HOME

WORK • MEDIA • POLITICS

TRANSPORTATION • TRAVEL

ORGANIZATIONS

Action is the antidote to despair.
—Joan Baez

MONEY

Banking

Credit Cards

Saving

Investing

FROM THE TIME we receive our first allowance as children, we learn the importance and power of money. Some people dedicate their lives to acquiring it; others feel that it is evil and avoid ever thinking about it. Either way, money ends up having power over their lives. Money is not inherently good or evil. It is just another way in which we shape the world around us. Money does not care if we use it to destroy the world or to rebuild it. It merely flows wherever we direct it.

Much of the money that passes through your hands is, at this moment and without your knowledge, aiding in the destruction of many of the things you hold dear in this world. For example, banks and mutual funds often invest in companies that pollute the Earth or violate human rights. This chapter will create possibilities for you to make sure that, behind your back, your money isn't harming what you love.

The banking section offers several opportunities for you to support community development in your own community and in economically impoverished areas across the nation, just by opening up a bank account. Credit card options provide simple tools so that you can support social change while you shop. The savings section provides useful tips on how to intelligently manage your money to support your most deeply held values. Finally, the investing section allows you to turn a profit while supporting responsible businesses and community-based development.

BANKING

When you open up an account at any bank, you may think your money sits idly in that account until you need it. At least that's what your monthly statement makes you think. In reality, to make a profit, banks constantly invest your money in all kinds of ventures. They may use your money for:
- funding a strip mine
- backing a union-busting corporation
- extracting petroleum in Burma using forced labor
- creating a factory-style hog lot that dumps thousands of gallons of waste into your local streams

Your money may very well be wreaking havoc on your community and the world without your knowledge. By taking control of your money, you take responsibility for directing its impact on the world.

❑ *Action: Investigate your bank*

Some banks serve the needs of diverse communities better than others. The Community Reinvestment Act (CRA) of 1977 outlawed the practice of 'redlining' — the systematic exclusion of poor neighborhoods from lending practices. It also mandated that each bank produce a statement of its community's needs and ways in which the bank is addressing those needs. Federal regulators assess the lending, investments, and services that the bank provides to its community and give it a rating, based on how well the bank is meeting the needs of its community.

Go into any bank and say, I would like to see your Community Reinvestment Act Performance Evaluation and the public comment file. The performance evaluation provides information about the credit needs of your community and reports how well the bank is meeting the needs of low- and middle-income people. The 20 to 40 pages of information may be slightly overwhelming, but don't worry. At the beginning of the report, federal regulators assess the bank's community responsiveness with one of the following four possible ratings:
- outstanding
- satisfactory (most common rating)
- needs to improve
- substantial non-compliance

If the rating is not 'outstanding,' make sure you tell the bank that you would like to see them improve. The public comment file will have any written correspondence regarding community involvement and is available at the main branch.

Federal Financial Institutions Examination Council (FFIEC)
www.ffiec.gov/cracf/crarating/main.cfm

FFIEC's website provides a searchable database, by city or state, for all financial institutions that are under the jurisdiction of the CRA. Ratings are easily comparable for banks in your area.

❏ *Action: Open an account at a socially responsible bank or credit union*

You will sleep better at night if you know that your bank is using your money to promote justice in the world. So how do you begin? Even with the CRA Performance Evaluation, it can be very difficult to rate the social and environmental impacts of an individual bank. Since banks typically invest their money in a wide range of corporations and individuals, you would have to evaluate every one of these entities to determine a bank's level of social responsibility.

Instead of putting your money in large corporate banks, whose overall impact is hard to determine, deposit your money in locally owned banks that have a strong commitment to contribute to their community.

A number of financial institutions dedicate themselves to making sure your money helps rather than hurts people. By placing your money in these institutions, you can rest assured that your money will help build new classrooms, renovate low-income neighborhoods, create small businesses, or aid needy families in buying their first homes. When you support a financial institution that is truly committed to its community, you are helping that community retain its wealth, instead of having it siphoned off through corporate banks to one of the world's financial centers. You are helping create a strong, self-sufficient economy in your community.

Don't be discouraged by the idea that you have too little money to make a difference. When combined with hundreds of other customers, these small amounts of money can make a big difference. Initially, to investigate banks and change your accounts requires an investment of time, but your choice will have positive consequences every day for years to come. Just think, you'll be helping the world even while you're at home sleeping!

AREN'T OUT-OF-STATE BANKS A HASSLE?!

If, after doing some homework, you can't find any socially responsible banking institutions in your area, don't worry. Most banking transactions today involve checks or Automated Teller Machines (ATMs), so having an out-of-state bank is not a hassle anymore. The only difference is that you won't be able to use ATMs to deposit your checks. If that's something you need, consider having two accounts: one in-state and one out-of-state.

BANKS The following Community Development Banks operate very much like normal banks, but their business is the permanent, long-term economic development of low- and moderate-income communities. Community Development Banks offer all of the services that the giant corporate banks do, including checking and savings accounts, certificates of deposit (CDs), money market accounts, lending, and FDIC insured deposits, but they provide one important additional service — a commitment to economic justice. Here are some of the best-known Community Development Banks:

ShoreBank
7054 South Jeffery Boulevard,
Chicago, IL 60649
☎ (800) 669-7725 ☐ www.sbk.com

 SHOREBANK

ShoreBank has been dedicated to the South Shore community in Chicago for many years. They use your 'development deposits' to reclaim neglected buildings, reinvigorate small businesses, and allow people to renovate their homes. ShoreBank also has offices in Detroit, the Upper Peninsula of Michigan, Cleveland, and Washington state.

ShoreBank Pacific
P.O. Box 400,
Ilwaco, WA 98624
☎ (888) 326-2265 ☐ www.eco-bank.com   SHOREBANK PACIFIC

ShoreBank Pacific is a subsidiary of ShoreBank of Chicago. They promote natural resource stewardship and community development, through their selective lending practices, to small- and medium-sized businesses that want to increase profitability in environmentally responsible ways. Checking accounts are not available at this time, but consider opening up a Certificate of Deposit (CD).

Elk Horn Bank and Trust
P.O. Box 248,
Arkadelphia, AR 71923-0248
☎ (800) 789-3428 ☐ www.ehbt.com

 ELK HORN BANK

Elk Horn Bank and Trust is a community development bank committed to the economic revitalization of distressed rural communities in southern Arkansas. They use your money to create jobs and support local businesses.

Chittenden Bank
Brattleboro, VT 05402, U.S.A.
☎ (800) 545-2236
💻 www.chittenden.com

Chittenden Bank's Socially Responsible Banking program offers you deposit account options that fund specific lending programs for affordable housing, conservation and agricultural projects, education, downtown revitalization, community facilities, and community-based businesses. You know your money is making a difference on a local scale.

Blackfeet National Bank
P.O. Box 730,
Browning, MT 59417-0730
☎ (406) 338-7000

When you deposit your money in Blackfeet National Bank, you will be furthering the development of the Blackfeet reservation economy. Take part in the strengthening of this Native American tribe and stand up in opposition to our country's horrendous history of genocide against indigenous people.

Wainwright Bank
63 Franklin Street, Boston, MA 02110
☎ (800) 444-2265
💻 www.wainwrightbank.com

Wainwright Bank uses over $140 million to support a variety of projects, including breast cancer research, housing for people living with AIDS, food banks, and the protection of wilderness areas.

Community Capital Bank
111 Livingston Street, Brooklyn, NY 11201
☎ (718) 802-1212
💻 www.communitycapitalbank.com

Community Capital Bank supports community development projects in New York City. Imagine the development that could happen if even one out of every 100 New Yorkers banked here!

Community Bank of the Bay
1750 Broadway,
Oakland, CA 94612
☎ (510) 271-8400
💻 www.communitybankbay.com

Community Bank of the Bay provides much-needed loans for the development of affordable housing, as well as loans to small businesses and non-profit organizations. They use your money to create positive social change in the Bay Area and beyond.

Louisville Community Development Bank (LCDB)
2901 West Broadway,
Louisville, KY 40211
☎ (502) 778-7000
🖳 www.morethanabank.com

Louisville Community Development Bank's mission is to revitalize 12 inner city neighborhoods of Louisville, Kentucky. They are accomplishing this goal of economic recovery by making targeted loans. In four years, they have made over $23 million in loans that have restored properties and created over 1000 jobs in the community.

CITIZENS FUNDS MONEY MARKET FUND

Citizens Funds is one of the most renowned socially responsible investing firms in the country. You can open a money market account and receive unlimited checking and a debit card. It also pays anywhere from 4 to 5% interest (the range for the last ten years) on the money in your account, and there is no minimum balance necessary if you have your paycheck deposited directly into your account. The real advantage of using this fund as your primary checking account is that you have the assurance that they invest your money only in businesses, banks, and government bonds that have passed one of the most rigid socially responsible selection procedures in the financial world.

Citizens Funds
230 Commerce Way, Suite 300,
Portsmouth, NH 03801
☎ (800) 223-7010
🖳 www.citizensfunds.com

CREDIT UNIONS A popular alternative to banks, credit unions are not-for-profit financial institutions with a mission to serve their communities. A credit union collects deposits and loans them to members at low interest rates. Most credit unions have specific membership criteria (usually you must be an employee of a certain organization or a resident of a certain area). Credit unions are an excellent alternative to large corporate banks. They consistently earn excellent ratings from consumers by charging lower fees and having better customer service. The National Credit Union Share Insurance Fund (NCUSIF) protects all federal (and many state) credit union deposits up to $100,000.

Community Development Credit Unions (CDCU) commit to investing in low-income neighborhoods (similar to Community Development Banks). They also provide low-cost financial services to low-income communities. CDCUs accept deposits from individuals and institutions outside of their usual field of membership. It is an amazing feeling to know that they are using your savings to reinvigorate low-income neighborhoods, instead of just padding the pockets of corporate bank CEOs.

Alternatives Federal Credit Union

301 West State Street, Ithaca, NY 14850,
☎ (607) 273-4666 🖳 www.alternatives.org

Alternatives works to make low-income communities more self-reliant. They base their philosophy on the premise that communities need a supportive financial network to keep their income within their community. Alternatives is dedicated to providing low-cost services to three main groups: (1) low-income families, (2) small business owners, and (3) non-profit organizations.

Self-Help Credit Union

301 West Main Street,
Durham, NC 27701
☎ (800) 476-7428 🖳 www.self-help.org

Since 1980, Self-Help Credit Union has financed $240 million worth of loans to assist low-income families (particularly minorities, women, and rural residents) to own homes, build businesses, and strengthen community resources. Self-Help's mission stresses that ownership is the key to economic mobility and security.

To find a Community Development Credit Union (CDCU) near you contact:

The National Federation of Community Development Credit Unions
☎ (212) 809-1850 🖳 www.natfed.org

To find other credit unions (both CDCUs and non-CDCUs) contact:

National Credit Union Administration
☎ (703) 518-6300 🖳 www.ncua.gov/other/custate.htm

Credit Union National Association
☎ (800) 358-5710 🖳 www.cuna.org

In Canada

Search for the nearest credit union at:

🖳 www.cuets.ca/links/html

Citizens Bank of Canada
P.O. Box 13133, Stn. Terminal,
Vancouver, B.C., Canada V6B 6K1
☎ (888) 708-7800 ▱ www.citizensbank.ca

Citizens Bank of Canada ⌂Ⅲ

Created by Vancouver City Savings Credit Union (VanCity), the largest credit union in Canada, Citizens Bank provides socially responsible telephone and Internet banking. Before they invest your money in a business, they consider the company's record on human rights, military weapon and tobacco production, the environment, and treatment of animals.

❑ *Action: Write checks that state your values*

For as little as $10, Message! Products will send you 200 personalized checks that include a beautiful background design and the logo of one of a number of progressive organizations. Not only are you spreading the message of your group every time you write a check (approximately six people see each check you write), but Message! Products donates a portion of the price of the checks to the organization you choose for your design. Since 1986, they have donated over $2.5 million to these organizations: Sierra Club, PETA, Human Rights Campaign, NOW, National Abortion and Reproductive Rights Action League (NARAL), and many others. These checks work just like the ones that banks issue, but you also get to share your values with the world as you use them.

Message! Products
☎ (800) CHECK-OK
▱ www.messageproducts.com

CREDIT CARDS

Credit cards are an increasingly popular method of making purchases in the U.S. and around the world. Watch out! Credit cards can be handy but they can also lead you down a fast track to debt. Studies have found that people spend significantly more money when they use a credit card than when they pay with cash. And as people spend more, they acquire more debt (and some credit cards charge almost 20% interest). Total credit card debt in the U.S. doubled from 1995-1999 — approaching $783 billion in the year 2000.[1]

❑ *Action: Cut up your credit cards*

There is a very simple way to avoid credit card debt — get rid of your cards! Start with cutting up all of your department store and gas company cards. You will not only save yourself the stress of having debt, but you will free up your resources for better things that reflect your values. If you think you might want a credit card for travel or emergencies, just keep one multipurpose card (Visa, Mastercard). Get rid of all the rest.

❑ *Action: Donate money while using your credit card*

A large number of activist organizations now have agreements with credit card companies. Each time you use your credit card, a small amount of money goes to their organization (or a group of organizations) — at no charge to you. Some of these organizations receive hundreds of thousands of dollars in extra funds each year that help them advance their efforts to make the world better. This is an incredibly easy, no-cost way to help organizations of your choice. Although the individual amounts may be small, they definitely add up. In addition, whoever sees your card also sees your organization's logo — another chance to spread your message. Call up your favorite organization and ask them if they have any contracts with credit card companies.

Working Assets   ☎ (800) 522-7759

Working Assets donates ten cents for each purchase on its credit cards to a pool of non-profit organizations that the cardholders select every year. In 2001, they anticipate donating $5 million to progressive organizations such as Greenpeace, Planned Parenthood, Amnesty International, Human Rights Campaign, and the ACLU. On top of the donations, you will be supporting Working Assets, one of the most socially responsible corporations in the world.

MBNA Sierra Club Card   ☎ (800) 523-7666

MBNA America donates 1/2% of all purchases made on a Sierra Club MasterCard to the Sierra Club plus $10 for each year you keep the card (there is no annual fee). This card results in hundreds of thousands of dollars every year being donated to the Sierra Club at no cost to the cardholders. Other participating organizations include Amnesty International and Clean Water Action. The donation rate may differ based on the participating organization.

> Experts estimate that U.S credit card spending by the year 2000 will exceed $1.5 trillion annually.[2] If just 1% of us make our purchases with the MBNA Sierra Club card, over $75 million would be generated for the Sierra Club to use to help save the environment.

Greenpeace MasterCard
☎(800) 790-1441

The Greenpeace MasterCard is a biodegradable credit card, made primarily from a plant-based polymer. Most credit cards are made primarily from PVC that has many poisonous by-products, including dioxin. This card is 99.9% PVC-free, truly one of a kind. Greenpeace raised approximately $150,000 in 2000 from the use of this card.

Wainwright's Community Card MasterCard   ☎(800) 444-2265

Each time you use the Wainwright Mastercard, Wainwright donates 1% of your purchase price to various nonprofit groups, including the AIDS Action committee, the Boston Women's Fund, and the Boston Alliance of Gay and Lesbian Youth.

Chittenden Bank's Visa Card for Kids ☎ (800)-642-5181

Vermont National Bank, one of the socially responsible banks we mentioned earlier, issues a Visa card that donates 1% of your purchases to various children's organizations. The benefiting groups include The Lund Family Center, Make a Wish Foundation, Vermont Campaign to End Childhood Hunger, and Camp Ta-Kum-Ta, a camp for kids with cancer. This card is especially neat because not only are you supporting great organizations, you are supporting a socially responsible bank as well.

In Canada

Citizens Bank Shared Interests VISA ☎ (888)-708-7800

Every time you use your Shared Interest VISA, Citizens Bank puts ten cents (Cdn.) into a donations pool to support not-for-profit initiatives for effecting positive social, economic, and environmental change. This comes at no cost to you. Card users vote to determine which groups get the donations. Citizens Bank also offers credit cards that raise money for Amnesty International and Oxfam Canada.

🖥 www.citizensbank.ca

SAVING

North Americans are addicted to shopping. It's no wonder, when you consider the amount of advertising companies expose us to on a daily basis. TV and magazines teach us that we should be thinner, wear more stylish clothes, and drive faster, fancier cars. It's not surprising that all of us, from time to time, confuse money with happiness. After enough of these purchases, you have a home full of stuff and a heap of debt.

> The average American saves a significantly lower percentage of his or her income (0.5%) than the average Canadian (1.2%), British (7.0%), Italian (11.5%), German (11.8%), Japanese (13.6%), and French (15.5%) citizen.[4]

The average American carries $8500 of non-mortgage personal debt, and each year the problem is getting worse.[3] The first step in escaping from the trap of consumer debt is to confront your urges to meet your needs, solve your problems, and enhance your life by buying things you don't need. Once you deal with our cultural obsession with possessions, it will be much easier for you to save your money.

> ### SAVING MONEY HAS THE FOLLOWING ADVANTAGES FOR YOU AND THE WORLD
> - You experience a sense of mental freedom formerly strangled by the shadow of debt.
> - You have more liberty to change jobs, work less, or take some time off to spend with your children or travel (to truly break out of the work-and-spend cycle).
> - You have the possibility of donating more of your money to organizations that are putting your values into action.
> - The fewer products you buy, the more money you save, and the less stress you cause upon the Earth's scarce resources.

❑ *Action: Keep track of your monthly expenses and income*

Most people in America look at their bank balance and say, Where did all my money go? Well, there's only one way to find out — keep track of your money.

How to calculate your income:

1. Add up 'after tax income' (your take home pay) from all paychecks.
2. Add up any interest on bank accounts.
3. Add up any other income (investments, property, etc.).

1 +2+3= Total Income

How to calculate your expenses:

1. Add up every check that you wrote for the month.
2. Add up every ATM cash withdrawal.
3. Add up every electronic withdrawal (credit cards, debit cards).

1+2+3= Total Expenses

Total Income – Total Expenses = Total Saved (or overspent)

If you keep track of this information for each month, you will be able to see if your lifestyle is financially sustainable. This process will not only empower you in your relationship with money but it will push you to reevaluate how you spend your hard-earned cash.

❑ *Action: Create a monthly and yearly budget*

It seems like such a simple idea to create a budget, yet few of us actually do it. Create categories for each of your major expenses, including rent/mortgage, food, car payment, clothing, etc. Write in the amounts you need for each and then compare this with your monthly income. Budget in your 'play money'

> If you are spending more than you can afford, consider tracking every penny that escapes from your wallet for a month. Reduce expenses that are not in line with your values.

— the money you can blow on whatever you want. Then plan to put whatever's left over in your savings. Having a budget takes away some of the power money has over our thoughts.

☐ *Action: Pay yourself at the beginning of the month*

Many people find that they don't have any money at the end of the month to save. If this is the case for you, take a percentage of your paycheck at the beginning of each month and designate it for savings — say 5 to 10%. Consider having your bank automatically take this amount from your paycheck and deposit it into a savings account or mutual fund. If you have less money in your checking account, it will increase your chances of saving money throughout the month.

SAVING RESOURCES:

📖 Dominguez, Joe, and Vicki Robin. *Your Money or Your Life*. Penguin, 1999. This wonderful book helps you gain control of your money so that your spending becomes an expression of your values. It has profoundly changed thousands of people's lives and given them the freedom to escape the bonds of money and enjoy the fruits of frugality.

INVESTING

As the stock market skyrocketed to its peak in 2000, more and more people leaped into the market to make their fortunes. Stories of blue-collar workers making thousands of dollars through online investing filled the news, encouraging everyone with a little extra cash to hop on board and get rich. Naturally, we all want to make as much money as possible through our investments, but have you ever wondered what happens to your money when you invest it? Many people worry about the financial results of their investments, but most forget to analyze the impact of their investments on the world. Your investments can support:

- the exploitation of workers in crowded sweatshops
- oil companies that destroy indigenous people's land
- chemical manufacturers that pollute the air you breathe
— OR —
- small business development
- environmentally friendly companies
- Bangladeshi women working their way out of poverty

It's your choice. Fortunately, there are several options for investing in ways that lead to a better world.

'Ethical investing,' 'values-based investing,' and 'socially responsible investing' are all terms that describe using a 'double bottom line' when choosing investment options. Generating a profit is the first bottom line. Making a positive contribution to the world is the second bottom line. For socially responsible investors, making the highest profit regardless of the social and environmental consequences is not a viable option.

Although you can do most investing by yourself, you may want to consider contacting a financial planner in your area who is well versed in socially responsible investing. They can help you make sound financial and ethical decisions (see Investment Resources).

❑ Action: Invest in socially responsible stocks

Screening is a process by which investors exclude from their portfolios companies that are involved in practices that the investor does not support (negative screens) or include companies that are doing things that the investor thinks are exceptional (positive screens). In this way, many investors are helping to support those corporations that are doing especially positive things for the world (for example, making extensive charitable contributions or having an excellent environmental record). Similarly, investors can withhold their support by excluding companies that act in ways that contradict the investors' values (for example, companies using sweatshop labor or producing nuclear weapons). When you own stock in socially responsible corporations, you are using your money to help manifest your values in the world.

> By 1999, U.S. investors controlled over $2 trillion (roughly $1 of every $8 professionally managed) in socially responsible investments — an increase of 82% from 1997.[5]

It can be challenging to determine which companies are socially responsible. After a little research, you will quickly come to realize that just as there are no perfect people, so there are no perfect corporations. The point is to do the best you can with the information available. Take into consideration everything you know about a corporation — any boycotts, awards, fines, and whether or not you feel good about the products they make. We've created a couple of lists to help you get started.

The following lists take into account: environmental impact, charity, diversity, working conditions, family benefits, community outreach, and current boycotts by organizations that are working for a better world. Each socially responsible corporation is followed by its corresponding stock symbol in parentheses.

Some of the most socially RESPONSIBLE corporations[6]:

American Express (AXP)	AT&T (T)
Avon (AVP)	Baxter International (BAX)

Body Shop (BDSPY)   Colgate-Palmolive (CL)
Fannie Mae (FNM)   General Mills (GIS)
Herman Miller (MLHR)   Hewlett Packard (HWP)
Horizon Organic (HCOW)   IBM (IBM)
Intel (INTC)   Interface Flooring (IFSIA)
Johnson & Johnson (JNJ)   Kellogg's (K)
Polaroid (PRD)   Quaker Oats (OAT)
Real Goods (RGTC)   SBC Communications (SBC)
Timberland (TBL)   Whole Foods (WFMI)
Wild Oats (OATS)   Xerox (XRX)

Some of the most socially IRRESPONSIBLE corporations:

Archer Daniels Midlan   Boise Cascade
Chevron Texaco   Coastal
Conagra, Inc.   Consolidated Stores
Dillard's   Dow Chemical
Exxon Mobil   Gateway
General Electric   General Motors
Genesco   Interstate Bakeries
Kohl's   Lockheed Martin
MCI Worldcom   Mercantile Stores
Mitsubishi   Monsanto
NCR   Nestle
Perry Ellis   Philip Morris
RJ Reynolds   Royal Carribbean
Royal Dutch (Shell)   Stone Container
TJX   Tosco
Tyson Foods   Union Carbide
Unocal

SOCIAL RESPONSIBILITY IS PROFITABLE!

You're probably thinking, Sure, investing in socially responsible stocks is great, but I bet you don't make nearly as much money. Actually, from 1990 to 1998, the Domini Social Index (made up of 400 socially responsible stocks) outperformed the S&P 500 — the most representative composite of U.S. stock values.[7]

❏ *Action: Be a shareholder activist*

If you own shares of a company's stock, you are in fact a partial owner of that company. This means that you have some unique privileges. If you find out that the company is engaging in practices that contradict your values, let them know you disapprove. Writing letters, calling, and stockholder voting are all important tools you can use to demand corporate responsibility. Check with the Shareholder Action Network (see below) for where to direct your complaints.

If you own at least $2,000 worth of stock for 18 months in a company, you also have the ability to shape corporate policy by proposing shareholder resolutions. You could call for divestment from countries rife with human rights abuses, increased usage of recycled materials, or more racial diversity in upper management. Even if your resolution is not adopted, you will have raised awareness of the issue you care about.

For more information on recent victories and upcoming resolutions contact:
Shareholder Action Network
1612 K Street NW, Suite 650,
Washington, DC 20006, U.S.A.
☎(202) 872-5313   💻 www.shareholderaction.org

❑ *Action: Invest in socially responsible mutual funds*

A mutual fund company buys stock and/or bonds from many different corporations and government agencies. When you buy a share of a mutual fund, you are in effect getting small amounts of stock shares and bonds from hundreds of different companies. This diversity of investments lowers the risk to the individual investor.

Much as with individual investors, most socially responsible mutual funds use their own unique screens to keep out corporations engaged in activities that are in opposition to the values of the fund. Many socially responsible investment groups, for example, refrain from investing in tobacco, alcohol, weapons, nuclear power, and corporations that are especially polluting or exploitative. Some also exclude companies that conduct animal testing. Many of these funds also seek out companies that promote equal opportunity, create beneficial and safe products, foster good labor relations, and are environmentally responsible. Each mutual fund uses different screens, so do some comparison shopping and ask for each fund's prospectus.

Citizens Funds
230 Commerce Way, Suite 300,
Portsmouth, NH 03801
☎ (800) 223-7010   💻 www.citizensfunds.com

Citizens Funds is known for its diversity of fund choices and rigorous social screens. Along with the usual standard social screens they also consider Community Reinvestment Act ratings and the AFL-CIO boycott list.

Domini Social Investments
P.O.Box 959,
New York, NY 10159-0959
☎ (800) 762-6814   💻 www.domini.com

The Domini 400 (an index of 400 screened companies) is a standard in the ethical investment industry. They are also the leader in using shareholder resolutions to promote ethnic diversity, environmental sustainability, and fair wages and working conditions in the corporate world.

DEVCAP Development Capital
209 W. Fayette Street,
Baltimore, MD 21201–3443, U.S.A.
☎ (410) 468-3922   🖥 www.devcap.org

Globally Responsible Investing

The DEVCAP Shared Return Fund is a unique socially screened mutual fund that provides an opportunity to investors to share a portion of their annual return to help support micro-enterprise programs in developing nations.

For contact information, recent performance, social screens, and investment guidelines for socially responsible mutual funds contact:

Social Investment Forum
☎ (202) 872-5319   🖥 www.socialinvest.org
SocialFunds.com
☎ (802) 348-7790   🖥 www.socialfunds.com

In Canada

Ethical Funds
☎ (604) 714-3800   🖥 www.ethicalfunds.com

If you want to invest in mutual funds that support lesbian and gay rights, women's rights, and the environment, then check out the following. Each fund is extremely dedicated to supporting its issues.

Issue		
Lesbian and Gay Rights	Women's Rights	Environment
Fund		
Meyer's Pride Value Fund	Women's Equity Mutual Fund	New Alternatives Fund
Contact		
☎(800) 410-3337 or 🖥:www.pridefund.com	☎(800) 385-7003 or 🖥:www.womens-equity.com	☎(800) 423-8383 or 🖥www.newalterna-tivesfund.com

---

❏ *Action: Invest in community development loan funds*

Investing in community development loan funds is perhaps the most powerful way to use your money to make the world a better place. Community investment helps support low-income housing development, provides small business loans (often to minorities and women), and creates lasting change in communities that need it most. Investing in community development funds is an especially effective way to fight poverty because:

- the people living in poverty, who know their situation the best, decide how to use the loans to most improve their lives
- loan programs for the very poor, when properly administered, teach and reinforce entrepreneurial behavior and self-sufficiency rather than promote dependency. They create lasting change.
- borrowers demonstrate a remarkable ability to work their way out of poverty
- funds spread social change beyond the individual loan recipient by creating jobs, which feed families and fight poverty in general.[8]

Micro-credit lending offers loans as small as $10! In Bangladesh or Latin America, your investment could help a woman buy a sewing machine to start her own business or give a fruit grower the opportunity to purchase his own fruit cart to sell his produce. Without the help of these small loans, people must rent equipment or work for others, perpetuating their poverty.

> Find out more about micro-credit from the Grameen Bank at
>
> www.Grameen.org

Community development loan funds are federally unregulated and uninsured. However, loan funds often use grant money and pre-funded loss reserve to protect your investment, making the risk very minimal. Community investment is a great supplement to other higher-rate investments. A small portion of your savings can make an enormous difference in someone's life.

Here are some Community Development Loan Funds that you can invest in:

Calvert Social Investment Foundation
4550 Montgomery Avenue, 1000 N,
Bethesda, MD 20814
☎ (800) 248-0337
💻 www.calvertfoundation.org

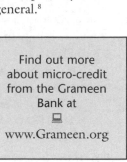

Calvert Foundation promotes community development and micro-lending throughout the U.S. and the world. They require a minimum $1000 investment and offer returns of 0 to 4%.

Nicaraguan Credit Alternatives Fund (NICA)
P.O. Box 1534,
Madison, WI 53701
☎ (608) 257-7230 💻 www.wccnica.org

The NICA Fund, a project of the Wisconsin Coordinating Council on Nicaragua, addresses the root causes of poverty by providing low-income Nicaraguans with loans for small business, farming, and cooperatives. This fund is a fantastic opportunity to help people of the second poorest country in the Western hemisphere maintain some control over their own well-being. The fund requires a $2,000 minimum investment for a minimum of two years, and returns range from 0 to 6%.

ICE's Revolving Loan Fund
57 School Street, Springfield, MA 01027.
☎ (413) 746-8660
💻 www.iceclt.org/loanfund

The Institute for Community Economics invests in affordable housing ($2.2 million in 1999), focusing on economically depressed areas. Since 1979, the fund has loaned over $30 million to those in need. The fund has a suggested minimum investment of $1,000 for one to ten years, and returns range from 3 to 5%.

For information on over 100 community development investments all across the U.S. contact:

National Community Capital Association
☎ (215) 923-4754   💻 www.communitycapital.org

❑ *Action: Invest your pension in a socially responsible manner*

For the fortunate among us who have a pension, there are some socially responsible alternatives to the traditional investment strategy. TIAA-CREF, a nationwide financial system primarily for employees in higher education, created the Social Choice Account based on customer interest. Also at the beginning of 2001, the $170 billion California Public Employees Retirement System applied human rights, labor, and environmental criteria to their overseas investments.[9] See if at your work you can secure your financial future at the same time that you protect future generations. Follow these simple steps:

- Find your pension administrator. Check your pension statement for a phone number.
- Find out if she or he offers a socially responsible alternative. Your administrator should immediately be able to tell you Yes or No.
- If the answer is Yes, great. Ask to have your pension invested in the alternative plan.
- If there is no socially responsible alternative, say that you would like one and ask to whom you can speak about it.
- Once you've switched your pension, tell your coworkers about it.

INVESTMENT RESOURCES

📖 Brill, Hal, Jack A. Brill, and Cliff Feigenbaum. *Investing with Your Values: Making Money and Making a Difference.* New Society Publishers, 2000.

This comprehensive book provides a model of investing that ties in with a sustainable society. The authors detail a broad array of investment options. It also includes ratings for the level of social responsibility of various mutual funds.

💻 *www.NaturalInvesting.com*

📖 Co-op America's *Financial Planning Handbook*

This inexpensive concise handbook gives you a good introduction to investing, provides socially responsible alternatives, and includes a directory of socially responsible financial planners across the country. It's free with a Co-op America membership. *RealMoney* newsletter from Co-op America is also a great resource (*www.realmoney.org*).

☎ (202) 872-5307   💻 www.coopamerica.org

The Social Investment Forum (SIF)

The SIF is a national non-profit organization that promotes socially responsible investing. Their website provides contact information for banks, loan funds, and mutual funds. Their guide to socially responsible financial planners is included in Co-op America's *Financial Planning Handbook* (see Co-op America).

☎ (202) 872-5319   💻 www.socialinvest.org

In Canada

SocialInvestment.ca

Canada's online Resource for Socially Responsible Investment

💻 www.socialinvestment.ca

SHOPPING

What to Buy

Who to Buy it From

Buying Guide

SHOPPING IS A CHERISHED RITUAL in the United States. A weekly pilgrimage to the local mega-mall has become more common than attending religious services. We often use shopping to meet our emotional needs. If we are happy, we go buy ourselves something to celebrate. If we are sad, we go buy something to make ourselves feel better. If we feel lonely, we go to the mall. If we fall in love, we go buy the person something to show our love. Surprisingly, for all the time we Americans think about and spend shopping, we haven't put much thought at all into how all of these purchases affect the world around us.

Every product on your favorite department store's shelf is made of a collection of natural resources that humans have extracted or harvested from the Earth. These raw materials were then transported, processed, and transported again to the store where we see them on the shelf — all with the integral help of our fellow human beings.

This chapter is about transforming the way you look at shopping. It will help you to consider the social and environmental impacts of the products and services that you buy. It will then be up to you to decide how these social and environmental considerations fit into the other factors that are important to you (price, quality, color, features). This may sound a little overwhelming, but in fact we've done a lot of the leg work for you to make sure your decision is as simple as possible. The following suggestions will help you use your purchasing power to support your community, the planet, and the businesses that you would like to see flourish — ones that create safe and positive work environments for employees, pay fair wages, nourish their communities, create quality products, and practice environmental sustainability on a daily basis.

❑ Action: Shop less

For some of us, we shop whether we need something or not. Shopping has become entertainment. Resist the urge to go shopping! When you get bored, do something creative instead of going to the store and buying things you don't need. You'll end up saving hundreds of dollars and hours, avoid accumulating more clutter, and give the planet a much-needed breather.

> When all facets of one person's life are taken into account, it takes almost 120 pounds (54.5 kilograms) of natural resources per day to maintain the lifestyle of the average American.[1]

❑ Action: Buy less stuff

Sometimes it seems as if people in our society are in a contest to see who can fill their house with the most stuff. Although our culture trains us to be consumers, there are many, many benefits to being frugal. Remember, everything you own owns you. Everything you buy you must maintain, store, repair, clean, and perhaps pay insurance on. Our stuff quickly becomes a psychological burden. The more you buy, the more money you need, which increases your work time at the expense of your family and friends. Finally, all of our stuff takes natural resources to produce, making everything we buy environmentally costly. Here are a few pointers to help you buy less stuff:

- ✓ **Fix broken things** Our disposable culture encourages us to replace broken items even when they are relatively easy to fix. Just because you can afford a new lawnmower doesn't mean you shouldn't try to fix your old one.

- ✓ **Reuse stuff** You can reuse many so-called disposable items, such as paint brushes, sandwich bags, and plastic containers.

- ✓ **Borrow from friends** Borrowing saves resources, money, and time and also helps build community. Check out books, movies, and CDs from your local library. Ask your friend if she has a pipe wrench, since you only need it for a day or two.

- ✓ **Ask yourself, Do I really need it?** Advertising makes us feel as if we'll be left out if we don't have the latest gadget or name brand clothing. When it comes down to it, we don't need much of what we buy.

- ✓ **Take a shopping list** Plan ahead before you shop. Decide exactly what you want before you go; otherwise fancy displays, colorful packaging, and salespeople might convince you to buy something you don't need.

- ✓ **Avoid impulse buys** Companies actually design their stores to encourage impulse buying. Do you really need any of that junk that surrounds you in the check-out line? One powerful technique to avoid impulsively buying big purchases, such as a new stereo, is to wait two weeks before you buy it. If you still really want it, then get it.

❏ *Action: Treat workers with respect and courtesy*

No matter where you shop or what you are buying, be sure to treat the employees (and other customers) with dignity, respect, and friendliness. Being treated like a fellow human being is far superior to being treated like an inanimate object or a subordinate. Show your appreciation when someone goes above and beyond the call of duty. Even though it can be difficult, be sure not to take your anger out on workers for policies and products that they did not create. You can complain about a purchase or policy while treating the other person with respect.

WHAT TO BUY

We grow up buying things unconsciously, never giving a second thought to how our purchases affect the world. There are ten basic questions you can ask yourself about any product before buying it:

1. Can I find it used?
2. Will it last a long time?
3. Is it reusable or at least recyclable?
4. What are the item and its packaging made from?
5. How will I dispose of it?
6. Is it toxic?
7. What conditions do the workers who made it work under?
8. How much will it cost to maintain it?
9. Is it a good value?
10. Will my buying it contribute to a better world?

You probably can't answer every one of these questions about every product. That's OK. The point is to increase your awareness and do your best. You won't become a conscious shopper overnight.

> To get 1 ounce (28 grams) of gold, you must excavate 700 tons (635 metric tons) of rock and dirt. Two pounds (one kilogram) of cyanide are subsequently released into the earth during processing.[2]

Five Things to Avoid Buying

1. Precious Metals or Gems	environmentally devastating resource intensive threatens indigenous cultures
2. Tropical Woods: Teak, Mahogany, Rosewood and Ebony	rainforest destructive resource intensive threatens wildlife
3. Styrofoam Products	non-biodegradable toxic production process non-recyclable
4. Products Tested on Animals	many alternative products waste of animal lives animal suffering involved
5. PVC Products	non-biodegradable toxic production process difficult to recycle

❏ *Action: Buy used*

Buying used products is a great way to lessen the demand for natural resources. Buying used books, for example, saves trees as well as money. Some of the more popular used items besides books include compact discs, clothing, and cars. But you can also easily find used appliances, computers, bikes, baby clothes, toys, and furniture. Check out garage sales, thrift and second hand stores, pawnshops, and the classifieds.

When you buy a used item you:

✓ conserve the energy and resources that would have been used to supply you with a new item

✓ promote a sustainable rather than a throwaway society

✓ retain your money for more fulfilling activities

Five Things to Put on Your Shopping List

1. Compact Fluorescent Light Bulbs	less electricity saves money lasts ten times longer
2. NiMH (Nickel Metal Hydride) Rechargeable Batteries	reusable 1000 times less toxic saves money
3. Cloth Napkins and Dish Rags	less waste saves money reusable many times
4. Low-Flow Shower Head	less water used saves money
5. Good Quality Shoes	fewer resources used better labor conditions last longer

eBay   💻 www.ebay.com

eBay is the popular Internet auction site where any registered user can buy or sell virtually anything. It's likely someone is selling exactly what you're looking for, no matter how obscure. You can register and search for free. eBay is also a great place to get rid of the stuff you no longer need.

DON'T GET SUCKERED IN BY SALES

Virtually every occasion gets its own sale: we have Father's Day sales, Labor Day sales, after-Christmas sales, 4th of July sales — the list goes on and on. North America is sale crazy. If you get the Sunday newspaper, you receive a huge stack of colorful inserts advertising cheap goods. Sales are clever ploys to get you to buy stuff you don't need. Just because you can get a brand-new Thighmaster for $19.95 doesn't mean you need one!

❏ **Action: Buy durable products**

In North America, we demand cheap goods and we get what we pay for. The saying, They just don't make things like they used to, is true judging by the amount of broken and worn-out junk clogging our landfills. In the long run, it's better to spend a little more money for more durable goods that you don't have to repair or replace all the time. Every time you replace a broken item, you use more natural resources.

It only takes a little research to determine a product's quality. You can find issues of *Consumer Reports* at your local library that you can use to compare models' reliability and quality.

❏ **Action: Buy reusable products**

If you had to stand in the middle of a landfill surrounded by mountains of garbage as far as you could see, breathing in the stench of rotting refuse, you would quickly reconsider buying disposable products. It's easy to throw things away because we never have to see them again; our garbage just 'disappears.' By purchasing reusable items, you save landfill space, money, and natural resources that go into more disposable products.

❏ **Action: Buy products with eco-packaging**

Product packaging sometimes requires more resources than the product itself. Some important questions to ask yourself before you buy are What is the packaging made of? and What will I do with it when I'm done? Whenever possible, buy products with less packaging (for example, buy in bulk), packaging made from recycled materials, packaging you can recycle, or biodegradable packaging.

AVOID	BUY
Disposable razors	Reusable razors
Disposable batteries	Rechargeable batteries
Paper towels/paper napkins	Dishtowels/cloth napkins
Disposable dishes and silverware	Washable dishes and ware
Bottled water	Water filters
Bleached paper filters	Cloth or metal coffee filters
Plastic baggies and wrap	Tupperware
Aerosol air fresheners	Natural fresheners
Battery-powered watches	Solar or self-winding watches
Disposable cameras	Digital or 35mm cameras
Disposable chopsticks	Reusable chopsticks

❑ *Action: Read the label*

If you find yourself uncertain about a particular product's environmental and social effects, or you are trying to decide among a number of brands that are offering relatively similar goods, it's time to check the product label. Key words may help you to make a more informed decision about your purchase. Here are a few examples of labels to keep an eye out for:

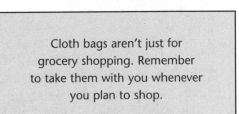

Cloth bags aren't just for grocery shopping. Remember to take them with you whenever you plan to shop.

Recyclable This label is almost meaningless. Almost everything is either theoretically recyclable or biodegradable. This may be an attempt to 'greenwash' the product.

Biodegradable An important label to look for when buying cleaning products like detergents. Be aware that this term has a history of abuse by some corporations. For example, despite what the label may say, there are no plastics that are biodegradable, period.

Recycled Content A percentage of recycled content is a good start, but this can include all kinds of materials (such as sawdust) that are merely by-products that are used rather than thrown away in production. Post-consumer content is the real key label to look for.

Post-Consumer Content   The percentage of post-consumer recycled content is the actual percentage of material that comes from what we traditionally think of as 'recycled' sources. This is where all that recycling you do at home or at the office shows up.

Soy-Based Inks Most of the traditional inks used in the process of printing are at some level toxic to the environment. Soy-based inks are much more eco-friendly.

Unbleached or Non-Chlorine Bleaching Most paper products that pass through our hands are bleached using chlorine, one of the most environmental destructive substances known. More recently, there has been a trend to bleach paper products without using chlorine. These less toxic alternatives provide the whiteness we all like with much less of an environmental impact.

PLASTICS

Not only do plastics produce pollution when they are manufactured but, unlike glass and aluminum which can be recycled virtually forever, plastic can usually only be recycled once, if that. Also, while the market for many recycled materials remains robust, recycling plastics currently has very tenuous economic benefits.

BEST   Avoid plastic items as much as possible. If you are going to buy plastic items, buy things that will last for five years or more.

BETTER   If you must buy disposable plastic products, make sure they are narrow-necked bottles with a #1 or #2 and recycle them when you are done.

WORSE   Some recycling centers are beginning to accept certain #5 containers, such as plastic tubs commonly used for margarine or yogurt. Not all #5 plastics are recyclable.

WORST   #3, #4, #6, #7, and any plastic item that lacks a number will end up in a landfill for sure. Avoid them at all costs. PVC (#3) is especially harmful.

#1 (PETE) plastic soda bottles
#2 (HDPE) plastic milk jugs, shampoos, bottled water
#3 (PVC) shampoos, mouthwashes
#4 (LDPE) toiletries
#5 (PP) margarine tubs, yogurt containers, syrups
#6 (PS) medicinal products
#7 all other plastics

Not/Never Tested On Animals Although companies can abuse this term by contracting out their animal testing, as a rule it is a label worth looking for — especially when shopping for personal care products. Some products may use the phrase 'Cruelty Free' instead.

CFC Free/Ozone Friendly It is important to make sure when buying aerosol products that you purchase items that contain no CFC's or other ozone-destructive gases. In addition, many propellants in aerosol products contribute to more toxic levels of air quality for people. Seek out non-aerosol based pump sprays whenever possible.

Made in the U.S.A./Made in Canada/Union Made Although a product made in the U.S.A. or Canada doesn't guarantee that sweatshop labor was not used, usually the workers are treated and paid more fairly than they would be in the Third World. A union-made product guarantees that the workers involved in the process were not unfairly exploited for their labor.

Certified Organic The U.S. government recently agreed upon a set of national standards that certifies that various consumables have been made without the use of pesticides, genetically altered organisms, or irradiation.

GREENWASHING

Just because a product has 'green' or 'eco' in its title doesn't mean it is any better for the environment. Some companies 'greenwash' their products to improve their image, meaning they present environmentally friendly slogans without really changing their ways. For example, some companies that sell a type of product which never contained CFCs might label their products 'CFC Free' to attract more customers. To avoid greenwashed products, read the label carefully, looking for the terms listed in the previous section.

WHO TO BUY IT FROM

It is just as important to take into account who produces the items you purchase as the type of item being produced. Different companies manufacturing the same product can have radically different impacts on the environment, workers, businesses, and communities. This is where you can shape what kind of world you want to live in with one of the most powerful forces in society: your dollars. If you add up the amount of money you spend on goods and services per year and multiply that by the adult population of the U.S., you can see what kind of power we have available to change things for the better. Think of every purchase you make as a vote. Instead of voting for government representatives, you are voting for the kinds of companies and business practices that you would like to see succeed. Polluters or environmental pioneers, sweatshops or quality jobs: you choose one or the other with every dollar you spend. Reward companies that make a difference while making a buck, and keep your money out of the hands of those that are sacrificing our quality of life for quick profits.

FAIR TRADE

'Fair Trade' is a term used to distinguish companies and organizations who are committed to paying people in the Third World a living wage for their products while ensuring safe working conditions. Initiated in 1949 by American churches, the Fair Trade movement has grown almost as rapidly as global trade itself. A number of major organizations now provide public access to fairly traded goods (coffee, arts and crafts) through mail-order and Internet purchases. If you live in a large city, check their listings to see if there are stores nearby.

Global Exchange	🖥: www.globalexchange.org
Ten Thousand Villages	🖥: www.tenthousandvillages.org
Serrv	🖥: www.serrv.org
Fair Trade Federation	🖥: www.fairtradefederation.org

❑ *Action: Support locally owned independent businesses*

When you buy from large corporations, you support the increasing consolidation of wealth and power in the hands of the few. Chain businesses often take those dollars directly away from smaller local businesses that cannot afford to lose the income. By making your purchases at local business, you spread that wealth out to more local people and increase your community's standard of living. Local businesses tend to rely more on local suppliers and service providers, forming a kind of local economic web of interdependence that creates jobs and a thriving community. Every dollar you spend at a local business helps your community maintain its individual character, uniqueness, and diversity while supporting your neighbors in their quest for the good life. Look in the phone book for local alternatives to large corporate chains.

❑ *Action: Pay in cash at local businesses*

When you are shopping at a locally owned store don't use your credit card — pay in cash or by check. When you charge a purchase, the credit card company and the bank that issued the card take a percentage (often 2 to 3%) off the top (this is also true for debit cards). A business also has to pay a monthly fee for the ability to take different types of credit cards. When you pay with cash or check, you are making sure that the local business gets to keep all of their hard-earned money, instead of having to give a portion to the large corporation that issued the credit card.

❑ *Action: Boycott irresponsible companies*

Boycotts have traditionally been, and continue to be, one of the most powerful forces for changing corporate behavior. Organizations coordinate people nation- or worldwide to withhold their dollars until the executives agree to listen and accommodate the social and/or environmental concerns of their customers. To note some successes: boycotts have helped get General Electric out of the nuclear weapons business, helped save the lives of millions of Third World children, and helped bring an end to apartheid government in South Africa. Keep up to date on the latest boycotts by visiting the Boycott Action Network (www.boycotts.org). Boycotts often take a lot of time and dedication from organizers and protesters. If you agree with the motivation behind a particular boycott, be sure to avoid purchasing products from that company regardless of their overall ratings. Periodically check the status of boycotts to check on the progress of targeted companies.

Boycott Action News (BAN) 🖥 www.boycotts.org
BAN keeps you abreast of all the latest boycotts with news alerts, updates, and victories. Their lists include each company, the reason for the boycott, the products the company makes, and how to contact them (as well as the organizers).

Canadian Labour Congress (CLC) 🖥 www.clc-ctc.ca/boycotts/
CLC has a great page dedicated to informing you about current boycotts. Organized by products, the site includes other great information.

CURRENT MAJOR BOYCOTTS (2000)	
WHO	**WHY**
The Gap, Banana Republic, Old Navy	Redwoods logging and Sweatshop labor
Mitsubishi	Rainforest destruction
Boise Cascade	Old-growth logging
Nike	Sweatshop labor
Philip Morris, Nabisco, Kraft, RJ Reynolds	Cigarette health and false advertising lawsuits

❏ Action: Let companies know how you feel

Whether you are notifying a company of your dissatisfaction with their business practices or praising them for making positive changes, it is important to let them know that how they run their company matters to you, the customer. If you think that one letter could never really make a difference to a big corporation, consider this: Wal-Mart will consider changing policy with as few as 20 letters from their 70 million customers![3] Here are some recommendations to make your letter powerful.

- Tell them that you will stop/start buying their products because of their behavior.
- Make sure that the letter is addressed to the CEO of the company and 'cc' to newspapers, watchdog groups, and government representatives.

- Mention how many other people and organizations share your views and alert the company to the possible effects of a boycott.
- Request environmentally friendly products.

❏ *Action: Shop at home*

There are a number of advantages to shopping at home, either through catalogs or on the Internet, rather than driving to a nearby store or mall. It is less time intensive; you are less apt to be taken to impulse buying; salespeople can't pressure you; and you have access to products that you just won't find in your area. The following list contains some of the best websites and catalogs for finding products that are useful and at the same time make a difference.

Real Goods

Looking for a mail-order company that cares about the environment and can supply you with many household items you might need?

Real Goods is one of the most respected environmental companies around, carrying everything from rechargeable batteries to non-toxic cleaning products. Call them for a catalog or check out their website to find out more.

☎ (800) 762-7325   💻 www.realgoods.com

Greater Good and **Shop for Change**

Internet shopping portals are websites that you choose to start from whenever you decide that you're going to shop online. When you link from those sites to your shopping sites, a certain percentage of your purchase price goes to an organization of your choice, without any extra cost to you. They are where you should start when doing all of your online shopping, no matter what you're looking for. By starting your shopping at Greater Good's site, 5 to 15% of what you spend will go to the charity of your choice at no cost to you. Also try Shop For Change, run by Working Assets, which gives 5% to a whole range of organizations doing good work.

💻 www.greatergood.com   💻 www.shopforchange.com

❏ *Action: Buy products from environmentally and socially responsible companies*

Figuring out who are the good guys and the bad guys in the corporate world can be a time-consuming process. What's more, when you finally get it all sorted out, you still have to change your purchasing habits to better reflect your values. We've tried to take out that initial hardship by doing much of the research for you with our Better World Buying Guide. After thorough investigation, cross-comparisons and synthesis, we've created a list of good and bad companies that is both practical and up-to-date.

Our list rates companies on a relative scale from POOR (the most social-ly irresponsible) to EXCELLENT (the most socially responsible). We've con-sidered research that rates these companies on many issues, including: diversity of employees and management, charitable contributions, commu-nity involvement, working conditions, involvement with oppressive regimes, environmental stewardship, corporate citizenship awards, and on-site daycare.

Three Ways To Use Our Socially Responsible Shopping List:

1. Go through each product category and see if you can make product choices that would be more socially conscious than what you are buy-ing now.

2. Pick out at least one product category and commit yourself to buying from a company rated EXCELLENT. We've provided web addresses for those products in the EXCELLENT category that you may not be able to find locally.

3. Avoid as many products as possible made by companies in the POOR category.

We've used over 20 different sources to rank products and companies. Here are some of the most valuable sources of data:

- *Council on Economic Priorities* (www.cepnyc.org) and *Shopping for a Better World*

- *Multinational Monitor* magazine (www.essential.org/monitor)

- *Business Ethics* magazine (www.business-ethics.com)

- *Boycott Action News* (www.boycotts.org) and *Boycott Action Quarterly*

- *Co-op America* (www.coopamerica.org) and *Co-op America Quarterly*

We consider our list to be the most comprehensively researched and up-to-date list available. *Note that all companies/products listed in parentheses are at the bottom of their rating category.*

SHOPPING FOR A BETTER WORLD

If you are looking for the ultimate guide to shopping with a social con-science, nothing comes close to *Shopping For A Better World* ($5.95), put out by the Council on Economic Priorities. Their research on rating the respon-sibility of companies that produce consumer goods has resulted in the most extensive set of ratings available anywhere. See their work at:
🖥 www.responsibleshopper.org

THE BETTER WORLD BUYING GUIDE

SUPERMARKETS	DEPARTMENT STORES
SUPERMARKETS	DEPARTMENT STORES
BANANAS/FRUIT	CLOTHES
BEVERAGES	COMPUTERS AND SUPPLIES
CEREAL	ELECTRONICS
CLEANING PRODUCTS	SHOES
COFFEE	TOYS
GENERAL FOOD	
ICE CREAM	
PAPER PRODUCTS	
PET FOOD	
PHARMACEUTICALS/	
PERSONAL CARE	
SOAPS AND COSMETICS	

S U P E R M A R K E T S

Supermarkets

EXCELLENT	Wild Oats, Whole Foods, local markets
GOOD	(A&P), (Safeway), (Von's), (Giant Food)
FAIR	Kroger, Ralphs, City Markets, Food 4 Less, King Soopers, Save-Mor, (Albertson's), (Lucky's), (Osco), (Savon)
POOR	(Wal-Mart), (Winn-Dixie), (Thriftway)

CONTACT INFORMATION
💻 www.wildoats.com 💻 www.wholefoodsmarket.com

Bananas / Fruit

EXCELLENT	Any organic brand
GOOD	Chiquita, Dole
POOR	Del Monte

Beverages

EXCELLENT	Odwalla, Horizon Organic, Honest Tea
GOOD	**Pepsi:** Mountain Dew, Slice, Tropicana, All Sport, Aquafina, Mug Root Beer; (Celestial Seasonings); (**Anheiser-Busch:**Budweiser, O'douls, Michelob)
FAIR	**Coors:** Naked Juice, Five Alive, Fruitopia, Powerade, Surge, Gatorade, Sunny Delight, (V8); (**Coca Cola:** Sprite, Dasani, Hi-C, Minute Maid)
POOR	Country Time, Kool-Aid, Tang, Lipton, (**Miller:** Genuine Draft)

CONTACT INFORMATION: 💻 www.odwalla.com
💻 www.horizonorganic.com 💻 www.honestea.com

Cereal

Look for:	Organic Non-GMO
GOOD	**General Mills:** Cheerios, Wheaties; (**Kellogg's:** Crispix, Rice Crispies)
FAIR	**Quaker:**Oats, Cap'n Crunch
POOR	(**Post:** Grape Nuts, Raisin Bran); (**Nabisco:** Shredded Wheat)

Cleaning Products

Look for:	Phosphate Free Non-Petroleum No Chlorine Biodegradable Non-Toxic Ammonia Free Non-Aerosol Not/Never Tested on Animals
EXCELLENT	Seventh Generation, Ecover, Allens Naturally
GOOD	**SC Johnson:** Windex, Pledge, Shout; **Colgate-Palmolive:** Ajax, Murphy's Oil Soap, Fab; (**Proctor & Gamble:** Cheer, Dawn, Tide)
FAIR	**Clorox:** Pine-Sol, S.O.S., 409, Tilex, Liquid-Plumr
POOR	**Unilever:** All, Wisk

CONTACT INFORMATION: 💻 www.seventhgen.com
💻 www.ecover.com 💻 www.allensnaturally.com

Coffee

Look for: Organic Shade Grown Bird Friendly Fair Trade
            Cooperative Sustainable

EXCELLENT	Equal Exchange, Thanksgiving Coffee Co., Adam's Organic, Café Campesino, Green Mountain
GOOD	(**Starbuck's:** Frappuccino)
FAIR	(**Procter & Gamble:** Folgers, Millstone, MJB)
POOR	**Nestle:** Hills Bros, Nescafe, Taster's Choice; (International Coffees), (Sanka), (Master Blend), (Maxwell House), (Brim), (General Foods), (Gevalia), (Yuban), (most store brands)

CONTACT INFORMATION:

🖥 www.equalexchange.com 🖥 www.thanksgivingcoffee.com
🖥 www.adamsorganiccoffees.com 🖥 www.cafecampesino.com
🖥 www.greenmountaincoffee.com

General Food

EXCELLENT	Newman's Own, Eden Foods, Horizon Organic, Stonyfield Farms
GOOD	**General Mills:** Bisquick; **Pillsbury:** Green Giant; Betty Crocker; Frito-Lay; (**Kellogg's:** Eggo, Pop-tarts); (**Proctor & Gamble:** Jif, Pringles)
FAIR	**Quaker:** Rice-a-Roni, Aunt Jemima; Hershey's; **Campbell Soup:** Prego, Pepperidge Farm; (**Best Foods:** Skippy, Boboli, Mazola), (**H.J. Heinz:** Weight Watchers, Ore-Ida, Stouffers)
POOR	Nestle; Del Monte; **Lipton:** Ragu; **Borden:** Classico; Tyson; Bird's Eye; Hunt's; **ConAgra:** Healthy Choice, Banquet, Van Camp's, Peter Pan; **Interstate Bakeries:** Hostess, Wonder, Roman Meal; (**Nabisco:** Oreo); (Post); (**Kraft:** Tombstone); (**Smithfield Foods:** John Morrell)

CONTACT INFORMATION

🖥 www.newmansown.com 🖥 www.edenfoods.com
🖥 www.horizonorganic.com 🖥 www.stonyfield.com

Ice Cream

EXCELLENT	Ben & Jerrys, Newmans Own
GOOD	Haagen-Dazs, (Starbucks)
FAIR	Dove
POOR	Borden, Meadow Gold, (Breyer's), (Good Humor)

Paper Products

Look for:	Post-Consumer Recycled Content Non-Chlorine Bleaching
EXCELLENT	Seventh Generation
GOOD	**Kimberly-Clark:** Kleenex, Scott; (**Proctor & Gamble:** Charmin, Puffs)
FAIR	Mead; International Paper; **Fort James**: Brawny, Northern, Dixie; **Georgia Pacific:** Angel Soft, Coronet; (Weyerhauser)
POOR	Boise Cascade; Westvaco; (Stone Container)

CONTACT INFORMATION 🖳 www.seventhgen.com

Pet Food

GOOD	**Colgate-Palmolive:** Science Diet, Hill's; (**Proctor & Gamble:** Eukanuba, Iams)
FAIR	(**H.J. Heinz:** 9-lives, Kibbles 'n Bits)
POOR	**Ralston-Purina:** Meow Mix, Purina, Butcher's Blend; (**Nabisco:** Milk-Bone)

Pharmaceuticals / Personal Care

Look for:	Non-Aerosol Not/Never Tested On Animals
GOOD	**Johnson & Johnson:** Band-Aid, Tylenol, Stayfree, Carefree, Imodium A-D, Mylanta; **Kimberly-Clark:** Huggies, Pull-ups, Kotex, Lightdays; (**Bristol-Myers Squibb:** Bufferin, Excedrin); (**Pfizer:** Ben-Gay); (**Procter & Gamble:** Pampers, Luvs, Nyquil, Pepto-Bismol, Scope, Tampax)
FAIR	**Warner-Lambert:** Listerine, Lubriderm; **Schering-Plough:** Coppertone, Dr. Scholls; **Gillette:** Oral B;

(**SmithKline Beecham:** Oxy, Milk of Magnesia, Tums, Sucrets)

POOR   **American Home Products:** Advil, Anacin, Chapstick, Robitussin; (**Pharmacia & Upjohn:** Cordaid, Dramamine, Kaopectate, Rogaine, (**Chesebrough-Ponds:** Vaseline, Q-tips)

Soaps and Cosmetics

Look for: Non-Aerosol Not/Never Tested on Animals

EXCELLENT   Tom's of Maine, The Body Shop, Seventh Generation, Kiss My Face, Aveda, Aubrey Organics, Ecco Bella

GOOD   **Avon:** Skin So Soft; **Colgate-Palmolive:** Irish Spring, Softsoap, Speed Stick, Colgate; **Johnson & Johnson:** Neutrogena; (Ban); (**Proctor & Gamble:** Clearasil, Cover Girl, Ivory, Oil of Olay, Pert, Secret, Sure, Vidal Sassoon, Crest, Old Spice)

FAIR   **Pfizer:** Barbasol; **Gillette:** Right Guard; (**Helene Curtis:** Suave, Finesse, Degree); (**Dial:** Breck, Tone)

POOR   **Alberto-Culver:** VO5, St. Ives; **Estee Lauder:** Clinique; (Revlon); (**Chesebrough-Ponds:** Dove, Ponds, Brut, Lever 2000)

CONTACT INFORMATION
- www.tomsofmaine.com
- www.bodyshop.com
- www.seventhgen.com
- www.kissmyface.com
- www.aveda.com
- www.aubreyorganics.com

DEPARTMENT STORES

Department Stores

EXCELLENT   (Ikea)

GOOD   (Target); (Mervyn's); (Dayton's); (Hudson's); (Nordstrom)

FAIR   JC Penney; Macy's; Bloomindale's; (Sears); (Yonkers); (Sak's 5th Avenue)

POOR   Sam's Club; Kmart; Weinstock's; Joslin's; Kohl's; Ward's; Filene's; Foley's; Lord & Taylor; Dillard's;

> Service Merchandise; (Wal-Mart); (Marshall's);
> (TJ Maxx)

CONTACT INFORMATION

💻 www.ikea.com

Clothes

Look for: Made in U.S.A. Organic Recycled Content

EXCELLENT	Deva Lifewear; Eco-Organics; Maggie's Organics; Grass Roots; GAIAM; Savers; Buffalo Exchange; Hempy's; Knowsweat; Natural Selections; Tomorrow's World; Under the Canopy; Wildlife Works
GOOD	Patagonia; Timberland; Levi's; Eileen Fisher; Cutter & Buck; (LL Bean); (Liz Claiborne); (Bass); (Van Heusen); (J. Crew)
FAIR	Land's End; Nicole Miller; Champion; Nike; Hanes; Eddie Bauer; (Benetton); (The Gap); (Banana Republic); (Old Navy)
POOR	The Limited; Esprit; Guess; Wrangler; Lee; Polo; Fruit of the Loom; Victoria's Secret; Talbot's; Brittania; Structure; Express; Lerner; BVD; Gitano; Ralph Lauren; Russell; Jansport; most discount brands; (Perry Ellis); (Calvin Klein)

CONTACT INFORMATION

💻 www.devalifewear.com   💻 www.eco-organics.com
💻 www.gaiam.com   💻 www.g-roots.com
💻 www.organicclothes.com   💻 www.savers.com
💻 www.buffaloexchange.com   💻 www.hempys.com
💻 www.knowsweat.com   💻 www.organicselections.com
💻 www.tomorrowsworld.com   💻 www.underthecanopy.com
💻 www.wildlife-works.com

For the latest information on clothing companies, check out the Clean Clothes Campaign at www.cleanclothes.org.

Computers and supplies

GOOD	IBM; Hewlett Packard; Xerox; (Sony); (Sun); (Intel)
FAIR	Compaq; Micron; Apple; (Dell)
POOR	Microsoft; (Gateway); (NCR)

Electronics

GOOD	Panasonic; Sony
FAIR	Sanyo; Sharp; Toshiba
POOR	(Mitsubishi)

Shoes

Look for:	Made in U.S.A. Recycled Materials Hemp Content
EXCELLENT	Eco-organics; Birkenstock; Eco Dragon; (Red Wing Shoes)
GOOD	Timberland; New Balance: Made in U.S.A. models; (Reebok); (Rockport)
FAIR	Nike, Adidas, Stride Rite, Keds, Sperry, Champion, (New Balance), (K-Swiss), (Puma)
POOR	LA Gear; Converse; Florsheim; Van's; Saucony; Skechers; Foot Joy; (Brands from department stores and discount shoe stores)

CONTACT INFORMATION
🖳 www.eco-organics.com   🖳 www.birkenstock.com
🖳 www.ecodragon.com   🖳 www.redwingshoe.com

Toys

EXCELLENT	Natural Toys
GOOD	Toys R Us; (Mattel); (Fisher Price); (Hot Wheels); (Matchbox); (Tyco)
FAIR	(Disney); (Hasbro); (Milton Bradley); (Tonka); (Parker Bros)
POOR	KB Toys

CONTACT INFORMATION
🖳 www.naturaltoys.com

* For a free pocket-size copy of this shopping guide go to
www.betterworldhandbook.com

FOOD

Buying Groceries

Eating

Planting a Garden

A S WE GO THROUGH THE DRIVE-THROUGH at our favorite fast-food joint or pop a frozen dinner into the microwave, we seldom think about where our food came from, how it was produced, and how our demand for it affects the rest of the world. We're usually thinking about taste, price, and convenience. Our fast-paced culture encourages us to eat at fast food chains, shop at one-stop supermarkets, and buy instant meals encased in layers of packaging. Though the familiarity of Burger King and Pizza Hut is sometimes comforting, and supermarkets and prepackaged meals are often convenient, they all have very real downsides that we often overlook. Cities lose some of their individual character when they all have the same restaurants. Prepackaged meals take the creativity out of food and leave behind tremendous waste. Cooking and eating degenerate from enjoyable, sacred experiences to little more than pit stops for maintaining our physical selves. Most of us love to eat, but few of us consider how this love can make our lives more fulfilling and the world a better place.

This chapter will give you some suggestions on how your grocery shopping, your eating habits, and the growing of your own food can make a difference in the world. What we eat is one of our most ingrained habits, and it can be a difficult area to change. Choose to follow only those suggestions that are reasonable for you. As in the rest of the book, gradual change is often longer lasting and thus makes more of a difference in the long run than abrupt change. Focus on changes that are reasonable and sustainable for you.

BUYING GROCERIES

❑ Action: Buy organic food

Organic foods are available in almost every grocery store, including many of the major chains. You can find everything from organic produce, pasta, and eggs to milk, meat, and herbs. What does the 'organic' label mean? In order to earn the U.S. Department of Agriculture (USDA) organic label, producers may use no chemical pesticides, growth-enhancing chemicals, or genetic modification on their crops. Farmers who raise animals organically avoid steroids, hormones, and antibiotics; use organically grown grains as feed; and generally treat livestock better than do non-organic, corporate feedlots.

Organic food may be more expensive than non-organic. If this is a concern for you, start out by buying a few organic items that differ little in price from conventional foods. Remember, there are reasons some foods are cheap: employers may pay workers lower wages, chemicals tend to increase crop yields, and organic foods are often not produced in the same massive volumes as non-organic foods. Your budget may allow you to purchase only a few items of organic food, but small changes are what ultimately shift whole industries! Organic foods are the fastest-growing segment of the food industry, and prices are quickly dropping as consumer demand rises.

> **BY BUYING ORGANIC FOODS YOU:**
> - lessen cruelty to animals
> - avoid health-threatening chemicals
> - prevent damaging pesticides from entering the environment
> - help maintain fertile soil
>
> *Such a small choice has many positive effects!*

❑ Action: Reduce food packaging by buying in bulk

Have you ever bought a box of snacks and discovered that you have to tear through three layers of cellophane and cardboard to get at the food? All of this packaging ends up somewhere, sometimes taking hundreds of years to biodegrade. By purchasing bulk items and those with less packaging, you save energy, resources, and landfill space all in one fell swoop. Most grocery stores have a bulk food section.

❑ Action: Bring your own cloth bags

"Would you like paper or plastic?" What a perplexing question for the environmentally conscious consumer. Hmmm…paper uses up forests, but plastic comes from petroleum, a non-renewable resource. It's actually a trick question because the real choice is not even listed — the cloth bag. It is reliable, reusable, has sturdy handles, and will even get you a small discount at many stores. Shopping with reusable bags helps to save trees and other natural resources right from the start. Buy a couple of bags and take them wherever you go. Check out your local grocery store for bags to purchase.

> You may want to keep some extra bags in your car trunk just in case you forget!

❑ Action: Support local growers and grocers

If you live in a small town, you may have noticed that it's pretty tough for small, locally owned grocers to stay in business. Supermarket chains can charge less for their food because they carry such a tremendous volume. Small grocers have a tough time competing. Supporting local grocers and farmers offers several advantages over supermarket shopping. First, you are supporting your local economy rather than a multinational corporation. You can see that your purchases are directly benefiting members of your own community. Second, shopping locally enables you to find out more about the food you buy, such as where it comes from and how it is produced. Producers at a farmers' market are usually more than willing to share how they grew their crops. By educating yourself about your food, you may be able to avoid pesticides and other chemicals large companies often use. Third, local grocers are more likely to stock locally grown food, which cuts down on the tremendous amount of energy wasted and pollution created in the transportation process. Finally, shopping at a farmers' market, joining a food cooperative, or being involved in community supported agriculture is often less expensive than shopping at a supermarket.

> The food on an average American's dinner plate has traveled 1400 miles (2250 kilometers).[1]

FARMERS' MARKETS

Farmer's markets are locally run, seasonal, open-air markets that showcase local growers. Many farmers' markets also feature local artists' wares. Farmers' markets help build community by allowing growers and consumers to educate and support each other one-on-one. They support family farmers and allow you to purchase fresh food that hasn't spent weeks in storage or on transport trucks. To find the farmers' market nearest you, contact:

U.S. Department of Agriculture, Agricultural Marketing Service
☎ (202) 720-8998 🖳 www.ams.usda.gov/farmersmarkets

FOOD COOPERATIVES

Food cooperatives (co-ops) are non-profit food businesses owned by their members. A food co-op is a group of people who order food together in bulk. No one owns the co-op, and members make decisions together, often purchasing organic, locally produced, and healthful foods. You get exactly what you want at a reduced price, avoid corporate grocery stores, and build community with your fellow members. To find the food cooperative nearest you, contact:

Common Ground Food Co-op
☎ (217) 352-3347   🖳 www.prairienet.org/co-op/directory

COMMUNITY SUPPORTED AGRICULTURE (CSA)

Community Supported Agriculture creates partnerships between farms and communities of consumer-supporters who help produce, harvest, and consume the food. This direct relationship lowers the cost for consumers, cuts out the corporate middleman, reduces food travel time, and ensures that growers make enough money to survive. Members often help tend or harvest the crops, creating a more direct relationship between consumers and their food. Most CSAs practice organic or bio-dynamic farming to help maintain soil fertility and produce healthy foods. To find the CSA nearest you, contact:

Robyn Van En Center for CSA Resources
☎ (717) 264-4141 Ext.3247   🖳 www.csacenter.org

❑ *Action: Support socially conscious food companies*

Some food companies are trying to make a difference. These companies consistently show their dedication to a clean environment and a just workplace. You can support good companies by *buy*cotting them — consistently choosing to buy their products over others. To find an extensive ranking of companies and how we evaluate them, read the SHOPPING chapter. Use the following short list of food companies and grocery stores to send a message with your dollars; they'll hear you loud and clear.

Food Companies

The Best	*The Worst*
Newman's Own	Tyson Chicken
Kellogg's	Hormel, Dinty Moore
General Mills	Nestle, Carnation, Libby's
Ben & Jerry's	Kraft, Maxwell House,
Quaker Oats	General Foods, Post, Nabisco

Supermarkets

The Best	*The Worst*
Whole Foods	Food Lion

Wild Oats   Albertson's
                                   Wal-Mart

To keep up to date on the best and worst food companies, visit the following website: 💻 www.cepnyc.org and www.boycotts.org.

RESOURCES

Shopping for a Better World. Council on Economic Priorities, 2000.
💻 www.cepnyc.org

For a simple, pocket-sized book that will help you choose great companies, we strongly recommend *Shopping for a Better World*, considered the bible of socially conscious shopping. It rates companies on several criteria, including environmental record, workplace opportunity, community outreach, animal rights, donations to charity, and many more.

EATING

Eating is perhaps the daily ritual we most take for granted. Although changing our eating habits may seem difficult, even small changes will produce significant results. Being conscious of where our food comes from, how it is produced, how it affects our bodies, and how it affects the lives of others reconnects us with the world around us.

❑ *Action: Prepare and eat food with others*

Think of how you can make meal time the most meaningful and enjoyable part of your day. Preparing and eating meals with others can be emotionally and spiritually satisfying. Imagine if everyone experienced eating as a sacred activity and a way to build a sense of community with others and a connection with the world around us. Be creative with your meals! Try new recipes and prepare meals without any instructions. Don't forget to turn the TV off so that you can fully enjoy your meal with your friends and family.

> Try to avoid using disposable dishes, utensils, and napkins whether you are at home, at work, or on a picnic. Keep a set of silverware with you in your bag, backpack, briefcase, or purse.

❑ *Action: Support locally owned restaurants*

When you eat at locally owned, non-chain restaurants, you benefit your community in the same ways as when you buy locally. Have you ever driven cross-country and noticed towns that look strikingly similar to the last 27 you passed: one Burger King, one Bank of America, one Wal-Mart, and one Texaco station? Having McDonald's and Taco Bells everywhere around the world eliminates much of the cultural variety that we all value. Over half of the U.S. population lives within a three-minute drive to McDonald's.[2]

Avoiding chain restaurants prevents the 'McDonaldization' of the world by preserving the uniqueness of your town. Plus, you may have noticed that many local restaurant owners take more pride in their service and how their food tastes!

❑ *Action: Eat more fruits, vegetables, grains, and raw foods*

The U.S. Department of Agriculture, National Research Council, the National Cancer Institute, and the American Cancer Society all recommend that you eat generous amounts of fruits and vegetables for your health.[3] Plant foods contain fiber, antioxidants, vitamins and minerals, low amounts of fat, and no cholesterol; while meats contain cholesterol, high amounts of fat, no fiber, and many artificial and toxic chemicals.

When you eat raw foods such as fruits, nuts, vegetables, and sprouted grains, it allows your body to access the maximum potential vitamins and minerals available from the plant. Raw foods also require fewer natural resources to produce and prepare. Check out   www.living-foods.com to learn more.

❑ *Action: Eat less meat*

If, like many of us, you grew up in a typical American household, you may believe that a meal just isn't a meal unless it's served up with a fair-sized piece of meat. For many of us a meat dish is the meal; the bread, salads, and vegetables are just side dishes. Our insistence on eating meat every day, often several times each day, creates problems for the environment, workers, our own health, and other people around the world. And due to modern factory farming techniques, it also causes the unnecessary suffering of animals. For one or more of these reasons, millions of people have already reduced the amount of meat

> Animal agriculture causes 80% of the world's annual deforestation.[8]

they eat![4] In fact, two out of every three people in the world lead healthy lives eating primarily meatless diets.[5] Once you learn about the environmental, hunger, labor, and health issues surrounding meat, you may want to join them!

To give you an idea of the different impacts each kind of meat has on the world, take a look at the Overall Impact Assessment — a symbolic representation of the relative impacts of each type of food based on environmental damage, resource consumption, and worker treatment. As you can see, beef has the most overall negative impact on the world. In fact, reducing your beef consumption may be the single most powerful action you can take in this whole book! Read on to find out why.

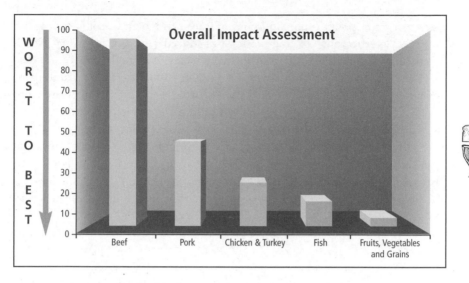

THE ENVIRONMENT

By eating less meat you help preserve the environment. Meat production consumes a tremendous amount of natural resources and creates a great deal of waste. In fact, we use about one-fourth of the Earth's land to graze cattle![6] A reduced demand for meat would mean we could use this land to raise grain, which would feed more people with greater efficiency, and we would help protect the world's grasslands from overgrazing. At the same time, there would be less incentive for the people of Central and South America to create grazing land for cattle by burning down rainforests. Closer to home, cattle grazing has eliminated or severely threatened more plant species in the western U.S. than any other cause and is the number one cause of soil erosion on western public lands.[7] That trend could be slowed or halted if we all lowered our demand for meat.

> ### USING OUR NATURAL RESOURCES WISELY
> Raising livestock for meat is one of the most inefficient uses of land. One acre (0.4 hectares) of land could produce 50,000 pounds (22,680 kilograms) of tomatoes, 40,000 pounds (18,144 kilograms) of potatoes, 30,000 pounds (13,608 kilograms) of carrots or just 250 pounds (113 kilograms) of beef.[9] To produce a year's supply of beef for a family requires over 260 gallons (1,182 liters) of fossil fuel, or approximately one gallon (4.5 liters) of gasoline per pound (454 grams) of grain-fed beef. Finally, it takes 2,500 gallons (11,365 liters) of water to produce one pound (454 grams) of beef; to produce one pound of wheat requires 25 gallons (113 liters).[10]

Though not as destructive as beef production, hog and chicken production cause their own environmental problems. Hog waste has become a major source of water pollution in a number of states. In North Carolina alone, 2.5 tons (2.3 metric tons) of hog waste is produced annually for every North Carolinian.[11] Spills have occurred in many states, contaminating our waterways and killing fish. It takes about 660 gallons (3000 liters) of water to produce a pound (454 grams) of chicken.[12] Farmers also often apply waste from chicken factories to crop fields as a form of fertilizer, which produces similarly destructive results as the runoff ends up as water pollution.[13]

Commercial fishing presents us with a different kind of environmental challenge: the misuse of our marine resources. The U.N.'s Food and Agriculture Organization estimates that, due to wasteful fishing practices, 57 billion pounds (27 billion kilograms) of sea life is caught unintentionally every year and thrown away.[14] The Environmental Defense Fund reports that 13 of the world's 17 major fishing grounds are depleted or in serious decline, due to overfishing.[15]

EATING SEAFOOD RESPONSIBLY

Based on research done by The Audubon Society on responsible commercial fishing practices, we have created a guide to make sure that your seafood choices will help ensure the long-term preservation of sea life.[16]

EXCELLENT	Mahi Mahi, Pacific cod, catching your own
GOOD	Catfish, Crawfish, Pacific halibut, Pacific pollock, Salmon [wild Alaskan only], Striped bass
FAIR	Calamari, Clams, Crab, Lobster, Mussels, Oysters, Sole, Tuna
POOR	Flounder, Grouper, Haddock, Marlin, Orange Roughy, Salmon [all other], Scallops, Sea bass[Chilean],Shark, Shrimp, Snapper, Swordfish

For more detailed information, check out Audubon's *Seafood Guide* online at 💻 www.audubon.org/campaign/lo/seafood/index.html.

WORLD HUNGER

Nearly 29% of us, or 1.6 billion people, are undernourished.[17] The Food and Agriculture Organization reports that more than 800 million people go hungry each year.[18] Between 40 and 60 million people starve to death each year, many of them children.[19] Despite these startling statistics, we feed 72% of all grain grown in the world to livestock.[20] In fact, due to the high demand for beef in the First World, agribusiness has transformed much of Central and South America's agricultural land into pastures for raising beef that gets exported to the United States, Australia, and Europe. The end result is that the wealthy of the world eat grain fed beef while over a billion people go hungry each day due to a lack of grain.

> ## TREATING WORKERS FAIRLY
>
> Americans who work in meat-packing and processing plants face some of the poorest working conditions. Most workers can afford little or no health care, yet their repetitive motion, high speed, physically demanding, assembly line jobs injure one-third of all workers every year — the highest injury rate of any industry.[21] When these workers can no longer function effectively, they are laid off in lieu of new, healthy workers. This has led to one of the highest turnover rates of any job in the U.S. Most packing plants are non-union and pay as little as $5 per hour.[22] Hog farms provide particularly dangerous workplace environments. Seventy percent of swine confinement workers suffer from respiratory ailments, such as chronic bronchitis.[23]

HEALTH

Many of us have already begun to realize the health benefits of eating less red meat. Diets high in saturated fats and cholesterol have been implicated in numerous medical studies as significantly contributing to a high rate of heart attacks, cancer (such as breast and colon cancer), and strokes.[24] The average U.S. man eating a typical meat-based diet has a 50% chance of dying from heart disease, the number one killer of people living in the U.S.[25] In addition, the vast majority of factory farms use antibiotics, hormones, and other drugs in beef, pork, and chicken production. Each year in the U.S. alone, contaminated chicken kills at least 1,000 people and sickens as many as 80 million others.[26]

ANIMALS

Unfortunately, the image of the small, family farm stocked with a fairly content variety of animals no longer corresponds to the reality of modern livestock conditions. Many animals live in less-than-humane factory farms their entire lives. Most breeding sows are kept in crates for almost their entire lives and 71% of pigs suffer from pneumonia.[27] More than 90% of chickens and eggs are raised on crowded factory farms.[28]

> A common myth is that substantial amounts of meat are essential to provide our protein needs. Actually, the average American gets almost twice the amount of protein necessary each day.[29]

BREAKING A PATTERN

Though there are many compelling reasons to reduce our meat consumption, we may find it difficult to break a pattern we've had since early childhood. The first step might be to not eat meat one day each week or to eat it only for dinner. Remember, it is important to make changes that are right for you. Gradual transformations that you feel comfortable with will likely last. Sudden, drastic changes often lead to frustration and giving up entirely. Think of reducing the meat in your diet as an opportunity rather than as a restriction. You have the chance to explore many new recipes you may not have considered before.

ALTERNATIVES

If you want to cut back on your meat but think you'll miss the taste, consider meat alternatives. Soy chicken nuggets, burgers, sausage, bacon, hot pockets, lunchmeat, ground beef, hot dogs, and chicken patties are all readily available in your local market. There are also healthy alternatives to dairy products, such as milk, cheese, and ice cream that tend to be easier on the planet and taste good, too!   Morningstar Farms, Eden Foods, Rice Dream, Gardenburger, and Fantastic Foods are just a few good brands too look for.

> **By eating less meat you can:**
> • help conserve our natural resources
> • contribute to the well-being of people in the Third World
> • improve your overall health
> • lessen cruelty to animals

PLANTING A GARDEN

There is only one way to know, without a doubt, where your food comes from and how it is processed — by growing it yourself. You may be thinking that you don't have the time, the space, or even any idea where to begin. Gardening is much easier you think, and with a little creativity you can garden just about anywhere. You can easily turn part of your lawn into a garden, even if it's just a small spot next to your house. Perhaps most importantly, gardening can be a tremendous source of relaxation, pride, fulfillment, and connection with the Earth.

❑ *Action: Plant an organic garden*

You can plant an organic vegetable garden that maintains the integrity of the earth. You get to eat and marvel at the fruits of your labor.

The following tips are vital to a healthy garden. If you follow them faithfully, you shouldn't need expensive and harmful fertilizers and bug killers.

- **Rebuild your soil** Healthy soil is the key to gardening. The best thing you can do is add compost from your compost pile. If possible, buy or gather manure from non-intensive/organic farms. Avoid the manure from factory feedlots that is often sold at your local greenhouse or hardware store. Maintain a healthy mineral balance in your soil by adding rock powders. Ask your greenhouse operator about the needs of soil in your particular area and buy only 100% organic fertilizers and humus.
- **Rotate crops** Certain plants require more or less of particular nutrients

in the soil. By planting each of your crops in a different spot every year, you won't deplete a nutrient in one particular area of your garden. Your plants will thrive.

- **Water early in the morning** Water your garden early in the morning so the soil and plants have time to absorb it before the sun makes the water evaporate. Drip irrigation systems can save 50% of your lawn water usage.[30]

- **Introduce beneficial insects** Ladybugs, green lacewings, and trichogramma wasps help control other pesky insects. Ask your local greenhouse how to order your new friends.

- **Hoe and weed your garden** Once each week you should take the time to pull weeds in your garden. Hoe to break up the soil and allow oxygen to get to the plants' roots more readily. Weeding and hoeing are good exercise and a chance to be outdoors, rather than a chore. Plus, you're doing the Earth a favor by avoiding weed killers.

RESOURCES

CFS Specialties, Inc.

CFS Specialties makes 100% organic fertilizers for both lawn and garden. ☎ (800) 822-6671   🖳 cfspecial.com

Gardens Alive! Catalog

The *Gardens Alive! Catalog* is a great source for organic gardening supplies (including fertilizers, weed and pest controls, lawn care products, etc.).Write *Gardens Alive!*,   5100 Schenley Place, Lawrenceburg, IN 47025, U.S.A.
☎ (812) 537-8651

❏ *Action: Be an urban gardener*

If you live in a place without space for a garden, you have several options. First, many cities offer community garden plots. Call your local parks and recreation department. You can share a space (and the work!) with a friend. Second, you might be able to set planters outside your door or near your building. You can grow a few tomatoes or some flowers in a planter. Third, window boxes provide a small area to grow a few green pepper plants or a few onions. Finally, if you don't have the space or resources for these suggestions, try growing a few herbs in small pots. Some fresh basil or garlic tastes great in many dishes. For more information on community and urban gardening, contact:

American Community Gardening Association
☎ (215) 988-8785   🖳 www.communitygarden.org

PERSONAL

Extraordinary Living
Emotional Well-Being
Spiritual Well-Being
Physical Well-Being
Reflection

SOME PEOPLE MAKE THE WORLD a better place simply through their way of being. Think of someone who inspires peace by his or her presence. Imagine a person in your life who makes you smile just by walking in the door. Envision someone with the outlook of a child, free of concerns, encountering the world with a fresh, open mind. These kinds of people touch us in a way we may not fully understand.

In this book, we explore ways to bring your actions in line with your values in each aspect of life. Each of us can also create a personal way of being in the world that makes it a better place for us, our families, and our communities. We can make changes in the different spheres of our lives and alter how we experience our lives, moment to moment, hour to hour, and day to day.

The Personal chapter encourages you to take action to make your own life extraordinary. Powerful social change begins with powerful individual change. Just think how remarkably different the world would be if more people led fulfilling personal lives. With this in mind, we offer suggestions for transforming your personal consciousness, developing emotional and spiritual well-being, maintaining physical health, and taking time for reflection.

EXTRAORDINARY LIVING

Most of us are mildly content with our lives. Sure, we can imagine some ways life could be better, but overall we get into a comfortable groove and coast along. But what if there was something better? What if certain ways of living could take us beyond our ordinary lives, into a realm of extraordinary possibilities? The actions in this section will empower you to push the limits of your happiness to new heights and make the world a better place simply by your presence.

❑ *Action: Don't sweat the small stuff*

Isn't it crazy how the smallest problems can cause us the greatest frustration? If there's one thing we know for certain, it's that reality is almost never how we expect it to be. In fact, our expectations can cause us a great deal of suffering. We can minimize our suffering by being flexible. Not sweating the small stuff doesn't mean not having any expectations. It simply implies an understanding that reality may not meet our expectations — and that's OK. It means paying attention to our reactions, thinking about them, and making a choice to be flexible. Pretty soon it becomes automatic. And remember, as the old cliché goes, almost everything is small stuff.

❑ *Action: Think and live in color*

Perhaps you've had a friend who was extremely unhappy with his job. He agonized over what to do about his dissatisfaction, quickly concluding he could either quit or just stick it out. How many times in our lives do we reduce important decisions or opinions to two options? It's very easy to get stuck at one of two extremes. We've been trained to think in terms of good/bad, right/wrong, black/white. But that's not the way life is! Not only does black and white thinking reduce our own options, it also makes us more judgmental: if I'm right, they must be wrong. Intolerant thinking is evident in many of our society's current conflicts: the abortion debate, affirmative action, gun control, lesbian and gay rights.... You name it, people are entrenched at an extreme that dehumanizes the 'other side.' There are always more than two sides. Try thinking in color. Be open to those who are different than you, explore your options, step outside the norm, and avoid the trap of either/or solutions.

❑ *Action: Commit to a creative life*

Most of us equate creativity with artwork and artists. But creativity applies to all spheres of life, from shopping to family and from food to community. A creative person is able to view ordinary situations in a unique way, create possibilities where there seem to be none, and act outside of the expected or normal realm of action. Creativity is not something some people are born with while others are not. It takes practice. Creative people have to have a commitment to creativity.[1] Take time to explore your creativity in whatever situation you find yourself. Here are a few suggestions:

- Plan a creative party.
- Find a creative way to take a mini-vacation.
- Create your own board game.
- Write your own nursery rhyme, prayer, or riddle.
- Create a way to run all of your errands without using your car.
- Invent a process to teach kids about drugs, sex, or violence.

At least once each week, take time to let your creative energies flow: write, draw, paint, take a dance class, sculpt, play music, cook a new meal, sew — whatever makes your heart sing to the heavens! We are a creative species, meaning we gain fulfillment from bringing our imaginations and skills to life. When you consistently give your creativity an outlet, it will improve your everyday experience. If you don't schedule creative time into your life, chances are you won't take the time.

LIVING OUTSIDE THE BOX

We live in a box. We have an image of how things should be, how we should act, and what is possible and impossible. These images make up the box we live in, the box that limits our possibilities. Consider the American dream: overwork at a job you probably dislike, get rich, buy a bunch of stuff, move into a huge house, have 2.5 kids, retire, and play golf. This dream doesn't allow for much flexibility or individuality, and many of us won't ever be in a position to achieve it.

We generally don't stray too far outside the box society creates for us. Instead, we follow the patterns we've learned from our culture, family, the media, and our friends. Often these patterns aren't as fulfilling as living outside the box might be. Check out these examples, then use your creativity to break out of your box.

✓ Next time you're at the coffee shop, pub, or restaurant, pay for someone else's order.

✓ After work, greet your partner with a dance instead of Hello.

✓ Go for a walk in the rain without an umbrella.

✓ Be the most gracious driver on the planet.

✓ Bike to work in your work clothes, even if you look a bit rumpled when you get there.

✓ The next time you must give a presentation at work, school, or wherever, focus on making it a totally unique experience.

✓ Leave an extra large tip for someone who has given you good service.

❑ *Action: Conquer your fears*

Have you ever really thought about what you're afraid of? Not the big fears, such as flying, spiders, or heights, but the little fears that affect you daily. How many times have you wanted to try something new but faltered because you fear failure? Singing in a choir, writing for the local newspaper, taking a dance class — you name it, someone's afraid of it.

Fear prevents many of us from living extraordinary lives. It limits us, keeping us from our full potential. To live a truly extraordinary life, we must learn to face and manage our fears, because they'll never completely go away. And after you face a fear, you often realize you had nothing to be afraid of.

Common Fears

- I'm not good enough.
- People won't like me.
- They'll think I'm (stupid, unprepared, boring, etc.).
- I'm not a good public speaker.
- People won't like my (artwork, proposal, new idea, etc.).
- I can't do it as well as that person.
- She/he won't find me attractive.
- I'd like to try that, but I probably can't do it.

There will certainly be times when we confront our fears and things don't go our way. If you're not failing once in a while, you're probably not taking the risks necessary to live an extraordinary life! But personal growth and fulfillment require risk, stretching into new territory. So take on your fears and revel in the process.

❑ *Action: Slow down and live in the moment*

Do you write a 'to do' list each morning then rush around all day doing your tasks and checking them off? Sometimes we go so fast that we focus more on how many checks we have than on how to experience the day one moment at a time. At the end of the day, we have a list of scratched-off tasks, but we feel sort of empty. Slowing down and doing less is an important key to fulfillment.

✓ **Be Present** We spend so much time worrying about the future and thinking about the past that we don't fully experience the present. The measure of a fulfilling life is the quality of experience, not the quantity. Focus on whatever you are doing in the moment. Do one thing at a time. Be present to the people around you — it will improve your performance in whatever you do and make your relationships incredible. Choose a few things to do each day, take your time, and do them well.

✓ **Learn to say NO** How many times have you agreed to do something that you knew you really didn't have time for? Perhaps your friend asks you to go shopping or help paint her house on a day you'd rather spend relaxing at home. Many of us have difficulty saying No, and for good reason: we like to help people out and we enjoy being with friends. Too much of a good thing, however, quickly turns fun or helping into an unpleasant burden. Practice saying No to some of the things that take up your time. And don't feel that you always need an excuse! Saying No allows you to put yourself more fully into those activities you choose to do.

❏ Action: Own less stuff

We are a nation of people with insatiable desires for stuff — newer cars, faster computers, stylish clothes, better stereos. Unfortunately, rather than bringing fulfillment, material possessions often create discontent — you're never happy with what you have. More is always better, right? Wrong. After we meet our needs and have a few comforts, extra purchases can actually become burdens to our existence. Everything you own, owns you. You must maintain it, fix it, insure it, wash it, dust it, and worry about it getting stolen or becoming obsolete. Searching for happiness at the car showroom or in the department store will not bring long-term fulfillment (but it will lead to long-term debt).

The acquisition of possessions also keeps our focus on ourselves: what can I get for me? By moderating your desire for material possessions, you liberate your mind from the burdens that come with ownership and free up your energies to live your most deeply held values and make the world a better place.

❏ Action: Treat others as humans, not as objects

Do you ever take the opportunity to talk to the cashier at your grocery store? How about the janitor that cleans your workplace? It's amazing how we treat many of the people in our lives as objects rather than as humans. We see the driver of the car in front of us or the people ahead of us in line as obstacles to us getting something done or as people we would rather not interact with. You can counteract these attitudes by smiling or talking to people in your life you normally wouldn't communicate with. Go out of your way to help people, both strangers and friends. Have patience, especially with folks just doing their jobs. The secretary or receptionist of a business you call isn't responsible for the company policies you may disagree with. The telemarketer that calls during dinner is just doing her or his job, too. There's no point in treating these folks poorly. By treating people like humans instead of objects you are making the world a more humane, loving place.

A good place to start is with smiling. Have you ever noticed how a smiling, cheerful person can instantly brighten your day? Try smiling at people you meet throughout your day — strangers and friends. Who knows, maybe your good cheer will be the turning point for someone who is having a bad day!

❏ *Action: Be the change you wish to see in the world*

As you read this book, chances are that you are beginning to construct a powerful vision of how the world could be a better place. Most of us imagine a more peaceful, caring, and just Earth. You might wish people were more kind, that there were less racism, or that kids received a better education. You can actually be a powerful source of change by living as a citizen of the world you wish to see.

WHO ARE YOUR HEROES?

Many people in our lives have a huge effect on us: teachers, family members, friends, leaders. We often unintentionally take these people for granted. Take this opportunity to reflect on some of these folks. Choose ten people who have made a powerful impression on your life. Then think about how each one of them had such an effect on you — what was it about them? Just imagine, you can have the same powerful effect on people in your life! Now that you've recognized these amazing people, tell them how great they are! Call or write them. You will rock their world.

Create ways that you can bring your better world into being. Here are a few examples:

✓ You wish people had a greater sense of community? Go out of your way to create community where you live.

✓ You envision a more accepting world? Demonstrate acceptance in your daily life.

✓ You believe kids should be a higher priority? Make children a huge priority in your life by spending quality time with them.

One of the most powerful ways to create change around you is through patient, personal example. Your powerful example will create change in others; we guarantee it.

❏ *Action: Live passionately*

People that live with passion seem to have a glow about them. They stand out from the crowd. Sometimes we worry so much about failure, what people will think of us, or if we should have done things differently that we live a mediocre life. To live passionately means to go all out once we make a decision and live full steam ahead. If we fail, then we learn something.

To live passionately also means that we dedicate ourselves to ideals that we are passionate about. Decide what you want your life to be about and then create it! Are you about giving unconditional love to children, bringing beauty into the world with your artwork, singing your heart out at Carnegie Hall, or writing a book that you hope will change the world? Whatever you choose (and it may change over time), make it the reason you get up in the morning. You'll know if you get it right, because it'll make you feel truly alive.

❏ Action: Expand your circle of compassion

Did you know that more than six million children die of malnutrition every year?[2] Or that many inner city kids attend class in hallways and bathrooms because their school has a classroom shortage? Have you heard that 17 to 70 million animals die each year in unnecessary medical and product tests?[3] It's easy to become so wrapped up in our own lives that we fail to recognize the suffering of other living beings.

It is our privilege to ignore others' suffering. Many of us simply tune out the suffering that goes on around us. It's not that we don't care, it's that we simply feel overwhelmed and helpless. Plus, we've got our own problems to deal with, right?

None of us can give our full attention to all the world's problems. However, tuning out and turning off our compassion is the easy way out. Rather than insulating yourself from the world's struggles, try to learn as much as you can. Really think about and empathize with people. We feel very compassionate toward our family, friends, and pets. What if we expanded this circle of compassion to include strangers, people in other countries, animals, and even the whole planet?

> Until we expand the circle of our compassion to all living beings, we will not ourselves find peace.
> — Albert Schweitzer

Compassion produces actions that affect the world. If you attempt to empathize with hurricane victims in Central America or earthquake survivors in India, you're more likely to send aid than if they were just another news item in the 'World' section of the paper. If you develop compassion for women in abusive relationships, perhaps you'll support your local women's shelter with supplies, time, or a donation. If you recognize that the animals that endure cosmetic testing aren't all that different from the animals you keep as pets, maybe you'll buy better cosmetics.

HELP VICTIMS OF NATURAL DISASTERS

When a disaster strikes, people need basic necessities, such as food, clothes, and shelter. They also usually need medical supplies, mental health support, and a feeling of community to overcome their sense of isolation. You can donate to many organizations that help victims of natural disasters. You could also set up a disaster relief collection through your workplace, religious group, or civic organization. Monetary donations are important, of course, but your time and skills are equally important and sometimes more necessary for relief. For information on recent natural disasters and links to disaster relief organizations, see <www.disasterrelief.org>, contact your local Red Cross, or call (800)HELP-NOW. Often it takes disasters to make us realize that we truly are interdependent members of the global community.

EMOTIONAL WELL-BEING

Do you ever feel burnt out? Not just physically but emotionally? Sometimes we spend so much time meeting our material needs (working, maintaining a household, etc.) and the needs of others that we neglect our emotional needs. In many ways we are fragile creatures. All of us fall out of balance. It is crucial that you look after your emotional well-being for your own sense of peace and for your effectiveness as an unstoppable agent of social change.

❏ *Action: Forgive yourself*

Have you ever met someone who is constantly putting herself down? Perhaps she is so stuck in self-guilt and frustration that happiness and fulfillment are the furthest things from her mind. We are often our own worst critics.

Constant criticism and guilt are terrible burdens to bear. They stop us, make us less effective, and prevent growth. Guilt never saved anyone. And our self-criticism sets a bad example for others. If we are negative about ourselves, we send the message that others can be, too. Although it benefits us to reflect on and learn from our mistakes, wallowing in self-blame does not. It is when we can transform negative feelings into action that the world is better off. Practice forgiving yourself. It will allow you to keep momentum in your life. And it will be easier for you to forgive others. We all make mistakes. Set a good example by learning from yours, forgiving yourself, and moving on.

BE AWARE OF NEGATIVE 'SELF-TALK'

How many times have you caught yourself putting yourself down in your head? We send ourselves negative messages like, I'm such a screw up; I'm ugly; and If only I was as smart as her. Practice catching and destroying these thoughts as soon as they arise. Your mood will skyrocket.

❏ *Action: Manage your stress*

Stress prevents us from leading fulfilling lives and creating a better world. Most of us manage to overfill our days with tasks and commitments, both enjoyable and tedious: walk the dog, set up a dental appointment, prepare for a dinner party, stop at the grocery store, meet your friend for lunch, drop off a book at the library, check and answer e-mail and phone messages, ask for time off next weekend, etc. Let's face it: we get stressed out.

Stress is our body's response to demands, challenges, and changes. Stress isn't the events we normally think of, such as traffic, nasty coworkers, and work deadlines; it's our reaction to these events. Both 'positive' events (marriage, vacation, new job) and 'negative' events (illness, divorce, a death in the family) trigger stress. Too much stress has a negative effect on your effectiveness and can lead to serious medical problems, such as ulcers, asthma, heart attacks, and strokes.[4]

How you can manage your stress

✓ **Decrease or stop using caffeine!** Decreasing or eliminating caffeine from your diet can be one of the easiest and most effective ways to decrease your stress. Caffeine is a stimulant that creates a stress reaction in the body. Pop, chocolate, coffee, and tea all commonly contain caffeine. It can take time to kick a caffeine habit, and going cold turkey might give you headaches. Try decreasing your intake by one drink each day until you're at zero. Then go three weeks without any caffeine. The results will amaze you.

✓ **Laugh!!** Laughing is a great way to relieve stress. Try to find the humor in any situation — the world is an absurd place.

✓ **Think positively.** Positive thinking opens you up to see more opportunities for changing your situation. Again, particular events are not inherently stressful; our interpretation of them creates our body's stress reaction.

✓ **Learn to let go of things outside of your control.** As much as we'd like to think we have some degree of control over everything, we really don't. Learn to recognize when you can make a difference and when you need to step back, take a deep breath, and disengage.

✓ **Go away for the weekend.** Sometimes we need to physically separate ourselves from our typical surroundings in order to rejuvenate our energy supply. Go camping or go on a short trip someplace nearby and just relax.

✓ **Give your time to something or someone you believe in.** Although it's not necessarily relaxing, it can be very therapeutic and re-energizing to give your time to a cause or person you believe in.

✓ **Vent your frustrations.** Just telling someone what's stressing you out can take a huge burden off your shoulders. Often all we need is someone to listen for a few minutes. Some people write out their frustrations. Either way, you'll rid yourself of some stress energy.[5]

A few more stress-relieving actions that we expand on in a later section include regular exercise, getting enough sleep, and relaxing and/or meditating. Don't let stress keep you from creating the life you want to live and the world you want to live it in.

STRESS RESOURCES

📖 Davidson, Jeff. *The Complete Idiot's Guide to Managing Stress.* Alpha Books, 1996.
As the title suggests, this guide offers simple ways to reduce your stress level, both at home and at work.

SPIRITUAL WELL-BEING

The technological advances of the 20th century were truly amazing. On the one hand, scientists produced an astounding body of knowledge, placing a robot on Mars, producing faster and smaller computers, and increasing our life expectancy via medical breakthroughs. On the other hand, our knowledge produced weapons that contributed to a century of bloodshed, industries that crippled our natural environment, and a profit-driven society that left much of the world's population in poverty. The number of Americans reporting that they were 'very happy' didn't increase from 1957 to 1994.[6] What's gone wrong? Perhaps we've focused so much on the knowledge we produce that we've lost sight of the wisdom necessary to guide it. Knowledge alone will not make the world a better place. We need wisdom to direct our energies to where they're most needed.

Ask Yourself Timeless Questions

Many questions have been important to humans for eons. These questions form the foundation of our search for wisdom, making them a logical place to start. They give direction, meaning, and motivation to our lives.

- ✔ Why is there suffering in the world?
- ✔ What is my purpose in life? Why am I here?
- ✔ What does it mean to live a 'good' life?
- ✔ What would I regret if I died today?
- ✔ Is there a power greater than us?
- ✔ What is my responsibility to my fellow human beings?
- ✔ What is my responsibility to animals and the Earth?

❏ Action: Read a book of wisdom

Sometimes it seems as though each generation attempts to create its own moral system from scratch, as if previous generations had little to offer. In fact, many wise people have pondered significant human questions for thousands of years. We don't have to start over; we can add to their accumulated wisdom.

You don't have to be a follower of a certain religion or belief system to benefit from its teachings. In fact, the commonalties among the world's major faiths are astounding. For example, many faiths address the perils of over-consumption:

Buddhist: "Whoever in this world overcomes his selfish cravings, his sorrows fall away from him, like drops of water from a lotus flower" (*Dhammapada*, 336).

Islamic: "Poverty is my pride" (*Muhammad*).

Christian: It is "easier for a camel to go through the eye of a needle than for a rich man to enter the kingdom of God" (*Matthew* 19:23-24).

Confucian: "Excess and deficiency are equally at fault" (*Confucius*, XI.15).

Hindu: "That person who lives completely free from desires, without longing ... attains peace" (*Bhagavad-Gita*, II.71).

Jewish: "Give me neither poverty nor riches" (*Proverbs* 30:8).

Taoist: "He who knows he has enough is rich" (*Tao Te Ching*).

American Indian: "Miserable as we seem in thy eyes, we consider ourselves ... much happier than thou, in this that we are very content with the little that we have" (*Micmac chief*).

Take the time to read, ponder, and discuss with others some of the ideas in these books:

Baghavad-Gita The *Baghavad-Gita* is one of the main Hindu spiritual texts. Written in verse form, it chronicles a discussion between the warrior Arjuna and Krishna, a Hindu deity.

"For him who has conquered the mind, the mind is the best of friends; but for one who has failed to do so, his mind will remain the greatest enemy."[7]

Tao Te Ching Written by Lao-Tzu over 2,500 years ago, the Tao or The Way offers incredibly profound insights into increasing one's spiritual level of being and harmony with the universe.

"Nothing in the world is as soft and yielding as water. Yet for dissolving the hard and inflexible, nothing can surpass it. The soft overcomes the hard; the gentle overcomes the rigid. Everyone knows this is true, but few can put it into practice."[8]

Bible The most sacred book of the Christian faith, the Bible offers a variety of insights in its many verses, including powerful thoughts on love, forgiveness, judgment, greed, and faith.

"Love your enemies, do good to those who hate you, bless those who curse you, pray for those who mistreat you. If someone strikes you on one cheek, turn to him the other also."[9]

Quran The Muslim Quran (Koran) uses lessons and stories of past communities to illustrate great moral teachings on many aspects of life. It discusses law, rights and obligations, and social concerns.

"Seest thou one who denies the Judgment (to come)? Then such is the (one) who repulses the orphan, and encourages not the feeding of the indigent. So woe to the worshippers who are neglectful of their prayers, those who (want but) to be seen, but refuse (to supply) (even) neighborly needs."[10]

Torah As the Jewish holy book, the Torah teaches about the power of tradition, community, compassion, and a deep love of God.

"Surely you should divide your bread with the hungry, and bring the poor to your home; when you see the naked, cover him; and do not ignore your kin."[11]

For more great sources of wisdom, check out the Personal Resources section at the end of this chapter.

❏ *Action: Foster your spiritual side*

Spirituality has always been a vital part of human existence. It connects us to something outside of ourselves, helps explain the unexplainable, and gives meaning and direction to our actions. The fostering of your spiritual side recognizes our need to connect with the eternal life force that binds us to each other and to all life on earth.

✓ Take a hike, focusing specifically on the interconnectedness of life around you.

✓ Volunteer for a local organization, with the clear intention of making a deep connection with those you help.

✓ Seek the divine, the sacred, and the humanity in every person.

✓ Cherish the wonder and miracle of life.

✓ Appreciate the cycle of life and death.

✓ Gather with others and support each other's spiritual quests.

❏ *Action: Live your life as a prayer*

Living out spiritual faith is difficult, particularly with all of the distractions modern society offers. Throughout the book, we've explored ways to integrate different aspects of our life based upon our fundamental values. The same principle applies to spirituality. Ask yourself what are the core values of your spiritual life. Perhaps love, peace, forgiveness and justice are among them. Now ask yourself how you can live out these values on a daily basis, thus living and being your spirituality. Faith can be a powerful part of making the world a better place.

PHYSICAL WELL-BEING

Not satisfied with being the 'land of the free,' America has become the land of the inactive. Over one-half of us are overweight.[12] Americans are eating more and exercising less than in the past — the perfect combination for increased heart disease and stress, high blood pressure, and diabetes. To be an effective force for making the world a better place, we need to foster a healthy mind, healthy emotions, and a healthy body.

❏ *Action: Exercise regularly*

How much time each day do you spend exercising? How much time do you spend watching TV, typing at a computer, or sitting at a desk? Many of us spend far more time sitting than getting our heart rate up. According to the American Medical Association, "More than 60% of American adults do not get the recommended amount of physical activity, and nearly half of American youth are not active on a regular basis."[13] The results of our increasingly sedentary lifestyles are:

- Greater risk for heart disease and stroke
- Greater risk for cancer
- Increased risk for non-insulin dependent diabetes mellitus
- Decreased strength and endurance
- Greater tendency to excess weight and obesity

The AMA recommends that you exercise your large muscle groups 30 to 60 minutes each day, three to six times each week. If this amount of exercise isn't possible, even 20 minutes three times a week will improve your health.

Aerobic exercise is vital to your health. It increases the capacity of your heart, lungs, and circulatory system. For maximum effectiveness, aerobic exercise needs to be rhythmic and continuous and to involve the large muscle groups (primarily located in the lower part of your body.) Some examples of good aerobic activities include walking, jogging, cycling, aerobic dance, and stair climbing. Some activities combine upper and lower body movements: cross-country skiing, rowing, and swimming can lead to even higher levels of aerobic capacity.

Hints on maintaining momentum

✓ **Find someone to exercise with.** It's fun, and you can make commitments to each other that you can help each other keep.

✓ **Get rid of your scale.** The scale doesn't measure your commitment to exercising, and a number can't tell you your well-being. Scales discourage many of us.

✓ **Keep an exercise journal.** Keep track of how much weight you lift, how far you walk, or whatever you do. This lets you see your progress, motivating you to keep improving. Every so often, take time to assess your progress.

✓ **Make exercise a priority.** Schedule exercise into your day and make it a habit like brushing your teeth. Even on those days you've had a long day at work, force yourself to get some exercise. It'll help you unwind.

✓ **Make exercise entertaining.** Listen to music or a book on tape. Vary your workout once in a while. If you exercise at home, move the TV where you can see it.

❏ *Action: Get enough sleep*

In our fast-paced world, many of us don't get enough sleep. The average person needs around eight hours of sleep each night but often gets much less. Lack of sleep forces us to function at less than our full potential. How much sleep do you need? John W. Shepard Jr., M.D., of Mayo Clinic's Sleep Disorders Center says, "We define an adequate quantity of sleep as that amount which, when you attain it on a steady basis, produces a full degree of daytime alertness and feeling of well-being the following day."[14] The benefits of enough sleep are huge: it's easier to have a positive outlook, and you'll have increased energy, clearer thinking, and better health. In fact, too much or too little sleep contributes to shorter life expectancy.[15]

❏ *Action: Eat healthy*

After a long day at work, it's often easier to eat processed, instant foods rather than prepare a nutritious meal. Though this may seem more efficient, it is ultimately counterproductive. Our bodies are our greatest resource. To skimp on food and pollute ourselves with substandard junk is a big mistake in the long run. Your body is, as the saying goes, a temple.

Here are a few basic tips for creating a healthy diet.

- Replace snacks, such as potato chips, candy, and ice cream, with foods such as raw vegetables, fresh fruit, or a mixture of raisins and nuts.

- Replace coffee, tea, soda, and liquor with fruit juice or water.

- Eat more fresh fruits and vegetables! You've heard this since you were a kid, now find a way to make it a reality. Fruits provide vitamin C, which helps prevent heart disease and certain cancers, lowers stress, and boosts our immune systems.[16] Vegetables contain nutrients that protect us from many health problems such as heart attacks and irregular blood sugar levels.[17]

- Eat a variety of foods, avoid too many sugars, eat plenty of whole grains, avoid foods high in fat and cholesterol, and stay away from too much salt and sodium.

THE 'NOT-SO-IDEAL' BODY IMAGE

Society creates an ideal body shape that few of us can live up to: the incredibly slender woman and the remarkably muscular man. Corporations use advertising to make us feel ugly so that we buy their products to become 'beautiful.' Many people, particularly young women, starve themselves in an effort to attain the societal image of perfection. Remember that we make up ideals; they aren't necessarily the best way for us to be. So as long as you're healthy, try to be satisfied with your body as it is.

REFLECTION

In our fast-paced society, we rarely take time to reflect on our lives. We're constantly moving on to the next thing. Reflection gives you time to recognize what you've accomplished and really appreciate what you experienced. It also provides an opportunity for you to grow, express concerns, reconsider your priorities, and record interesting and creative ideas.

❏ *Action: Keep a journal*

One of the best ways to reflect is by keeping a journal. Write, draw, or paint whatever is on your mind. Many of us have a preconceived idea of what a journal should be: a special book that you write deep thoughts in every day. But a journal can be whatever you want it to be. Write in it once a day, week, month, or year — whatever's valuable to you. Use a spiral notebook or purchase a hardcover drawing book with blank pages. The journaling process, however you choose to do it, is a very valuable way to reflect on your life.

❑ *Action: Center yourself*

Centering is the practice of mindfulness, a way of paying attention to the moment. It is calming, rejuvenating, and balancing — not some weird religious activity practiced by people who want to escape the world. It's simply an easy way to bring yourself back into balance. Although there is no right way to center yourself, some general principles are helpful:

✓ **Stillness** Choose an area or room where you will be comfortable sitting still and where there's not a lot of activity around you.

✓ **Quiet** If possible, choose a quiet place where you won't be interrupted.

✓ **Deep breathing** Focus on your breathing. Keep your mouth slightly open, breathe in slowly through your nose, hold it for a second or two, then slowly let the breath out through your mouth.

✓ **Affirmation/focus** Some people like to focus on one particular thought or image, such as love, God, or silence. Others repeat a meaningful phrase in their heads.

✓ **Emptying the mind** It's nearly impossible to free your mind of all thought, but with practice you can come close. Let your thoughts, any thoughts, come and go as they please. Always return your focus to your breath or mantra.

You can center yourself wherever you are. Some people practice rush hour centering during their commutes. Throughout the day, especially during particularly stressful times, you may want to take brief, calming breaks where you stop what you're doing, close your eyes, and take several deep breaths. Centering time can be one minute or an hour or more. A focused mind and relaxed spirit will substantially improve your day.

❑ *Action: Step out of your comfort zone*

Most of us like to be comfortable. We like to feel safe, in control, and unafraid. Unfortunately, comfort rarely creates growth, fulfillment, or a better world. It is often during times of discomfort that we grow the most, and turbulence often creates social change. There is something very powerful about intentionally taking on uncomfortable experiences.

What makes you uncomfortable? Teenagers? Very sick people? Poor neighborhoods? Racism? Often our discomfort is a signal of something we could work on. While we're in our 'safe zone,' we have little reason to really stretch into something new. Visit a place you normally would be afraid to go, take a class in something that you are nervous about, volunteer with a population that makes you uneasy — whatever will push you into new ground.

❏ *Action: Examine your stereotypes*

Even though we like to think we are completely accepting of people and their differences, our society often teaches us to think poorly of racial and ethnic minorities, women, lesbians, gay men, immigrants, youth, and a host of other groups. Accepting that we have stereotypes is crucial to creating a more tolerant world, where people from diverse backgrounds feel valued and safe. It is not easy to examine our prejudices — it forces us to face our dark side. However, becoming aware of stereotypes is the first step toward challenging them.

❏ *Action: Reconnect with nature*

We are part of a living, breathing planet that sustains our bodies and nourishes our spirits. Most of us feel a need to connect with nature on some level, hence the prevalence of 'weekend warriors' who leave the city for the tranquillity and adventure of nature. Appreciating nature means more than going out to play in it, though. Create a meaningful way to reconnect with your natural surroundings. Some suggestions include:

✓ sitting on your patio for 15 minutes each evening, listening to the sounds around you
✓ taking more hikes
✓ connecting with a tree
✓ finding a tranquil spot in the woods and practicing centering
✓ appreciating the life that surrounds you when you're in nature. You notice things you wouldn't normally.

❏ *Action: Reconsider your priorities*

If you don't consciously choose to spend time on what's really important to you, the little things will consume your priorities. Make a list of your top priorities and compare it to a list of how you spend your time. You may be surprised to learn that you spend relatively little time on some of your top priorities. Consider focusing your energies on your most important priorities to give them the attention they deserve — strengthening your relationships, reading, exercising, volunteering, enriching your spiritual life, exploring new things, taking a class, spending time outdoors, pursuing hobbies.

❏ *Action: Write a personal mission statement*

If someone asked you what exactly do you stand for, could you tell him? Writing your own personal mission statement can be a powerful way for you to reflect on who you are and who you'd like to be.

✓ Make a list of your core values.
✓ Ask yourself how these values tie together.
✓ Write a statement that encompasses your core being, values, and goals.

Try to keep it under one page.

Here is an example of a personal mission statement:

I am committed to living a creative, peaceful, compassionate life. Life, to me, is a spiritual journey; I intend to constantly examine my life, stretch into new experiences, and grow personally. There will be highs and lows on this path, but I will try to live an intentional life, staying in the moment and maintaining a peaceful existence. I will never lose sight of my connection with others. I hope that everything I do in some way makes the world a better place. True happiness comes from meaningful connection, and often service, to others.

A personal mission statement gives direction to your life. You can revisit it anytime to reaffirm your sense of purpose, evaluate where you're at now, or change your mission to include new insights.

PERSONAL RESOURCES

  📖 Anderson, Sherry Ruth, and Patricia Hopkins. *The Feminine Face Of God*. Bantam Books, 1991.
A book about the spiritual life of women that "shows how many women have redefined traditional beliefs and rediscovered their own unique spiritual heritage."

  📖 Cameron, Julia. *The Artist's Way: A Spiritual Path to Higher Creativity*. J. P. Tarcher, 1992.
Composed of a 12-week program of exercises and activities, this book helps you overcome any obstacles that stand between you and a completely creative life. It also links creativity and spirituality in a unique way. If you like this one, consider *Vein of Gold: A Journey to Your Creative Heart* by the same author.

  📖 Covey, Stephen. *7 Habits of Highly Effective People: Powerful Lessons in Personal Change*. Fireside, 1990.
This book has sold over ten million copies for a reason: it teaches personal effectiveness by encouraging you to see the world in a new way. It will help you live with fairness, dignity, and integrity.

  📖 Duerk, Judith. *Circle Of Stones — Woman's Journey To Herself*. InnisFree Press, 1999 [1989].
Myths and stories make this book an exciting journey for women to discover their sacred selves within. A great read, *Circle of Stones* searches for the roots of femininity and the power of women.

  📖 Elgin, Duane. *Voluntary Simplicity: Toward a Way of Life That Is Outwardly Simple, Inwardly Rich*. Quill, 1993 [1981].

This book will help end your enslavement to products and work. It advocates balance, not poverty, and connects personal growth to simple living.

📖 Hanh, Thich Nhat. *The Miracle of Mindfulness: A Manual on Meditation*. Beacon Press, 1987 [1975].

Thich Nhat Hanh, an exiled Vietnamese Buddhist monk, offers a guide to meditation that transcends sitting in the lotus position. He offers a variety of interesting activities designed to increase your mindfulness.

📖 Hesse, Herman. *Siddhartha*. Shambala Publishers, 2000.

This novel tells the story of Siddhartha's quest for enlightenment. Hesse illustrates the basics of Buddhist thought in a simple but profound story.

📖 McGrane, Bernard. *The Un-TV and the Ten Mile Per Hour Car*. Small Press, 1994.

The *Un-TV* is a truly wacky book filled with experiments that will totally shift your consciousness. The engaging activities will encourage you to see the world in a fresh, new way.

📖 Millman, Dan. *Way of the Peaceful Warrior: A Book That Changes Lives*. Kramer, 1985 [1980].

Dan Millman writes about his days as a college gymnast searching for ultimate happiness. An extremely engaging story with powerful insights applicable to everyday life.

📖 Neihardt, John G. *Black Elk Speaks*. Bison Books, 2000.

Black Elk was an Oglala Sioux medicine man born in 1863. Black Elk, speaking through Neihardt, describes his vision of spiritual values, a vision he was determined to pass on to the world before he died.

FRIENDS AND FAMILY

Building Strong Relationships

Giving Gifts

Children

MANY FORCES IN TODAY'S WORLD work against strong relationships with our friends and families: consumerism, overworking, individualism, and our fast-paced society. Even though our families and friends are the most important people in our lives, these factors often lead us to neglect our relationships and take our loved ones for granted. Ask yourself, How can I take a more active, intentional role in creating extraordinary relationships? You'll amaze yourself with the possibilities you create.

One of the most significant ways you can have a positive impact on the world is through your family and friends. With a little effort you can transform your relationships into meaningful connections that provide a nurturing environment for love and personal growth. When supported by loving relationships, you will also create a solid foundation on which to make the world a better place.

Each of us creates what family means for us. Family can mean parents and children, a single parent and children, a couple without children, gay or lesbian couples with or without children, extended family, friends living together, loved ones who live in another state — you name it. Each of us knows who our loved ones are; this chapter is about them.

This chapter addresses several important aspects of relationships, including ways to create strong relationships, gift giving, and raising children. Hopefully it will spark your creativity and help you act toward your family and friends in a way that spreads love and compassion in the world. Imagine a world where everyone committed to creating strong, loving relationships — that's a world we want to live in.

BUILDING STRONG RELATIONSHIPS

Great relationships don't just happen; we have to create them. We all know that certain ways of acting with loved ones strengthen relationships and other ways stymie growth. The following actions are central to the strength of all relationships — friends, siblings, or life partners.

❏ *Action: Make time for loved ones*

It takes time to build strong relationships. You can't create meaningful relationships in the ten minutes between meetings or the hour between errands. It takes effort and it takes commitment. Your boss is never going to get on your case when you neglect your friends and family. You must make your relationships a priority if you want them to prosper.

Instead of scheduling the items on your to-do list, schedule in your real priorities. If you find that you are neglecting the people who are important in your life, schedule them into your busy life. It's easy to neglect your loved ones when they don't carry much importance on your calendar.

Reunions, parties, and potlucks are great ways to build community, whether they are for extended family or for your college buddies. Everybody loves them but most people don't take the time to plan them. They can be very cheap if you stay at home and have a potluck. Get-togethers can be spontaneous, too. Throw an impromptu barbecue with your neighbors or play an after dinner volleyball game.

> Mark a 'date night' on your calendar or set aside one weekend a month as a 'couple weekend.'

❏ *Action: Check in*

Sometimes we get so caught up in the rat race that we forget to check in with the people that we care for. Write a letter, send an email, or pick up the phone. Just ask how they are doing and how their week was. You may even want to schedule a time every week or every month where you catch up with certain people in your life. Open and frequent communication is vital to healthy relationships.

❏ *Action: Practice deep listening*

Have you ever been talking to someone and noticed after a few minutes that she just isn't there with you? Interacting with people whose thoughts are elsewhere is completely annoying. Make sure that you are attentive to your loved ones when you are with them. When you're reading the newspaper, watching TV, being in a hurry, or worrying about what you have to do tomorrow, it detracts from fully experiencing the people you care for. One of the most powerful ways you can show people that you respect and care for them is to listen to them — truly listen to them, whether they are talking about their day at work, what movie they want to see, or cherished memories of a loved one. Deep listening creates a space for people to feel safe and grow.

❑ *Action: Resolve conflicts collaboratively*

Most people learn to deal with conflict in one of two ways:

avoid it at all costs

or

go for the jugular!

Avoiding conflict at all costs leads to resentment and allows little griev-ances to grow into huge problems. On the other hand, aggression leads to hot tempers, hurt feelings, and irrational decisions. It doesn't have to be that way. How would your relationships be more fulfilling and productive if you saw conflict as an opportunity for growth? Collaborative conflict resolution engages conflict so that the underlying problems truly get resolved while strengthening the relationship.

WHEN A CONFLICT OCCURS

1. Listen to their side of the story.
- actually listen (don't just be thinking of what to say next)
- ask questions to seek understanding
- restate their point of view in your own words
- remember the conflict is about an issue, not the person

2. Share your side of the story.
- seek to be understood, not to blame
- talk about yourself not about them
- share feelings

3. Work to find a win-win outcome.
- create options that would satisfy both people's interests
- don't just settle for a compromise

❑ *Action: Give unconditional love and support*

Think of a time when someone did something for you, expecting nothing in return, simply because they cared about you. Perhaps your partner surprised you with a lunch date, or perhaps a stranger helped you out when you had car trouble. It's an amazing feeling to know that someone cares enough to make you feel special simply because of who you are, instead of what you do.

Be sure to nourish the personal growth of the people you care for. Encourage them to follow their dreams and spend time developing their interests. Especially when your loved ones are thinking about major life-changing decisions, they need you to love and support them.

❑ *Action: Forgive others*

You've probably read stories of people who have visited a prison to forgive their child's murderer. Most of us have difficulty comprehending this level of forgiveness, even when we see that forgiveness helps the distraught parents move on with their lives. Although difficult, the ability to forgive is crucial to emotional well-being.

We're all human beings; others will hurt each one of us many times in our lives. When we enter loving relationships, we open ourselves up to vulnerability, disappointment, and hurt. There will undoubtedly be times when others take advantage of our vulnerability, causing us pain and anger. Grudges and resentment are difficult burdens to bear. They breed cynicism and distrust and often inhibit personal growth and transformation. Leo Buscaglia writes, "Forgiveness is an act of will...we either choose to forgive or we do not."[1] Choosing to forgive is a difficult but powerful process. Here are a few suggestions to make it easier:

- ☮ **Remember all aspects of the relationship**, not just the hurtful or negative incidents. It's easy to let the damaging parts of a relationship cloud the good times.
- ☮ **Put yourself in their shoes**. At some point, we've all hurt someone else. How would you want to be treated if you were in the other person's shoes?
- ☮ **Avoid using forgiveness as a source of power**. Don't use your forgiveness to get what you want. If you choose to forgive, then forgive unconditionally.
- ☮ **Remember what it's like to be forgiven**. You are giving the wrongdoer and yourself a tremendous gift, one that can be extremely empowering for everyone involved.

Forgiveness can be hard; that's OK. The price of not forgiving, however, is great.

GIVING GIFTS

Gift giving is often fun for both the giver and the receiver. Try to think of meaningful ways to express your love that also take into account the well-being of the planet and others around you. Here are a few suggestions for making your gift giving extra special.

❑ *Action: Give of yourself*

Instead of buying a ready-made card and present, why not give something that more powerfully shows how much you appreciate the person? Show them that they are worthy of your time and energy, not just your money. Try making the birthday card yourself, writing a song or poem, cleaning the house for them, or giving them a 'coupon' for a back rub or romantic evening together. In other words, put yourself into the gift.

❏ *Action: Donate money for someone*

Eventually, many of us get to the point where we don't need or even want any more stuff. Show that you truly understand your loved one's deepest values by donating money to an organization that is struggling for something that they believe in — instead of buying something that will go straight to the storage closet. Most organizations will send out a small newsletter or magazine on a regular basis throughout the year so that your loved one can see what kind of powerful changes their gift is creating in the world.

Alternative Gifts International

The Alternative Gifts catalog highlights 30 humanitarian projects by which you can honor your loved ones with a donation while empowering people in crisis and protecting the Earth. Examples include: providing solar powered water systems in Honduras, helping female workers in the Maquiladoras (Mexico-U.S. border factories) learn about their rights and their health, and helping provide literacy training in Senegal. Your loved ones receive a gift card in the mail indicating your gift.

☎ (800) 842-2243   💻 www.altgifts.org

Protect-an-Acre

A handful of organizations have programs for adopting an acre of rainforest. Your donation to these organizations helps develop infrastructure to protect the rainforest for generations to come. In return, you will get information about the specific impact of your donation, as well as a certificate to acknowledge your help.

☎ (415) 398-4404   💻 www.ran.org/give/paa

❏ *Action: Buy socially responsible gifts*

Consider buying gifts that are more in line with your values. For example, if you value non-violence, buy your nephew a toy that encourages cooperation rather competition. Or if you want to prevent eating disorders, buy your niece a stuffed animal, not a Barbie doll. If you are an environmentalist, consider buying someone reusable canvas shopping bags or another gift that will help them lessen their environmental impact. It's tempting to get all our gifts at a superstore such as Wal-Mart or K-Mart, but your shopping dollars are extremely important to locally owned shops and craftspeople (besides, if you shop locally, you might find something unique!). Other gift ideas are:

- creative supplies (paints, drawing pencils, journals, etc.)
- subscription to an alternative magazine (see the MEDIA chapter)
- items made by Third World artisans and workers

Ten Thousand Villages

Ten Thousand Villages is a non-profit organization that sells handicrafts made by unemployed or under-employed people of the Third World. They promote fair trade (livable prices and wages), reinforce cultural traditions, and support ethical and humane work environments. Contact them to find out where the store nearest to you is located.

☎ (717) 859-8100   🖳 www.villages.ca

❏ Action: *Simplify the holidays*

Unfortunately, multi-million dollar marketing campaigns have slowly transformed our most cherished holidays into frazzled shopping frenzies. Many of us spend so much time worrying and being anxious that the holidays seem more like a chore than a blessing — not to mention the extra weeks we have to work to pay off our shopping debts. Take time to fully appreciate the meaning of the holidays by slowing down, focusing on what's really important, and cutting back on the amount of money and time you and your family spend in shopping malls. Be creative with your family and find ways to share generosity without giving in to the ploys of Madison Avenue. Simplifying the holidays is a great way to improve your relationships, save the Earth's resources, save some money and frustration, and help halt the commercialization of our most honored times together. Be sure to talk with your family at least a few weeks in advance about your desire to simplify the holidays. Here are some ideas:

> Wrap your gifts in newspaper or put them in a reusable gift bag or box!

✓ Set dollar limits on gifts.
✓ Pick names out of a hat so that each person only buys one gift.
✓ Take some of the money saved on gifts and donate it to a favorite charity (try this at work, too).
✓ Have each person share a treasured family memory.
✓ Give of yourself instead of just buying something.

RESOURCES

Center for a New American Dream
Check out their 'Simplify the Holidays' Campaign for more ideas.
🖳 www.newdream.org/holiday

CHILDREN

Many people describe the experience of giving birth and raising children as the most amazing and meaningful experiences in their lives. The responsibilities of child-rearing are also extremely challenging. Much of our children's potential is shaped by their experiences during the first few years of life. The following actions address important issues that parents should consider when raising their children as kind and compassionate members of the human family.

❑ *Action: Limit your number of children*

In 2000, 78 million more people were born than died. That means the world's population grew by about 2-1/2 people every second (that's births minus deaths!).[2] We've got to slow our population growth. The Earth already bends under our collective impact. We can choose to limit our family size to zero, one, or two children. You may think that the 'population problem' only exists in China and India, but North Americans use so many resources that an extra North American has a vastly greater environmental effect than does a person born in a developing country.

> The U.S. uses 120 pounds (54 kilograms) of natural resources per person per day, and the average American consumes as much energy as:
>
> | | | |
> |---|---|---|
> | | 2 | Germans |
> | | 6 | Mexicans |
> | | 12 | Chinese |
> | | 29 | Indians |
> | or | 117 | Bangladeshi[3] |

❑ *Action: Adopt*

Americans adopt more than 100,000 children each year.[4] Although this seems like a lot of children, many remain without permanent homes. By adopting a child, you provide him or her with a safe, stable home — essential ingredients for a happy, healthy childhood. Adoption is also an ecologically beneficial way to have kids; rather than producing more children and requiring more resources, adoption enables you to support a child already here. After determining your desired family size, consider adopting some or all of your children. If you want three kids, consider having two yourself and adopting one. Adoption is one of the most powerful gifts you can give.

National Adoption Information Clearinghouse (NAIC)

NAIC is a division of the Department of Health and Human Services. It is a government-run national organization that can answer virtually all of your questions regarding

National Adoption Information Clearinghouse

adoption, including international adoption and adopting children with special needs.

☎ (888) 251-0075 💻 www.calib.com/naic

The Center for Family Building

The Center for Family Building is a good example of an adoption agency with a "progressive, enlightened outlook on adoption."  They offer a great deal of information to both birth parents and adoptive couples, and many of their staff have personal experience with adoption.

💻 www.centerforfamily.com ☎ (847) 869-1518

❑ *Action: Be a foster parent*

By the end of 1995, about 494,000 children were in foster care in the US.[5] Children in foster care often have special needs or have been abused or neglected and are especially in need of your help. Adoption agencies usually have information on how you can be a foster parent.

❑ *Action: Start a babysitting club*

In the past, people relied more on friends and neighbors to help with child care. Unfortunately, we often don't know our neighbors well or feel bad about burdening them with our children. Instead, we create several worries for ourselves by hiring a babysitter: is he/she competent? How much can I afford to pay? Will I be able to find a babysitter for tonight?

Many other parents face these same issues. Why not create a group of friends to share babysitting responsibilities? Start with the groups you already belong to, such as a work or religious community. Announce your idea and pass around a sign-up sheet to see who might be interested.

❑ *Action: Spend quality time with children*

Our children deserve our time. Some parts of our culture are creating an increasingly hostile environment in which to raise children. Images of violence and excessive consumerism are daily fare for the young in our country, and these images are hard to compete with as parents. The most effective way to raise children is to spend time with them. It shows them that you love them, and it increases the influence you have on their values.

> The average parent spends less than three hours each day with her or his children[6]

Many adults gripe about children's lack of values. Actually, everyone is teaching your children values: your TV is doing it; their friends are doing it; and you are doing it. If they see you one hour a day and they watch four hours of TV messages — guess whose values are going to win out? It is essential that you play a significant role in the creation of your child's values. When you make your children a priority in your life, it leads them to have a sense of belonging and security that is essential to healthy maturity.

❑ *Action: Express affection*

'I love you' are three of the most powerful words in our language. It's important that family members, both kids and adults, know we love and care about them. Express your love for each other as much as possible. We all like to hear I love you. Teaching a child how to love another person through your own·example may be the most powerful impact that you can have on them.

BE A RESPECTFUL SPORTS FAN

You've probably seen news stories about parents at kids' sporting events who belittle and berate young players, shout at other parents, and even start fights with sports referees. As absurd as this sounds, it seems to be a growing trend. In one of the worst cases in July 2000, one father beat another father to death at their sons' hockey game.[7] Don't be an obnoxious parent at kids' sporting events. Make sure and model good sportsmanship, civility, and positivity at any sporting event, especially one involving kids. Remember, it's just a game!

❑ *Action: Model peace*

Given our war-torn, gun-toting world, it's no wonder that kids often resort to violence to solve their problems. The single most important action you can take to help kids (yours or others') develop into peaceful people is to model peace yourself. As kids learn, they take mental notes on our every little action, no matter how insignificant. The most important modeling you do may be to use discipline as a teaching tool instead of as an expression of anger. If applied in a clear and consistent manner, discipline can be a powerful tool to teach about your family's core values. The following non-violent actions are particularly significant:

- Model good conflict resolution skills.
- Avoid physical punishment
- Control your temper.
- Give coaching, not criticism.
- Be patient.
- Have your child think about what she or he did.
- Explain why the behavior (not the child) is unacceptable.
- Help clarify the purpose behind household rules.

❏ *Action: Teach caring and giving*

One of the most important values we can instill in our children is the obligation to help others and make a positive contribution to the world. So much of our culture tells our children to do whatever feels good or exciting at the time without thinking of the consequences to themselves or others. Teaching the value of treating others as we would like to be treated goes a long way to building a world that we would all like to live in.

Be creative in encouraging your child to think of others and to give part of their time and money to charitable causes. Volunteer as a family — it's a wonderful way to bond while doing good deeds for others. Children who grow up helping their parents volunteer will likely continue to make service a priority throughout their lives. By teaching your child alternatives to violence and selfishness, you are taking a large step to making the world a more loving, peaceful place. Here are a few suggestions:

✓ Serve at a soup kitchen.

✓ Create a holiday gift tree for underprivileged children.

✓ Donate gifts to your local homeless or women's shelter.

✓ Make holiday decorations for your local retirement home.

✓ Do yardwork for the elderly in your neighborhood — for free.

✓ Participate in any community clean-up programs.

✓ Go on a litter patrol. Make it even more fun by creating a search team, with a child as team leader.

❏ *Action: Model flexible gender roles*

We teach kids early on what it means to be a boy and what it means to be a girl. Gender differences are especially evident in the division of household labor: women generally clean, cook, do laundry, and sew; men typically handle home repairs, heavy yard work, and auto maintenance. Also, our culture teaches that men are the heads of the household and therefore are responsible for important family decisions. Dividing up work and decision making are fine, but doing so on the basis of gender limits our opportunities. Strict gender roles prevent girls and boys from becoming whole people who can express a broad range of emotions and succeed at a broad range of tasks. Consider the following gender-empowering actions:

• Show that it's OK for both women and men to show emotions.

• Trade off on household tasks: scrub the bathroom one week, mow the lawn the next.

• Demonstrate that both men and women can make big decisions.

• Teach boys how to cook and girls how to fix the sink.

• Avoid guiding your kids to gender specific play; encourage them to value and engage in a variety of activities, regardless of gender.

❏ *Action: Teach an appreciation of diversity*

Racism, homophobia, classism, and sexism cause a great deal of suffering in our world. Kids are not born intolerant; they learn prejudices from adults and other kids. Going out of your way to teach kids tolerance and even appreciation of differences is a huge step in making the world a better place. They will model and teach what you have taught them — passing on your good lessons. Use real-world examples of racism and other bigotry to discuss how you and your kids can respond when such situations occur in your own lives. Keep in mind that if you don't consciously teach tolerance, children will likely learn and accept negative stereotypes from the media and their peers.

❏ *Action: Teach the difference between wants and needs*

As you are reading this, advertising executives are figuring out how to 'brand' your child with images of their products. They spend millions of dollars every year on TV commercials, product placements in movies, cartoon shows based on a product, and other forms of advertising meant to confuse your child about what is really important in life. You can help your child define what is really meaningful (spirituality, friends, family, a clean environment) and what is only fleeting and superficial (the newest toys or fashions). Consider showing your love in more positive ways and only buy gifts on special occasions. Children are extremely observant. Don't wonder why your child demands a new toy every week if you are getting a new outfit every month or a new car every year.

> The average child watches 20,000 to 40,000 commercials every year.[8]

❏ *Action: Choose childcare that supports your values*

Choosing a daycare can be tough. Several issues concern all parents: safety, cleanliness, stimulating environment, child/caregiver ratio, and staff qualifications, for example. Remember, if your kids spend a significant amount of time there, you want it to be the best environment possible! Important questions to ask include: What kind of experience do you have caring for children? How have you learned about children and their development? What would a typical day be like for my child? Do you insure that each child receives individual attention? How many children are in the group my child would be in?

> Consider having a birthday party where no gifts are exchanged.

In addition to the standard concerns, you may want to consider asking some of the following questions about your childcare provider. Keep in mind that childcare providers are often overworked and underpaid and may have trouble implementing some of these ideas.

- Do they encourage cooperative activities over competitive and/or violent activities?
- Do the supervisors teach sharing?
- Is the daycare 'educational?'
- Are children disciplined non-violently?
- Do the caregivers teach children how to resolve their own conflicts collaboratively?
- Does the daycare foster creativity in the children in a variety of ways, or do the kids watch TV?
- How do the caregivers teach other languages, handle gender roles, and encourage cultural activities? Are there children of diverse ethnicity present?

> Consider choosing your local Boys and Girls Clubs as a childcare option. They offer kids a safe, fun environment with positive role models at a very low cost.

- Does the daycare do its best to reduce, reuse, and recycle? Does the daycare actually teach kids to value the Earth and be environmentally responsible?

❑ *Action: Limit TV watching*

Television is a direct pipeline that delivers gratuitous violence, cheapened sexuality, racial stereotypes, and a barrage of advertisements right into your home. None of us want to believe that TV has a negative effect on us. Unfortunately, experts conclude that television violence increases kids' aggressive behavior. TV viewing also leads to apathy, inactivity, desensitization to violence, and lack of imagination.

An easy way to limit your family's TV watching is to create a TV viewing schedule (yes, all the adults, too). Decide as a family how much Total Tube Time (including shows, movies, and video games) each person gets. Keep a log by the TV set for each person to monitor their watching. Encourage your kids to practice selective viewing by checking the TV guide to best use their allotted time.

A TV schedule serves several goals:

- You'll find out just how much TV your family wants to watch (it may be a lot).
- You'll see exactly which shows your children like and can reflect on which shows are really worth watching.
- You can compare the actual time you spent watching with your goal and work to cut your time to meet it.
- You won't watch things that aren't important to you just to be watching something.

❑ *Action: Choose alternatives to TV and video games*

It is essential for us to teach our children how to spend their time in ways that lead to learning, personal growth, strong friendships, enhanced creativity, and

---

PLANNING FAMILY TIME

1. Assess everyone's interests
Brainstorm general interests of each family member. Next, list everyone's interests on a large sheet of paper.

2. Brainstorm activities
Once you've assessed general interests, have each family member write down a few activities for each interest — their own and everyone else's.

3. Prioritize activities
Encourage each family member to list the five activities he or she would most enjoy doing as a family. As you share your favorites, imagine how you could combine different members' activities (for example, hiking and camping, or biking and picnicing).

4. Make commitments as a family
Now that you've created some things you'd like to do together, make commitments, on a calendar, about when you'd like to do each activity.

---

physical health. It takes creativity and discipline to use your time in a productive and positive manner — two skills which television, the primary waster of kids' time, does not teach. TV is addictive, and it encourages you to watch more and more while tuning out the rest of the world.

SOCIAL ACTIVITIES

Create a family tree, go to parades, play board games or cards, tell stories, enjoy just being together, team work

OUTSIDE ACTIVITIES

Play in the park, play frisbee golf, go bowling, go ice-skating, hike, build a snow creature, play basketball, hacky sack, fly a kite, play soccer, swim, bike, have a picnic, go sledding, play softball, run relay races, go bird watching, collect leaves, garden, play wiffleball, play croquet, play badminton

EDUCATIONAL ACTIVITIES

Visit museums, go to the public library, go to the theater, visit a planetarium, read, do crossword puzzles, do science experiments

CREATIVE ACTIVITIES

Create art together, play music together, write a poem, draw pictures of each other, color, write a short story, sing, arrange flowers, paint, journal, cook, play with sidewalk chalk, pursue other hobbies

---

Rarely does watching TV get a kid excited about life or build intimacy between friends or family. Instead of letting your kids lie on the couch all day watching cartoons, engage them in activities which get them actively participating in life. Get them outside — it will not only get them in shape but will help them appreciate our natural environment. Having fun with other family and friends leads to deeper relationships and a healthier mental state, just as experiencing creative and educational challenges leads to immense personal growth.

☐ *Action: Talk with your kids about TV*

Encourage critical TV viewing in your kids. Kids are in the process of learning about different types of people: men and women, whites and people of color, gay and straight, rich and poor. TV often distorts our perceptions of diversity and fundamentally shapes our ideas about what's really important in life. Consider asking:

- What is the difference between TV and reality?
- What are the stereotypes that TV perpetuates?
- What is the purpose of a commercial?
- How does TV exaggerate some characters' attributes?
- What is the show's message?

After watching a show with your kids, ask them what they thought of any scenes that could be used as an opportunity to discuss values.

TV RESOURCES

Merbreier, W. Carter, with Linda Capus Riley. *Television: What's Behind What You See.* Farrar, Straus and Giroux, 1996.
This wonderfully illustrated kids' book will teach your children and you everything from how TV images appear on our screens to marketing and setting up the stage for a sitcom. Very sophisticated, yet fun for all ages.

☐ *Action: Choose alternatives to violent toys and games*

Toy guns, swords, action figures, tanks, and warplanes have filled kids' toy boxes for years. Encourage your children to play with fewer violence-based toys by having a healthy balance of other items around. Stock art supplies, puzzles, building toys such as Lincoln Logs and Tinker Toys, dress-up clothes, and sports equipment, and make sure they are readily available.

At first glance, violent toys may seem like a 'boy issue.' Girls, however, engage in their own form of violence when they emulate dolls with impossibly shaped figures. Toys, in fact, play a large role in reinforcing typical girl and boy behavior, which is why making mindful choices is so important.

Most conventional board games teach kids the importance of winning; there can only be one winner and the rest of the players are losers. Pretty depressing, huh? Some games teach kids cooperation rather than competition and encourage helping versus hindering strategies. Some even teach

Looking for a good book to read to your children? Dr. Seuss is one of our all-time favorites. *The Sneetches and Other Stories* teaches about racism, *The Butter Battle Book* hints at the absurdity of the arms race nuclear disarmament, and *The Lorax* has great environmental themes.

good social skills, such as sharing, being polite, and understanding different points of view.

Video games get more gruesome every year. Watch any current video game and you're likely to see one character rip out the other's spine in a shower of blood. Gone are the days of Pac-Man and Breakout; Mortal Kombat and Doom are here to stay. Not only are games violent, they often portray women and minorities in stereotypical and demeaning ways (for example, women appear in skimpy outfits, people of color are portrayed as the enemy). There are, however, some games that not only avoid violence and stereotypes but are educational as well. Ask your local computer store about educational games. Before you buy a child a game, make sure you check the game's rating. The Entertainment Software Rating Board provides a useful website that allows you to enter the name of the game and receive a rating reflecting the game's violent and sexual content. You can also find a game's rating on its box.

Entertainment Software Rating Board
🖥 www.esrb.org

TEACHING POSITIVE PLAY RESOURCES

📖 Drake, Jane, Ann Love, and Heather Collins. *The Summer Games Book.* Kids Can Press, 1998.
This illustrated book offers indoor and outdoor games, land and water games, games for groups and games for one or two; in other words, a lot of games.

📖 **Family Pastimes**
RR4, Perth, Ontario, Canada K7H3C6
☎ (613) 267-4819   🖥 www.familypastimes.com
Family Pastimes is an excellent source for friendly and educational games. It is a family-run Canadian company specializing in cooperative games. Contact them for their Catalog of Cooperative Games.

📖 McGregor, Cynthia. *Everybody Wins! 150 Non-Competitive Games for Kids.* Adams Media Corporation, 1998.
This book offers games that will help you prevent hurt feelings, arguments, and disappointment.

📖 Milord, Susan. *The Kids' Nature Book: 365 Indoor/Outdoor Activities and Experiences.* Williamson Publishing, 1997.
Set up like a calendar, this book has a season-appropriate activity for every day of the year.

📖 Steffens, Charlie, and Spencer Gorin. *Learning to Play, Playing to Learn: Games and Activities to Teach Sharing, Caring, and Compromise.* Lowell House/Contemporary Books, 1998.
With over 60 entertaining activities, this book teaches how to play without hurting bodies or feelings while fostering cooperation and positive behavior. To order, contact Creative Spirit, 6062 East Beverly, Tucson, AZ 85711, U.S.A.   💻 www.joyinlearning.com

RAISING CHILDREN RESOURCES

📖 Hill, Linda. *Connecting Kids: Exploring Diversity Together.* Foreword by Rick Scott. New Society Publishers, 2001.
Over 200 games and activities teach kids to cherish diversity.

📖 Kivel, Paul. *Boys Will Be Men: raising our sons for courage, caring, and community.* New Society Publishers, 1999.
Teaches how to raise boys to be loving and happy while challenging racism, sexism, heterosexism, and consumerism.

📖 Martin, April. *The Lesbian and Gay Parenting Handbook: Creating and Raising Our Families.* HarperPerennial, 1993.
A useful guide for dealing with the special issues faced by lesbian and gay parents in raising their children.

📖 Miller, Jamie C. and Cam Clarke. *10-Minute Life Lessons for Kids: 52 Fun and Simple Games and Activities to Teach Your Child Trust, Honesty, Love, and Other Important Values.* Harperperennial Library, 1998.
This easy-to-read and inspiring book provides fun yet meaningful games that will help you discuss your values with kids.

📖 Popov, Linda Kavelin, John Kavelin, and Dan Popov. *The Family Virtues Guide.* New York: Penguin, 1997.
A guide to help parents teach 52 virtues (one for each week) to their children.

💻 The American Psychological Association. "Raising Children to Resist Violence: What You Can Do." www.apa.org/pubinfo/apa-aap.html

COMMUNITY

Neighborhood

Local Community

Community Issues

I T'S IRONIC THAT IN AN AGE of instant global communication, with our cell phones, email, and fax machines, many of us feel more isolated than ever. Virtually all of us want to feel a sense of community — it's comforting, safe, and fulfilling. In fact, community is an essential part of being human. More than just a physical place, a community exists when people care for each other's well-being, share their lives, and embrace the ideal of loving others as they would wish to be loved. Community is a process by which we open up and begin to embrace others as part of our extended family. Our local communities then become good models for caring about people around the world whom we may never meet — the beginnings of a global community. Community never just happens — we must create it.

Unfortunately, society teaches us to behave in ways that thwart our desire for connection: buy a house in the suburbs as far from neighbors as possible; don't ask your neighbors for favors; drive your own car rather than carpool; and look out for yourself first. We feel that our values as a people are eroding; violence is rising; and our nation is divided. We've responded to these beliefs in counterproductive ways. Despite our desire for connection, many of us move frequently rather than put down roots, and we take refuge in our homes rather than connect with our neighbors. As a response to fear of crime and perceived decline of social values, many people who actually yearn for community isolate and barricade themselves in protective, exclusive neighborhoods. Our instincts are to withdraw rather than to fully engage the world. Instead of reaching out, we close ourselves off.

But don't despair. Millions of people are showing us how to create the communities we want. Religious groups, communities of color, lesbians and gays, members of the simple living movement, and others are being proactive and redefining what community means. Out of necessity, they have created safe, supportive environments in which they thrive. Consider, for a moment, the awesome possibilities for your life and the world when you intentionally create community.

This chapter will inspire you to make your neighborhood and local community better places to live. Its concrete actions and resources will challenge you to make real your dreams of a community where everyone feels a sense of belonging and responsibility toward the common good. It is important to think of community not only as an end goal or a place to exist but also as a process and an ideal to reach. Have an exciting and wonderful journey in creating your world anew!

> We are faced with having to learn again about interdependency and the need for rootedness after several centuries of having systematically — and proudly — dismantled our roots, ties, and traditions. We had grown so tall we thought we could afford to cut the roots that held us down, only to discover that the tallest trees have the most elaborate roots of all.
> — *Paul L. Wachtel*

NEIGHBORHOOD

The creation of community starts at home. The quality of your relationships significantly shapes how you and your neighbors experience your lives. Living in a neighborhood where you can rely on other people and enjoy going outside feels great. There are many things you can do to make your neighborhood into a vibrant and welcoming place. We describe a few below to get you started.

❏ Action: Put down roots

Every year, about 42,000,000 of us pack up and move — that's about one out of every six people.[1] The average American moves 11.7 times in a lifetime.[2] Many of us move whenever we find a new job or can afford a bigger, so-called better house. A certain amount of mobility is beneficial (and even unavoidable), but moving every few years reduces the probability of developing meaningful community. It's difficult to justify investing time and effort to connect with a place that you know you'll be leaving soon. Yet putting down roots offers advantages that may outweigh taking a higher-paying job or a larger house in some other community. Long-term friendships and community ties are priceless.

❑ *Action: Get to know your neighbors*

Moving creates a great deal of stress. When new people move into your community, you can help create a sense of belonging by welcoming them. Try to greet new members of your neighborhood within the first week of their arrival. Each day that you wait to introduce yourself decreases the likelihood that you will have the courage to deliver a warm welcome.

A good way to start is to share food. Take over some extra vegetables from your garden, bake some muffins, or invite your new neighbors over for coffee or dinner. This is also a great opportunity to introduce them to other neighbors living around them — maybe you could have a block party. You can even create a list of common services, such as bus schedules, area parks, schools and churches, farmers' markets and/or locally owned grocery stores, a trustworthy mechanic, the nearest cheap movie theater, or good locally owned restaurants, for your new neighbors! Challenge yourself to meet people who may not fit the norm in your neighborhood, such as people of different races, social classes, abilities, ages, and backgrounds. Strike up a conversation and start building some real community.

❑ *Action: Help your neighbors and ask for their help*

Imagine waking up on a cold, snowy morning, looking out the window, and seeing that someone has already shoveled your sidewalk. What a great feeling! You can create that feeling in your neighborhood by helping your neighbors when they need a hand. Not only will you help your neighbors out and build community, you'll also find fulfillment that just doesn't come from watching TV or mowing your own lawn. Here are a few suggestions your neighbors will appreciate:

✓ Shovel snow off their driveway and sidewalk.

✓ Mow their lawn and feed their pets when they're out of town.

✓ Take your neighbor to the airport.

✓ Watch their kids so they can have a nice evening together.

✓ Help with home repairs and yard work.

✓ Split the cost of expensive power tools that you can both use.

✓ If you go to the farmers' market, buy them some produce.

✓ Borrow from and lend to your neighbors.

Even if you offer your help, you have little control over whether or not your neighbors ask you for help. Although almost everyone is willing to give help, very few people are willing to ask for it. Consider asking your neighbors for their help, to begin the process of establishing a community of people that can count on each other.

❏ *Action: Organize a neighborhood event*

Often our sense of community grows from our participation in events that bring local people together or that benefit the neighborhood as a whole. If your neighborhood lacks these kinds of events, you just might be the person who gets them going. You can begin to revitalize your community. Consider one or more of the following:

- Organize a local litter clean-up walk.
- Coordinate a blockwide garage sale.
- Set up an annual graffiti paint-over day.
- Throw a block party.
- Establish a Neighborhood Watch program
  (Check out www.ncpc.org/2neig.htm).
- Plan a 'TV-Turnoff Week' or a 'Buy Nothing Day' event
  (see Resources that follow).

To get started, type up a one-page flyer with a description of the event, a call for some help, and a contact number or email address where people can reach you. Make enough copies so that you can post one on each of your neighbors' doors, and prepare to set up a convenient meeting time to discuss the event. The rest is just a combination of good will and a little sweat.

TV-Turnoff Network's 'TV Turnoff Week'
For $15, TV-Turnoff Network will send you a 48-page organizer's kit — complete with posters, bumper stickers, alternative activities, articles, essays and much more — to start your own 'TV-Turnoff Week' in your community this April. 'TV-Turnoff Week' encourages people to dramatically reduce their television viewing in order to promote healthier and more connected lives, families and communities. Consider encouraging your local school to join in.
☎ (800) 939-6737   🖳 www.tvturnoff.org

Adbusters' **'Buy Nothing Day'**
Adbusters will send you sample press releases, posters, TV and radio commercials, and will connect you with like-minded members of your community to help celebrate 'Buy Nothing Day' — an international event on the Friday after Thanksgiving — to publicize the effects of over-consumption on our families, culture, and the planet. A growing number of activists in over 30 countries made 'Buy Nothing Day' an international success in 2000.
☎ (604) 736-9401   🖳 www.adbusters.org

❏ *Action: Plant a tree*

We owe the air we breathe to the plants and trees around us. Unfortunately, as cities and highways continue to grow, wilderness areas shrink. Planting trees is a fun way to repair some of the damage humans have done to the Earth and to learn how trees grow and thrive. Seedlings make great creative gifts. Go to your local nursery and pick out a tree appropriate to your eco-system.

American Forests
☎ (202) 955-4500   ▢ www.americanforests.org

LOCAL COMMUNITY

Take time to think about what makes your community unique and special. Is it the food, music, and art? The landscape, parks, and wildlife? Is it the old downtown and the local businesses? Is it the opportunities for recreation and local attractions? Is it the schools and community centers? The architecture, history, and ethnic diversity? Here are some suggestions for becoming more integrally involved in your community and making it a more spirited, compassionate, and beautiful place to live.

❑ Action: Participate in community organizations

You don't have to start your own organizations from scratch to create community. There are likely dozens of organizations that already bring people together in positive ways. You can participate or take an active role in maintaining these groups.

- Peace Centers
- Civic Organizations
- Free Clinics
- Service Organizations
- Retirement Homes
- Boys' and Girls' Clubs
- Youth Centers
- Churches/Synagogues/Temples/Mosques
- Rape Crisis Centers/Women Shelters
- YMCA/YWCA/Community Recreation Centers
- Volunteer Fire Departments
- City Sports Leagues

❑ Action: Volunteer in a soup kitchen, homeless shelter, or food pantry

A community is only as strong as its weakest members. Create a strong, caring community by serving those who most need your help, including the homeless and hungry. Food pantries, soup kitchens, and homeless shelters always need volunteers and resources. Many businesses and religious and civic groups commit to serving at a soup kitchen or food pantry once each month. Volunteer on your own or get your favorite group to commit with you.

❏ Action: Volunteer at your local animal shelter

Expand your circle of compassion to include other species by walking a dog or playing with a cat at your local shelter. It's likely that your under-funded, overworked animal shelter staff does not have enough time to give the animals the love and care they need. You can make a difference in animals' lives and have fun while doing it. Dogs are great icebreakers for communicating with strangers, and working with abused animals can be an incredibly healing experience.

SENIOR CORPS

Senior Corps is a great way for seniors to stay involved in their communities. Nearly half a million Americans over 55 donate their time to be foster grandparents, companions who help other seniors live independently, and volunteers in a variety of community organizations.

Corporation for National Service
☎ (202) 606-5000   💻 www.seniorcorps.org

❏ Action: Help Habitat for Humanity build homes

Habitat for Humanity, an ecumenical Christian organization, builds community by building homes with people who need assistance in purchasing their own house. The receiving family helps construct the home and pays for much of it through a no-interest mortgage. In this way, Habitat has built over 100,000 homes around the world!

You can help build community by raising money or volunteering at a site. Don't worry — there's a place for you even if you can't hammer a nail. More than likely there is Habitat construction happening in or very near your community. You may want to get your friends, religious group, business, or other groups involved with working or paying for materials.

Habitat for Humanity
☎ (912) 924-6935
💻 www.habitat.org

Habitat for Humanity® International

❏ Action: Get involved in your local schools

Ask most people what the long-term solution to their community's problems is and education will likely be at the top of their list. Yet few of us take time to be actively involved in our local school. Getting involved in your local school is an incredibly powerful way to make the world a better place! Engaged adults (not just parents) are crucial to successful schools and thereby to successful students. Contact your local school and ask how you can be of service. They will greatly appreciate your talents. Here are a few possibilities:

- Be a crossing guard.
- Chaperone a field trip.
- Donate money.
- Volunteer.
- Join the Parent Teacher Association.
- Coach a team.
- Participate in after-school activities.
- Attend school plays.
- Serve on the school board.
- Attend sporting events.
- Tutor kids.
- Be a mentor.
- Do a presentation about your career.
- Advise a student group.

TEACH FOR AMERICA (TFA)

In 1989, Wendy Kopp, a senior at Princeton University decided it was time to act. Troubled by the inequities in America's educational system, she started Teach for America, a national teacher corps which serves underprivileged school children and gives college graduates one of the most profound experiences of their lives. The program accepts recent graduates with any major for two-year commitments in over a dozen different rural and urban locations. TFA teachers earn regular teacher's salaries, which depend on the area of the country in which they work. To find out more about Teach for America, call: (800) 832-1230 ext. 225, or visit their website at: www.teachforamerica.org.

❑ *Action: Decommercialize your schools*

Corporations seeking to create brand recognition and brand loyalty at younger ages are now advertising to the captive and impressionable audience of kids in schools. Many companies even develop public relations materials disguised as academic lesson plans, teaching children to consume products they don't need. You can take a stand against corporate sponsorship in your school and keep education from becoming a corporate playground. You'll be protecting kids from corporations whose main motivation is hooking kids on their products for life.

"If you own this child at an early age, you can own this child for years to come," explained Mike Searles, president of Kids-R-Us, a major children's clothing store.[3]

✓   Survey the extent of commercialism in your school. Contact Corp Watch at (415) 561-6568 or www.corpwatch.org/trac/feature/education/commercial for a step-by-step guide.

✓   Ask your school to adopt the National PTA guidelines for corporate involvement (www.pta.org/programs/guidelines1.htm).

✓   Share your views by writing a letter to the editor, talking to other parents, or speaking up at a school board meeting.

RESOURCES

The Center for Commercial-Free Public Education

The Center for Commercial-Free Public Education offers great information and actions you can take to decommercialize your school. Their website includes sample press releases, letters to the editor, a resolution against commercialism in schools, and many other great resources to assist you.

☎ (510) 268-1100   🖳 www.commercialfree.org

❏ *Action: Create safe schools*

Unfortunately, violence in our schools has become all too common. Although school shootings make the news, fistfights and intimidation happen more frequently. Sharp divisions between social cliques lead to verbal harassment, hazing, bullying, and feelings of isolation. Differences in social class, race, ethnicity, gender, and sexual orientation make certain students especially vulnerable.

Many proactive schools are implementing violence prevention plans. Talk to your local school's principal to make sure your school has such a program. Refer administrators to the following resources and consider offering your help. By starting a violence prevention project, you could literally be saving lives.

As adults, we need to ensure our schools are safe spaces for all students. It seems that the last group it is acceptable to harass and slander is lesbians, gays, bisexuals, and transgendered (LGBT) people. Students hear an average of 25 anti-gay slurs each day. LGBT youth have a three-to-seven times higher rate of attempted suicide than other youth.[4] Make certain that your local school is taking action to curb this kind of violence.

VIOLENCE PREVENTION RESOURCES

Teaching Tolerance

The Southern Poverty Law Center's Teaching Tolerance Program is one of the most exciting education-based programs dealing with issues of equality, respect, and understanding. They offer a wide variety of free books, magazines, videos, and tool kits to educators and educational institutions that request them.

☎ (202) 467-8180   🖳 www.splcenter.org/teachingtolerance

Center for the Prevention of School Violence (CPSV)

The CPSV provides current school violence research, manuals for starting a Students Against Violence Everywhere group, educational campaign materials, and public awareness ideas.

☎ (800) 299-6054   💻 www.ncsu.edu/cpsv

SCHOOL VIOLENCE.
LET'S GET IT OUT OF OUR SYSTEM.
Center for the Prevention of School Violence

Parents, Families, and Friends of Lesbians and Gays (PFLAG)

PFLAG's Safe Schools program offers resources of all kinds. They offer concrete steps you can implement to make your schools a safe place for lesbian, gay, bisexual, and transgendered youth.

☎ (202) 467-8180   💻 www.pflag.org

❑ Action: Support local arts and culture

Artists reflect the soul of a community and help celebrate its spirit. Folk musicians who play on the street corner downtown add flavor to the city. Summer arts festivals demonstrate the character of a town. Supporting local arts is often an inexpensive yet meaningful way to connect with members of your community and learn something new. Consider the following actions:

✓ Go to museums and visit galleries featuring local artists.
✓ Go to concerts in the park.
✓ Give money to street musicians.
✓ Buy artwork from a local artist.
✓ Attend dance performances, local plays and school productions.

❑ Action: Participate in local, county, regional and statewide community events

Attend community celebrations, ethnic festivals, pow-wows, county and state fairs, music and arts festivals, community fundraisers, and street dances. It's a great way to get to know people beyond your immediate area and to discover which issues are important in their community. These events create an opportunity for a community's unique character to emerge. Plus a little creativity and fun is good for the soul!

❑ Action: Set up a sister city relationship

Sister city relationships build global community by sharing cultures and ideas, building cooperation, and creating opportunities for development. Cities in different countries pair up in long-term relationships; people from one city often exchange business and visit others in their sister city. Some cities, such as Boulder, Colorado, have sister city relationships with multiple cities in different parts of the world — a great way to form meaningful international relationships. Sister churches are similar. Almost every major religious denomination in the United States has a sister church program, which creates close relationships in the lives of church members across nations. Contact your local churches for more information. To help start a sister city program in your area, contact:

Sister Cities International

☎ (202) 347-8630 or (202) 393-6835

💻 www.sister-cities.org

COMMUNITY ISSUES

Tired of roads in your neighborhood that are laden with potholes? Sick of a school system that cut your kid's band program? Curious about who decides how much money to allocate for city parks? Find out what decisions your community leaders are making and let your voice be heard! Local politics has much more of a direct impact on your life than national politics, and you can have more impact at this level, as well.

When most people think of politics, they think of the President and the Congress, but many important decisions are made right at home within your city and county governments. Actually, local governments provide the most important forum for issues such as urban growth, open space protection, education, and transit. Local ordinances and planning have a profound impact on the quality of life in your community. Your involvement in local politics gives you a wide range of opportunities to improve your community for yourself and everyone else.

✓ Write a letter to the editor.

✓ Talk to friends and family about livable community issues.

✓ Collect petitions.

✓ Attend a city council meeting, school board meeting, or public hearing. To find out when and where city council or school board meetings are, check the community events listing of your local newspaper or look in the local government section in the phone book and give city hall a call.

❏ *Action: Stop urban sprawl*

If you've ever been in a metropolitan area, you've probably noticed how the city goes on and on and on, consuming surrounding open space and leaving a trail of Wal-Marts and Pizza Huts in its wake. For the past 50 years, development has spread unchecked, leaving us with irresponsible, frustrating urban sprawl. Sprawl destroys open space, increases traffic congestion, crowds schools, adds to pollution, costs taxpayers billions of dollars in subsidies, and steals our community's identity. You can fight sprawl by advocating responsible, smart growth that considers the environment and the community before profits. Don't forget that the flip side of stopping sprawl is actively creating a more livable community that people can enjoy for generations to come.

- Join Sierra Club's Stop Sprawl campaign. Ask about their stopping sprawl tool kit.
- Attend a city council meeting and demand that policymakers stop unchecked growth.
- Ask your local government to support public transportation rather than build more roads.
- Support unique local businesses over big cookie-cutter chains.
- Support public parks, open space, and local wildlife.
- Encourage the development of bike paths, pedestrian-only streets, traffic-calming devices, and mixed-use development.

Sierra Club
The Sierra Club is one of the largest, most outspoken groups fighting sprawl and advocating more livable communities. Check out the resources on their website or contact them by phone to obtain your own sprawl-fighting tool kit.
☎ (415) 977-5500   💻 www.sierraclub.org/sprawl

Sprawl Watch Clearinghouse (SWC)
SWC compiles resources and serves as a network for grassroots groups fighting sprawl. They feature a list of national organizations and up-to-date information about what's happening in your area.
☎ (202) 974-5133   💻 www.sprawlwatch.org

People around the world are wising up to the drawbacks of sprawl. Norway instituted a moratorium on the construction of suburban malls for five years to encourage inner city renovations.[5]

Streets for People
Streets for People is a how-to manual people can use to bring traffic calming to their neighborhood. Download it in its electronic form for free.
☎ (212) 629-8080
💻 www.transalt.org/info/streets4people/index.html

❏ *Action: Advocate for affordable housing*
The lack of affordable housing is one of our biggest problems. Wages are not keeping up with increasing housing costs. In 1999, the National Low Income Housing Coalition found that in no local jurisdiction in the U.S. could a full-time worker making minimum wage afford the Fair Market Rent for a one-bedroom apartment in her or his community. In fact, in 70 metropolitan areas, minimum wage workers would have to work over 100

hours each week to afford Fair Market Rent in their city![6] By advocating affordable housing in your area, you will join a movement that is dedicated to ensuring economic diversity and the fundamental human right of adequate housing. To find out how to demand affordable housing, check out the resources below.

National Low Income Housing Coalition (NLIHC)

NLIHC educates and organizes people to create affordable housing. Their informative publications influence policy.

☎ (202) 662-1530 ▭ www.nlihc.org

Local and State Affordable Housing Programs

To find affordable housing programs and homeless assistance providers for your state and community, contact the Department of Housing and Urban Development at (202) 708-1422 or www.dud.gov for listings and information. Your state or city office of housing can also be helpful, as can your local Public Housing Authority.

❑ *Action: Advocate for a community living wage*

Living wage campaigns rest on the premise that hard-working people should be paid enough to support themselves and their families. It's that simple. The income gap between the rich and the poor has soared in the past 20 years, and executive salaries have skyrocketed. In contrast, the average worker in 1998 made 12% less in real wages than in 1973.[7] And for the most vulnerable members of your community, the minimum wage still provides less buying power than it did in the early 1980s.[8]

A minimum wage increase would benefit the over ten million families who are trying to get by on meager incomes.[9] Fortunately, community activists are taking matters into their own hands, instead of waiting for Washington to help support poor families. A San Francisco living wage ordinance passed in 2000 guarantees wage increases and benefits for over 21,500 workers who contract with the city. Minimum standards are $9 per hour with a 2-1/2% raise per year; health insurance; and vacation, sick, and family leave time.[10] With your support, your community can join 50 cities and counties across the U.S. that have enacted living wage ordinances since 1994.[11]

ACORN
(see the ORGANIZATIONS chapter)

ACORN is a very active coalition of community groups dedicated to creating affordable and livable communities. They also happen to be the major force behind local living wage laws. Local branches in dozens of cities organize people into powerful voices for change.

☎ (202) 547-2500   ▣ www.acorn.org

❏ *Action: Advocate for increased school funding*

Virtually every politician who runs for office gives lip service to education, yet few take meaningful action towards improving our children's education. Americans consistently place education at the top of their priority lists, and a vast majority of us believe the government needs to increase funding to our schools. Each of us benefits when all kids receive quality education, regardless of whether they're our own kids or not. Money alone won't solve every school's problems, but lack of resources is severely hindering children's educations. Our leaders need to hear loud and clear that repairing dilapidated school buildings and buying textbooks is more important than building a new fleet of fighter planes or giving tax breaks to corporations. This is a great issue about which to make your voice heard at the local, state, and federal levels of government.

National Education Association (NEA)
The NEA advocates for school funding, better teaching, and fair teaching contracts. They also fight attempts to privatize public schools.

☎ (202) 833-4000   ▣ www.nea.org

COMMUNITY RESOURCES

📖 Shaffer, Carolyn R., and Kristin Anundsen. *Creating Community Anywhere: Finding Support and Connection in a Fragmented World.* G.P. Putnam, 1993.
This great how-to manual offers insights on how to create meaningful community and reclaim our connection to something larger than ourselves. It also offers tips on communication and tools applicable to a variety of communities, including your family and friends, your neighborhood, and your workplace.

HOME

Energy

Water

Trash

Lawn and Garden

Your Home

D O YOU REMEMBER your dad constantly reminding you to close the refrigerator or turn off the faucet? Or perhaps you remember your mom telling you to turn down the heat and put on a sweater to save energy. Our homes offer us great opportunities to conserve energy and water, as well as to reduce our trash. Many of us learned early on that conserving resources around our homes is important. Yet as adults our society encourages us to buy bigger and bigger houses that require unimaginable resources to construct and maintain.

In the past, many people settled in one place and lived there for 30 years or more. Their homes became almost sacred places, filled with the stories and memories of a lifetime. In today's highly mobile society, we've given up homes for houses — places in which to store our stuff and return for brief periods of rest between workdays.

The first half of the chapter addresses actions that save water and energy around the home. The rest of the chapter addresses typical home issues, such as recycling and composting, and maintaining a lawn and garden. Finally, we end with some tips on remodeling your current home and choosing where you want to live. Whether you live in an apartment, town home, condo, or house, you'll learn many easy ways to make your home, and therefore the world, a better place.

ENERGY

Our grandparents knew a time when electricity was a luxury. Today, electricity is so convenient that it is easy to forget it is often produced by the burning of non-renewable heavily polluting fossil fuels. Most of us are unaware of how generating energy affects the Earth, because to us it just comes out of a socket in the wall. In our world of coal-fired plants and nuclear reactors, home energy conservation translates into cleaner air, cleaner water, a safeguard against global warming, and the preservation of habitat from strip-mining and drilling — in all, a more sustainable society. And it doesn't hurt that saving energy saves us money, too.

❏ Action: Contact your local utility company to perform an energy audit

For a nominal fee, your local utility may send someone out to assess the best energy-saving changes that you can make to your home. Look on your utility bill for a contact number. They might even give you a price cut on energy-efficient purchases, such as compact fluorescent bulbs or a water heater jacket.

❏ Action: Use your appliances efficiently

When you are ready to purchase a new appliance, be sure to consider its impact on the environment. Most major appliances have clearly displayed 'Energy Guide' stickers that make it easy to compare individual models' energy efficiency. Consider buying the appliance with the lowest energy usage that meets your needs. Just by installing energy-efficient appliances, you can save over 50% of your energy consumption as compared to standard models.[1] Remember that even if you have to pay extra for the energy-efficient model, it will often pay for itself (and then some) in reduced energy bills for the years to come. Before you buy a new appliance, check with your utility company for possible rebates on energy-efficient models!

THE ENERGY STAR PROGRAM

By designating the most energy-efficient appliance models as 'Energy Stars," the Environmental Protection Agency (EPA) makes it easy for us to purchase energy-saving devices. When you are shopping for a new appliance, look for the Energy Star symbol directly on the item. If you want to make a thorough search for the most efficient appliance, check out the EPA's website. They rate household appliances, furnaces, air conditioners, office equipment, and windows.
☎ (888) STAR-YES   🖳 www.energystar.gov

Here are some easy tips for purchasing energy-efficient appliances and using your current appliances in a more efficient manner.

Heating System (The #1 User of Household Energy)

Heating our homes is an extremely energy-intensive endeavor. Efficient natural gas furnaces, pellet wood stoves, and electric space heaters (as a supplement) are great alternatives to inefficient electric furnaces and fireplaces. Ask for 'high-efficiency' furnaces that earn an AFUE efficiency rating of 90% or higher (compared to the minimum standard of 78% efficient). For heat pumps, an HSPF rating of 7.5 or higher is considered 'high efficiency'; the maximum available is 10.0. (6.8 minimum standard).

Tips for use:

✓ Replace your furnace air filters monthly and tune up your furnace annually.

✓ Turn down your heater's thermostat to 65°F (18° C) during the day and 57°F (14°C) at night. Install a programmable thermostat to allow the heat to kick in right before you wake up and just before you come home. Energy savings from programmable thermostats can reach 30-40%.[2]

✓ Let the sun heat your home. By opening your blinds during the day and closing them at night, you can save up to 7 gallons (32 liters) of heating oil.[3]

Air Conditioner

Every year, the energy used to cool the average air-conditioned home creates about 3500 pounds (1600 kilograms) of carbon dioxide (the leading greenhouse gas) and 31 pounds (14 kilograms) of sulfur dioxide (a leading cause of acid rain).[4] Consider alternatives or supplements to central air conditioners to cool your home including: a whole-house ventilating fan, ceiling fans, an evaporative cooler/swamp cooler (in arid climates), or room-size air conditioners (with an EER rating of at least 12).

For central air conditioners, seek out models with a SEER rating of at least 12 (17 is the highest available, with 10 being the minimum standard).

Tips for use:

✓ Set the A/C thermostat a little higher (78°F [25° C]) and turn it up even further any time you leave the house for more than a half hour.

✓ Shut your windows during the hot parts of the day and open them at night.

✓ Plant shade trees by hot spots, such as southwest-facing windows, or to provide shade for your air conditioning unit.

Water Heater (The #2 User Of Household Energy)

Solar water heaters are the most energy-efficient alternative to electric water heaters. They are considerably more expensive, but they pay huge dividends in reduced energy usage. You may also want to consider a tankless on-demand water heater that heats water as you need it. An on-demand model conserves massive amounts of energy (up to 50%), because it doesn't run throughout the night and day when no one is using it.[5] You'll also never run out of hot water! Call up any water heater dealer and ask about these energy-saving alternatives. When buying a gas-fired or electric water heater, look for energy-efficient models with an EF rating of at least .63 or .96, respectively.

Tips for use:

✓   Install a water heater jacket and insulate the connecting pipes.

✓   Turn down your water heater to 120°F (50° C) and ever lower when you go on vacation.

Refrigerator (The #3 User Of Household Energy)

The energy efficiency of refrigerators varies widely between models and brands — so be sure to compare Energy Guide stickers. The most important eco-tip is to buy the smallest refrigerator that meets your needs. Extra features often increase energy usage, too: a side-by-side refrigerator-freezer uses more energy than a top-bottom model (especially compared to models with the freezer on bottom), and automatic icemakers increase energy use by up to 20%.[6]

Suggested brands

Sunfrost and Conserve (see Jade Mountain in Home Resources section) refrigerators save 40-75% of the energy of a standard refrigerator. They cost more than other refrigerators but you'll save hundreds or even thousands of dollars in energy costs over the life of the fridge.

Tips for use:

✓   Clean the refrigerator coils once a year with a vacuum or rag.

Dishwasher

When you are looking for a dishwasher, look for the following energy-saving features: a booster heater that allows you to turn down your water heater, and lower levels of water usage (most models use between 8 and 14 gallons [16 and 64 liters] of water each use).

Suggested brands:

Explorer (about $750) and Asko (about $900) dishwashers use only 5 gallons (23 liters) of water and save about 65% of the electricity usage of the standard dishwasher.

Tips for use:

✓   Wash full loads.

✓   Use 'light wash,' 'air dry,' and other energy-saving cycles.

Washer and Dryer

The heating of water uses up to 90% of the energy consumed during clothes washing.[7] That's why it's important to find models that use less water and allow you to use colder temperatures. Front-loading washing machines use up to 50% less water than top-loading models.[8]

Suggested brands:
Asko, Equator, and Creda can use as little as 13 to 18 gallons (59 to 82 liters) per wash, significantly less than the conventional washer.

A gas-powered dryer can save you 50% in energy costs and will create less pollution than electric dryers.[9] Dryers with automatic moisture sensors can save up to 15% because they prevent the over-drying of clothes.[10]

Tips for use:
✓ Wash and dry full loads of laundry.
✓ Wash your clothes in cold water when possible.
✓ Let the sun dry your clothes (or put them on a drying rack).
✓ Don't over-dry your clothes.

❑ *Action: Weatherize your home*

- **Weatherstripping**: Install proper weatherstripping and caulking — it's a cinch and very inexpensive. Just check around your windows and doors for energy-wasting drafts. Ask at your local hardware store for tips.

- **Insulation**: Check with your local utility to determine the proper insulation for your home. The average household could reduce its energy consumption by 20-30% with proper insulation.[11]

- **Energy-efficient windows**: Substantially more heat escapes through your windows than through your walls. Double-paned windows are an option for cutting heat loss and your heating bill. Install storm windows in the winter for another great way to conserve heat. Thermal draperies that fit snugly in your window frame can also reduce lost heat by 50%.[12]

❑ *Action: Light your home efficiently*

Home lighting consumes approximately 25% of your annual home energy usage.[13] It's no wonder that figure is so high, when a normal (incandescent) 100-watt bulb turned on for 12 hours a day for one year requires 394 pounds (179 kilograms) of coal to be burned.[14] There are two easy steps to remember:

1. Turn off your lights when you aren't using them or when you can just let the sun shine in (it's free and naturally renewable).

2. Install compact fluorescent light bulbs in your most commonly used lamps and fixtures. Compact fluorescent bulbs are a great alternative because they last 10 times longer and use one-fourth the energy of incandescent bulbs. Compact fluorescent bulbs cost around $15, but over the life of the bulb, they will save you $45 (mostly from energy savings) and prevent the burning of 300 pounds (136 kilograms) of coal.[15] There are even torchiere lamps available that use compact fluorescent bulbs instead of energy-guzzling halogen bulbs.

❏ *Action: Choose an environmentally responsible electricity provider*

Currently, two dozen states have deregulated their utility industry (including California, New Jersey, and Pennsylvania), and it seems to be a growing trend. Unfortunately, utility deregulation removes many regulations that protect the consumer and the environment. If California's 2001 energy crisis is any indication of deregulation's consequences, we should be careful before deregulating any further. On the up side, deregulation gives consumers more choice in picking their energy provider. If you have a choice, be sure to shop around and take this opportunity to help create a more sustainable future. Pick the utility with the highest percentage of clean renewable energy (for example, wind and solar power). Whether or not your state's utility industry has been deregulated, be sure to contact them about any possibilities of purchasing clean, renewable energy.

WATER

As with electricity, water is easy to waste because we don't really see where it comes from. Water conservation is an important environmental issue for two main reasons. Saving water: (1) helps support wildlife habitat by replenishing local streams and lakes and (2) saves energy that would otherwise have been used to heat and purify the water at your local water treatment plant.

Fortunately, it is quite easy to conserve water at home. Up to 50% of home water usage comes from taps running unnecessarily.[16] To prevent wasting water, try to determine where the water in your home is escaping. The simple act of shutting off your faucet while you are washing your dishes or brushing your teeth may seem insignificant, but it quickly adds up to monumental conservation when multiplied by millions of people.

❏ *Action: Install faucet aerators and low-flow showerheads*

Faucet aerators reduce the amount of water you use, while still maintaining the water pressure. They are easy to install and are less than $10. Most large hardware stores carry them. A faucet aerator can decrease your water consumption from 4 gallons (18 liters) per minute to less than 1 gallon (4 liters) per minute.

The average showerhead uses up to 6 gallons (27 liters) of water each minute we shower.[17] By using a low-flow showerhead, you will cut your water consumption down to 1 to 2 gallons (5 to 9 liters) per minute (a more than 75% reduction), without significantly diminishing water pressure. Some showerheads even have a handy switch to turn off the water while you lather up. An outlay of $25 to retrofit one showerhead and two faucets will save you up to $100 per year on your utility bills and reduce carbon dioxide emissions by 580 to 3200 pounds (260 to 1450 kilograms).[18] Cutting the length of your showers is also an easy way to save water.

❏ Action: Transform your toilet into a water miser

Toilets use more water than anything else in our homes. The common household toilet can account for 40% of a home's indoor water use.[19] Astonishingly, we flush away around 19 gallons (86 liters) of water per person every day.[20]

A cheap way to reduce the flow in your current toilet is to fill a slim milk jug with water and place it in the toilet tank. This will displace some of the water, reducing the amount required to fill up the tank. Keep adding bottles and jugs until there is just enough water to effectively clean the bowl. Be sure that you don't impede the workings of the toilet's mechanisms. Also, don't use a brick as a displacement device, because it breaks apart and can cause plumbing problems. If you want to get fancy, you can purchase a water dam that partitions off part of your tank to reduce water use.

When you need a new toilet, buy one that is designed to conserve water. Older toilets use 5 to 7 gallons (23 to 32 liters) of water per flush, but ultra-low flow toilets can reduce a flush to 1.6 gallons (7 liters) or less (and still keep the bowl nice and clean).

❏ Action: Use environmentally friendly cleaners and laundry detergents

If your cleaning cupboard is like most people's, it's filled with tons of sprays, powders, and bottles of all colors and sizes. Chemical companies constantly try to sell us the latest great cleaners, detergents, deodorizers, and stain removers (for evidence of the effectiveness of marketing just look under your sink). Unfortunately, cleansers usually come in a non-recyclable plastic container, expose your family to hazardous chemicals, were tested on animals using horrific methods, and wreak havoc on local lakes and streams. Fortunately, there are ways of reducing our dependence on commercial cleaners.It's easy to make your own non-toxic cleaners, and they have many benefits for the world. Non-toxic cleaners:

✓   often clean just as well as many commercial cleaners

✓   take little time to prepare

✓   save you money

✓   reduce hazardous chemical and packaging waste

✓   protect you from harmful chemicals

Here is the line-up of non-toxic cleaning all-stars:
- water
- baking soda
- vinegar
- borax
- vegetable oil-based liquid soap
- washing soda (it's mildly toxic)

EVERYDAY SOLUTION FOR GETTING OUT TOUGH STAINS

General stains: 2 Tbsp (30 ml) Washing Soda in 1 C (250 ml) Warm Water

Fruit and wine: Pour salt or hot water on the stain and soak it in Milk before washing

Grease: Pour boiling water on the stain and dry with baking soda

Other stains: Try mixing salt, baking soda, cream of tartar, or shampoo with water

Eco-Fabric softener: Add 1/4 to 1/2 C (50 to 125 ml) Vinegar or 1/4 C (50 ml) Baking Soda or Borax during the final rinse. Vinegar even reduces static cling and lint!

CLEANING CHART

All-Purpose General Cleaners (replaces your 409 or Soft Scrub)

1/4 C (50 ml)   +   1/2C (125 ml)   +   1/2 C (125 ml) Vinegar   +   1 gal (4.5 liters) Water

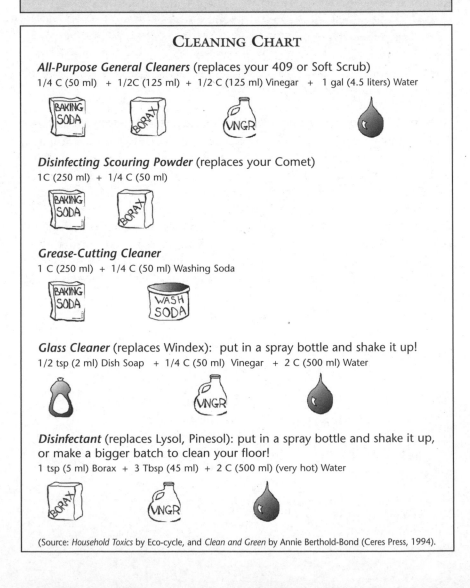

Disinfecting Scouring Powder (replaces your Comet)

1C (250 ml)   +   1/4 C (50 ml)

Grease-Cutting Cleaner

1 C (250 ml)   +   1/4 C (50 ml) Washing Soda

Glass Cleaner (replaces Windex): put in a spray bottle and shake it up!

1/2 tsp (2 ml) Dish Soap   +   1/4 C (50 ml) Vinegar   +   2 C (500 ml) Water

Disinfectant (replaces Lysol, Pinesol): put in a spray bottle and shake it up, or make a bigger batch to clean your floor!

1 tsp (5 ml) Borax   +   3 Tbsp (45 ml)   +   2 C (500 ml) (very hot) Water

(Source: *Household Toxics* by Eco-cycle, and *Clean and Green* by Annie Berthold-Bond (Ceres Press, 1994).

If you don't want to take the time to make your own non-toxic cleaners, companies such as Ecover, Seventh Generation, Bon Ami, Granny's Old Fashioned Products, Allens Naturally, and Ecco Bella make eco-friendly cleaners and detergents. Look for them at your local natural food store or in a natural products catalog.

Most conventional laundry detergents contribute to similar environmental and health problems. The two main ingredients to avoid in laundry detergents are phosphates and chlorine. Phosphates flow into our rivers and streams, wreaking havoc on algae levels and changing the composition of the ecosystem. Chlorine production and use damages the natural environment possibly more than any other single substance. Avoid chlorine at all costs! Fortunately, companies such as Seventh Generation and Ecover produce chlorine- and phosphate-free detergents for washing your clothes. Chlorine-free bleach is also available at any supermarket.

RESOURCES

Berthold-Bond, Annie. *Better Basics for the Home: simple solutions for less toxic living.* Three Rivers Press, 1999.
This book has everything from nontoxic ways to clean your fireplace and metal items to homemade car wax and furniture polish. A really fun book.

TRASH

The whole concept of throwing away something is really an illusion. You can't throw away anything — you can just relocate it. When we take our garbage out to the curb, we like to wash our hands of it. But it goes from our driveway to an incinerator or a landfill, where someone else has to deal with it. The average American throws away 4 pounds (2 kilograms) of waste every day — that's over 1 billion pounds (450 million kilograms) of trash, every day, just in the U.S.[21]

WHAT'S IN OUR TRASH?

Other 14%
Food 7%
Glass 7%
Plastics 8%
Metals 8%
Paper 38%
Yard Waste 18%

U.S. Environmental Protection Agency www.epa.gov, "Recycling," Sept. 29, 1997.

A number of actions will reduce your contribution to the enormous growth of solid waste and the overconsumption of natural resources in this country. The key to cutting your waste is to better understand what you are throwing away. How could you have prevented even buying what you are throwing away? Can you reuse or recycle it? Can you compost it?

❏ *Action: Reduce your junk mail*

Americans receive over 4.5 million tons (4.1 metric tons) of unsolicited junk mail every year — that's 34 pounds (15 kilograms) of useless mail for each person.[22] We discard about half of this mail before even opening it.[23] There are a few easy steps you can take to reduce the amount of junk mail you receive.

✓ Contact companies who send you unwanted mailings and tell them, "Take me off your list." (Use their business reply envelopes!)

✓ Ask telemarketers, " Please take me off your calling list."

✓ Obtain every variation of your name, address, and phone number (look at the labels on your junk mail for variations). Send them to the following addresses and ask them, "Remove me from your mailings and telephone lists."

Mail Preference Service
Direct Marketing Association
P.O. Box 9008,
Farmingdale, NY 11735-9008,
U.S.A.

Telephone Preference Service
Direct Marketing Association
P.O. Box 9014,
Farmingdale, NY 11735-9014,
U.S.A.

Equifax Options
P.O. Box 740123
Atlanta, GA 30374-0123, U.S.A.
☎ (800) 556-4711

Experion Consumer Opt Out
701 Experion Parkway,
Allen, TX 75013, U.S.A.
☎ (800) 353-0809

Trans Union LLC's Name
Removal Service
P.O. Box 97328
Jackson, MS 39288-7328, U.S.A.
☎ (800) 680-7293

In Canada:
Direct Marketing Association
1 Concord Gate, Suite 607,
Don Mills, Ontario M3C 3N6
Canada

If you want a really easy way to get off of junk mail lists, check out <www.newdream.org/junkmail>, type in your name and address, and it will generate the letters for you.

❏ Action: Recycle

Recycling is a commonsense way of saving resources. It decreases the amount of virgin materials and energy consumed and the

> For other tips on saving paper and wood products at home or office, check out www.woodwise.org.

amount of pollution created in the production process. Recycling also decreases the amount of landfill space needed to store our garbage.

Recycling at home is easy. There are three simple steps to get started:

> Remember the 'three Rs' of waste reduction:
>
> *first Reduce what you use, then Reuse what you can, and finally Recycle what's left over.*

1. Locate a collector or a drop-off site for your recyclables.
2. Find out what materials they accept.
3. Start recycling!

Many neighborhoods have curbside recycling programs in which trash haulers pick up your recyclables and keep them from going to the dump. Check your local Yellow Pages under 'Recycling' to see what services are available in your community. If you live in an apartment, consider asking your landlord to expand recycling services.

❏ Action: Compost your kitchen scraps and yard waste

Composting is nature's way of recycling organic matter by letting it decay and return to the soil. Think of composting as a recycling bin for your kitchen scraps and yard waste.

Two reasons to compost:

1. It significantly lessens your household waste (by about 30%).[24]
2. It creates a soil additive that helps grow healthy plants and flowers, reducing the need for harsh petroleum-based chemical fertilizers in your garden (you can also use it as a mulch).

All you have to do to start a compost pile is: find a 3-by-3-foot (1-by-1-meter) plot of land and start piling up your leaves, grass clippings, and food scraps.

To aid decomposition and avoid odors: (1) keep an even balance of leaves/dried grass and food scraps and (2) periodically use a pitchfork or shovel to mix up the pile. Especially in urban areas, many people buy a plastic bin to contain their compost pile (worm boxes work great for apartment dwellers). Ask at your local hardware or lawn store for more information.

DO compost	DON'T compost
vegetables and fruit scraps	meat
flowers and plants	bones
eggshells	fish
pasta and bread	large amounts of fats
coffee (and filters)/ tea bags	(salad dressings)
paper towels	dairy products
leaves/ grass clippings	weeds
straw/ sawdust	infected plants
fireplace ashes	charcoal
	trash

If you use the above tips, it will help produce quality compost and keep the critters away.

RESOURCES

   📖 Harmonious Technologies. *Backyard Composting: Your Complete Guide to Recycling Yard Clippings.* Harmonious Press, 1997.
A very readable book on composting yard waste and food scraps. It's got all the information you need to get started! Call (800) 247-6533 to order it for $6.95.

❑ *Action: Properly dispose of household hazardous waste*

Many substances in your home are considered household hazardous wastes. Unfortunately many people just throw these materials in the trash or dump them in the sewer. If improperly disposed of, these materials can poison wildlife or children, pollute your local stream, or injure sanitation workers.

> Be sure to take your used motor oil to a local service station, car parts store, or community disposal site!

Before disposing of any toxic substances in your home, be sure to call your community disposal site for household toxins. Just look in your Yellow Pages under 'Waste Disposal — Hazardous.' Hazardous waste drop-off sites usually accept paints, solvents, and other chemicals that you should not throw in the garbage.

Household hazardous waste

Motor oil, antifreeze, brake fluid, and other auto fluids	Pesticides
Batteries	Adhesives, caulk
Paint, thinner, stripper, varnish, stain	Chemicals and cleaners
Cosmetics	Weed killer
	Arts and crafts materials

LAWN AND GARDEN

Many North Americans enjoy landscaping their yards and tending to flower and vegetable gardens. As you care for your lawn and garden, be sure to also care for our Earth as a whole. There are many actions we can all take to balance our desire for a nice yard with the need to conserve water, energy, and toxic chemicals.

❑ Action: Xeriscape your lawn and garden

Xeriscaping means that you plant grasses, bushes, and shrubs that will thrive even if they don't receive very much water. This allows you to significantly reduce your household water consumption (especially if you avoid watering during the hottest parts of the day). Ask your local lawn and garden store for the varieties of plants that will work best in your area.

📖 Proctor, Rob. *Xeriscape Plant Guide*. Fulcrum Publishers, 1999.

This guide has detailed descriptions and pictures of 100 popular plants that require little water. It includes trees and shrubs, shade plants, vines and perennials, annuals, ground covers, and grasses.

❑ Action: Use a manual or electric lawnmower

Manual mowers are back (actually they never left). The only energy they require is your muscle power — with no air, water, or noise pollution. Current models cut well and are certainly the most ecologically friendly mowers available.

Believe it or not, you can also buy a mower that plugs into an electrical outlet. Small gasoline engines like those in lawnmowers are extremely inefficient and heavily polluting. In contrast, electric mowers are powered by electricity that has been generated at a power plant (which is much more efficient than your lawnmower's little engine). Electric mowers also cut down on noise pollution. These mowers are especially great for folks with smaller lawns. Don't worry, they teach you how to avoid running over the cord (and some electric mowers don't even need a cord!).

❑ Action: Don't bag your grass clippings

Buying and using a mulching blade for your lawnmower allows you to leave your grass clippings on your lawn. It will create a nitrogen-rich mulch that decreases the need for water and fertilizer and significantly reduces the amount of yard waste you send to the dump. You can purchase a mulching lawnmower blade at most hardware and department stores for under $10.

❑ Action: Avoid buying unnecessary power tools

Before you buy that leaf blower, electric edge trimmer, snow blower, or super deluxe giant-sized grill, ask yourself, "For what this costs and the resources it uses, will I really gain that much fulfillment from it?" and "Is there another way I can accomplish what this machine does?" A broom or rake, for example, can generally do whatever a leaf blower can (and you get a little exercise to boot). By avoiding unnecessary power equipment, you save money (purchase price, fuel, and maintenance), save space (avoiding clutter), reduce pollution, and preserve natural resources.

If, on the other hand, you decide a certain machine will make your life easier, consider purchasing and sharing it with a neighbor. Sharing tools saves money, fosters community, and helps reduce clutter. You can store the snow blower while your neighbor keeps a place for the mower.

REDUCE CHEMICAL FERTILIZERS

Americans use over 1/2 billion pounds (230 million kilograms) of chemical fertilizers on their lawns and gardens every year.[25] It isn't very appealing to think of all that gunk seeping into our groundwater supply. The prevention is to avoid lawn fertilizer and chemical weed killers entirely. Pull weeds by hand, wear golf shoes while you mow to aerate your lawn, and grow grasses and plants natural to the area. If you really think your lawn needs some fertilizer, check into organic fertilizers such as Naturall. Ask your local greenhouse or sod grower for more alternatives.

CFS Specialties, Inc.

CFS Specialties makes 100% organic fertilizers for both lawn and garden.

☎ (800) 822-6671 💻 www.cfspecial.com

YOUR HOME

Your home is more than a place to eat and sleep. It has the potential to be a sustainable, spiritual oasis that supports your desire to make a positive contribution to the world. Most of us like having a sense of home — somewhere we feel comfortable, can be ourselves, and experience a sense of belonging. Our choice of a home is such an important decision, because our physical surroundings influence us significantly every day. Take advantage of this opportunity and create a space that increases your energy and intensifies your enjoyment of life while respecting the natural environment.

❑ *Action: Live close to work*

Where we live largely determines how we get to work. If you live less than one mile away from your workplace, your chances of walking or biking to work grow exponentially. Living close to work will prevent pollution and save you time and money, since your commute is shortened.

❑ *Action: Live in a smaller home*

Many of us eventually want to own an enormous dream home to fill with all of our stuff. Unfortunately, they are more difficult to heat and cool, take up more natural space, and require more lumber and plastic to put together.

Also, big homes tend to tie up our time and money; they take longer to clean, require more repairs, and simply cost more to buy. The more money and time our homes demand, the less we have for other things we value, such as volunteering, spending quality time with our families, or giving to worthy causes.

> The size of a new house has almost doubled since the 1950s (from 1,000 to 1,950 square feet [93 to 181 square meters]) while the size of the average family has decreased.[26]

❏ Action: Arrange your furniture to encourage conversation

Many people circle their furniture around the TV as if it is a shrine. This leads to a knee-jerk reaction of sitting down and turning on the TV. Your likelihood of reading a book or having a quality conversation increases exponentially if your chair isn't staring right at the boob tube. Consider putting your chairs and couches in an arrangement that fosters communication. At the very least, put the TV in a cabinet or cover it up so it doesn't look so inviting.

❏ Action: Grow household plants

Plants improve the air quality in your home. They not only take in carbon dioxide and give off oxygen (that's what we breathe), but they also absorb many types of indoor air pollutants. Plants also create a warm living environment. And it is wonderful to be surrounded by living things, instead of exclusively by machines and appliances. Plants also give you the opportunity to be a steward for another living organism, since you get to feed, water, and watch them grow.

❏ Action: Sign up with a socially responsible long distance service

Working Assets

Imagine if every time you made a long distance call, some of your money went to doctors working in war-torn countries, women's literacy programs in the Third World, or the Educational Fund to End Handgun Violence. Working Assets is a long distance phone company dedicated to social justice and empowerment. They donate 1% of your long distance charges to a variety of non-profit organizations, from civil rights and environmental groups to peace and economic justice groups. One percent may not sound like much, but since 1986 Working Assets has donated well over $12 million to hundreds of organizations — $3 million in 1997 alone! They offer action alerts about a number of important issues with your phone bill, as well as free calls to your legislators every month, all at very competitive long distance rates.

☎ (800) 788-8588   ▣ www.workingassets.com

Earth Tones

If you are particularly passionate about the environment, consider Earth Tones, a long distance company similar to Working Assets that gives 100% of its profits to environmental groups. They also offer action alerts and free calls to government officials every month.

☎ (888) 327-8486   ▣ www.earth-tones.com

LONG DISTANCE TELEPHONE SERVICE	
EXCELLENT	Working Assets, Earth Tones
GOOD	AT&T
FAIR	Sprint
POOR	MCI-Worldcom

❏ *Action: Give away your clutter*

Many of us have a room, a basement, or a garage full of stuff that we don't use. Physical clutter not only fills up our homes, it fills up our minds, leading to anxiety and mental clutter. Why have a lot of stuff stored away when other people could be using it right now? Old TVs, clothes, and books will be appreciated by people who are less fortunate.

A few times a year, search through all of your storage space. A good rule to start with is if you haven't used it in the past 12 months, you probably don't need it. When you give away your extra stuff, you will not only be helping people get quality merchandise at cheap prices but you will help the environment by having your stuff reused.

❏ *Action: Consciously choose your community*

Most people put a lot of time and thought into picking the right home but never even think about choosing the right group of people to live with and around. When you consciously choose your community, instead of just happening upon it, your choice can lead to years of benefits. There are a lot of exciting possibilities for creating a living environment that supports strong community building.

Is it important for you to live:

- near a park for recreation?
- near bike paths for alternative transportation?
- in an area with a strong sense of community?
- in an area with low levels of traffic?
- in a racially and ethnically diverse neighborhood?

You also might want to consider some of the following non-traditional living environments to build a stronger sense of community.

Shared Housing Multiple families live in one home. You can rent out unused rooms to family, friends, or strangers. Shared housing is a great way to add some vitality to your house and help pay the bills.

Co-housing A concept that we imported from Denmark, co-housing combines the privacy of a single family dwelling with the sense of a strong community. Each family has its own unit with private rooms, living space, and a small kitchen. Communal spaces include a large kitchen, workshop, office space, children's playroom, and garden. Check out The Cohousing Network at: www.cohousing.org for more information.

Intentional Communities A fast-growing alternative to anonymous suburban life, intentional communities usually form around shared values such as environmentally sustainable living, vegetarian eating, or a certain spiritual path. Members often share cooking, gardening, and other chores. Check out The Fellowship for Intentional Community at: www.ic.org for more information.

RESOURCES

📖 McCamant, Katheryn, and Charles Durrett. *Cohousing: A Contemporary Approach to Housing Ourselves.* Ten Speed Press, 1994.
This is *the* book on co-housing. It is full of floor plans, pictures, and stories about co-housing communities around the world.

☐ *Action: Remodel with green materials*

Remodeling is an exciting activity for homeowners. As you plan your remodeling, consider your home's impact on the environment.

Here are some ideas to get you thinking:

✓ Use latex (water-based) paint instead of oil-based paint.

✓ Use adhesives with low levels of Volatile Organic Compounds (VOCs).

✓ Use second-hand building materials.

✓ Use recycled products (porches, fences, carpets, and benches can be made from recycled plastic).

✓ When buying wood, look for labels that indicate environmentally sustainable harvesting methods: Forest Stewardship Council (FSC), Scientific Certification Systems (SCS), or Smartwood.

✓ Install photovoltaic solar cells (known as PVs) on your roof (they are becoming more affordable every day).

HOME RESOURCES

📖 *Consumer Guide to Home Energy Savings.* American Council for an Energy-Efficient Economy, 1999.
Whether you are considering repairs or renovations, ACEEE's guide to energy savings will get you the information you need on energy efficiency

for appliances, insulation, windows, landscaping, lighting, and home maintenance. Available for $8.95.

☎ (202) 429-0063   🖥 www.aceee.org

Department of Energy's Home Energy Saver

Type in your zip code to find out the most cost-effective, energy-saving home improvement tips for your area.

🖥 www.homeenergysaver.lbl.gov

Jade Mountain

Jade Mountain is a retailer for all types of environmentally responsible products for the home. Everything from composting toilets and photovoltaic solar cells to energy-efficient appliances are available on their website. Their site is also a great source of information about a number of cutting-edge home technologies.

717 Poplar Avenue, Boulder, CO 80304, U.S.A.

☎ (800) 442-1972   🖥 www.jade-mtn.com

Rocky Mountain Institute (RMI)

RMI is a great resource for energy saving tips for the home, energy-efficient cars, and renewable sources of energy for the world.

1739 Snowmass Creek Road, Snowmass, CO 81654-9199, U.S.A.

☎ (970) 927-3851   🖥 www.rmi.org

📖 Schaeffer, John, ed., and Douglas R. Pratt. *The Real Goods Solar Living Sourcebook: The Complete Guide to Renewable Energy Technologies and Sustainable Living.* Real Goods, 1999.

This large book, now in its tenth edition, is the 'renewable energy bible.' It has detailed information on using the sun, wind, and water to make your home more ecologically sustainable.

🖥 www.realgoods.com

WORK

Workplace Relationships

Socially Responsible Workplace

Finding Your Work

D O YOU LOOK FORWARD to going to work in the morning, or is it a struggle to drag yourself out the door? For some of us, work is nothing more than putting money on the table, while others gain significant meaning from their jobs. The average person who works 40 hours each week for 35 years will work around 70,000 hours in their lifetime. Since we spend so much time working, we ought to consider how we can make our job engaging and fulfilling while actively contributing to a better world.

Somehow work has come to mean a place that keeps you from more enjoyable activities. Many of us are working for the weekend, struggling through a miserable job so that we can afford to escape for a while and play. Unless you consciously choose to pursue fulfilling work, society will likely push you toward monotonous, unsatisfying jobs. Imagine how your life would be different if your job was more than a way to maintain a lifestyle and you were genuinely excited to get to work because you were actively creating a better world each day.

When you integrate your work with your most deeply held values, it becomes a meaningful expression of who you are as a human being. This chapter will empower you with actions that transform your work experience, will help you choose a great job, create an extraordinary place to work, help workers out, and make your workplace socially and environmentally friendly.

❑ *Action: Limit your work time*

Have you ever noticed that when you meet someone, almost the first question out of your mouth is "What do you do?" This is a very open-ended question.

167

Your new acquaintance could answer, "I garden," "I write poetry," or "I try to be the best parent I can be." The answer, however, is always the person's work.

In our culture, work defines who we are: we are driven to be career focused. Our status and identity often come from our job's prestige and salary rather than from the quality of our relationships and the overall quality of our lives. Consequently, when we're offered a promotion that will increase our status and salary we tend to accept it without hesitation — despite the additional hours, stress, and responsibility.

The average American works 1,966 hours each year. That's 235 hours more than workers in the United Kingdom, 310 more than in France, 392 more than in Germany, and 414 more hours than in Sweden![1] Men worked on average 100 hours more and women 233 hours more per year in 1993 than in 1976. Almost 20% of Americans worked 49 hours or more each week. That's a full extra 8-hour day![2]

Even with the best of intentions, if you don't consciously limit your work time, work will creep in and take over all of your other priorities. How do extra meetings at work or overtime pay compare to your daughter's first soccer game or a special dinner with your significant other? We need to realize that the time we give our friends and family is more valuable than the things we give them.

We realize that many of you may not have the luxury of working less. Rising housing costs and stagnating wages restrict our opportunities to limit work time. However, simpler lifestyles create possibilities for many of us to limit work time and achieve balance between work aspirations and the rest of our lives. Working less will help you lower your stress, improve your health and sleep patterns, improve your relationships, provide time for civic and creative pursuits, and make your life more fulfilling. Consider asking for more vacation time instead of a raise next time around!

ARE YOU A WORKAHOLIC?

Do you regularly work through lunch?	Yes No
Have your long hours caused strain in your relationships?	Yes No
Does work interfere with your planned time off?	Yes No
Do you often think about work outside the office?	Yes No
Do you work more than 45 hours a week?	Yes No
Have you given up on your hobbies?	Yes No
Do you think about work while driving, falling asleep or when others are talking?	Yes No

If you answered Yes to a majority of these questions, you may want to consider if you work too much and how you might reconsider your focus on work.

❑ *Action: Take your lunch to work*

The cost of eating out each day adds up quickly and is often less healthy than making your own lunch. If you bring your lunch from home, you save money, packaging, time, and gas (if you drive somewhere for lunch). You can share with other people or have a picnic outside. Try to use reusable containers and utensils rather than plastic baggies and silverware.

WORKPLACE RELATIONSHIPS

Your experience at work has an enormous impact on your satisfaction with life. How content you are with your work and your relationships with your coworkers affects your quality of life even more than your salary. If you take time to create some community and a supportive work environment, everyone will experience daily benefits.

❑ *Action: Avoid gossip*

Nothing creates a hostile work environment more quickly than gossip. Few things feel worse than knowing people are talking about you, and the effects of talking behind people's backs are potentially devastating.

✓ Don't get reeled in by people who want to gossip. You can remove yourself from the situation or simply listen without adding to the gossip pool.

✓ Try to resolve conflicts immediately, before gossip and rumors begin, by dealing directly with the other person. You'll save yourself loads of trouble later by dealing with conflict now.

✓ Stay positive at work. People will have less to gossip about.

❑ *Action: Appreciate everyone in your workplace*

When we are young, our society teaches us which people deserve respect because of their jobs and which ones do not: doctors, lawyers, and professors are important people, while secretaries, janitors, and manual laborers are not. As adults, we often unintentionally reaffirm this hierarchy in the workplace by giving some people significant respect and treating others almost as if they were invisible. Be respectful of all people in the workplace and thank them when you notice their quality work. This includes the people who clean and maintain your workplace, those who install and fix your equipment, temporary workers, interns, customers, and delivery people. They all make integral contributions to your workplace. Consider taking them out to lunch, telling them how much you appreciate their work, or even giving them a heartfelt gift.

❑ *Action: Get to know your coworkers outside of work*

Although you may feel that you already spend enough time with your coworkers, consider spending some quality time with them away from work. You'll form more meaningful connections, they'll become more human to you, and working with them will be even more special. We all know what it's like to work in a stressful environment: tempers run short, deadlines make people jumpy, and we get annoyed and angry. Creating a sense of community at work helps us through the stressful times we all encounter. Here are a few suggestions:

- Enter a workplace softball team in your city's league.
- Go to the gym, on a hike, or for a bike ride together.
- Go dancing together.
- Organize a barbecue.

❏ *Action: Set up a workplace carpool*

Carpooling is a great way to reduce your impact on the environment and get to know your coworkers better. Put a sign-up sheet in your break room where people can list their names and addresses. Then determine who lives near each other and divide up driving times. Carpooling will also save you money on gas and maintenance.

❏ *Action: Make people from diverse backgrounds feel welcome*

In our increasingly global economy, we often find ourselves working with people from other races, regions, countries, and backgrounds. This is an incredible opportunity for us to exchange ideas, cultures, and experiences.

Entering a new workplace, however, can be extremely uncomfortable for a person who may be the only member of a certain ethnicity, nationality, or other group. If we truly value diversity and community, we must make sure that people from diverse backgrounds feel welcome. Here are a few suggestions:

This space respects people regardless of gender, race, sexual orientation, social class, ethnicity, age, or ability.

- ✓ Invite people to lunch.
- ✓ Talk to people; ask them about themselves.
- ✓ Have their family over for dinner.
- ✓ Offer to show them around town.
- ✓ Make a welcome basket.

❏ *Action: Brainstorm with coworkers about how to make a better workplace*

A nurturing and positive workplace doesn't just happen; you and your coworkers must create it. Everyone's input is important. Organize a social gathering where you begin the following process of creating a better work environment.

Process

1. Have each participant write several paragraphs completing the statement: "A workplace I would enjoy coming to every day would be ....."

Ask everyone to write for about five minutes.

2. Have each coworker use their writing to list five concrete things she likes about your workplace.

3. Now have everyone list five things they think could be improved.

4. Anonymously exchange lists. Have everyone read a list aloud to the whole group.

5. Discuss which of the improvements are most important, and make a master list.

6. Decide, as a group, to commit to making several items on the list a reality.

After you've put some of your ideas into action for a while, schedule a check-in meeting to reevaluate your goals and find out how everyone feels about them. Make adjustments and add new intentions if necessary. Remember, good communication is vital to an extraordinary workplace, just as it is in any relationship. You may want to hold check-in meetings several times each year.

SOCIALLY RESPONSIBLE WORKPLACE

You not only have the opportunity to create positive and supportive relationships with coworkers but also to help make your workplace more directly benefit your community and the natural environment. It may seem overwhelming to try to change the way your company or organization functions, so just take it one step at a time. First evaluate your own office or department and find manageable changes you can propose or implement. You may even inspire other coworkers who also want to make positive changes.

❏ *Action: Find out if your workplace encourages charitable giving*

Many companies offer their employees matching funds when they donate to charities. This is a way to double your impact on the world for free! Even better, a number of companies have started offering to take a specific amount (you decide how much) out of your monthly paycheck automatically and give it directly to the charity or charities of your choice. Ask your company if it has programs like this and if not, would it be willing to start some.

❏ *Action: Organize around community service*

Imagine the good things you and your coworkers could accomplish in your community if you pooled your talents, time, and resources.

Some companies actually allow employees paid community service days. The Body Shop, a popular bath and perfume franchise, compensates employees for up to two days of community volunteering each month.[3] Some business leaders are realizing that fostering good community relations improves employee morale and increases profits.[4] Encourage your employer to offer community service incentives.

✓ Organize a food drive for your community food bank.

✓ Raise funds to buy winter coats for homeless children.

✓ Sponsor a local kids' sports team.

✓ Get involved in the Big Brothers/Big Sisters program.

❏ Action: Know your rights as a worker

Part of the reason that employers are able to take advantage of employees is that workers are unaware of their rights. To find out the legal ins and outs of your rights as a worker you may want to do your own research on these topics: privacy (can your employer monitor your email, phone calls, and your work? Conduct background checks?), health benefits, overtime pay, sick leave, work standards, safety, and equal pay for equal work. When you demand that your employer respect your rights, you are sending a message that she or he must respect the rights of all workers.

Workplace Fairness

Workplace Fairness is a non-profit organization helping people with "understanding, enforcing, and expanding their rights in the workplace." They assist people who can't afford their own attorney. Contact them if you feel your rights have been violated.

☎ (800) 469-3474　💻 www.workplacefairness.org

❏ Action: Support your fellow workers

The American Dream of hard work leading to prosperity is not the reality for millions of people. Many working Americans have forgotten that we're all in this together — blue- and white-collar workers alike need to stick together.

Traditionally, unions have been the main means of uniting workers. Unions played a large role in creating many of the labor standards we take for granted today, including the 40-hour workweek and the minimum wage.

Unions are not a relic of the past. They are still the most effective avenue for millions of people in rich and poor countries to collectively stand up for fair working conditions, hours, and pay.

Despite the fact that belonging to a union is economically beneficial for most workers, union memberships have consistently declined in recent decades. In 2000, union workers earned 28% more than their non-union counterparts.[5] Learning about, joining, and supporting unions is an important way to support your fellow workers.

AFL-CIO (American Federation of Labor-Congress of Industrial Organizations)

AFL-CIO is a voluntary federation of 66 national and international labor unions. Contact them for information on union organizing and research about economic issues facing average Americans.

☎ (202) 637-5000   💻 www.afl-cio.org

> You can support your fellow workers by paying attention to strikes, not crossing picket lines, buying union-made products whenever possible, boycotting particularly worker-hostile companies, and joining a union (see the SHOPPING chapter for worker-friendly products).

❏ **Action: Confront injustices in the workplace**

There is nothing more frustrating than being singled out or harassed because of your sex, age, race, sexual orientation, or ability. Sexual harassment, racial discrimination, and homophobia have been pervasive problems in our society for many years. We have the power to confront injustices where we work; we can create a safe space for each of our coworkers. If you think injustices don't concern you directly, remember that your work environment has a huge impact on you; what affects others affects you.

Common workplace injustices:

- 'Gay' jokes
- Lewd sexual comments/unwanted sexual advances
- Expecting more from people of color and women
- Racial/ethnic jokes
- Inappropriate physical contact

How you can confront injustices:

- Don't laugh at sexist, racist, and homophobic jokes.
- Offer victims of injustice your support. If you are the victim, seek others' support.
- Tell people who act inappropriately that their actions or words make you uncomfortable. (You don't have to be confrontational, just direct.)
- Document the injustice. This is crucial, even if you presently do not wish to file a complaint.
- Talk to your union representative, if you have one.
- Talk to your employer or someone in human resources.
- File a formal complaint.

❏ **Action: Green your workplace**

We use a lot of resources at work, especially paper and electricity. Imagine all the resources your workplace uses, and then think of all the other companies out there using just as much if not more. By creatively reducing your workplace's resource use, you will make a huge impact on our environmental well-being. Use your imagination — every little bit helps!

The easiest way to reduce your workplace's impact on the environment is to reduce the resources you require. Send memos by email, turn off unnecessary lighting, print using a smaller font than you normally would, use energy-efficient office machines (look for the Energy Star sticker), and set your printers up to print using less ink and on both sides if possible.

There are many opportunities to reuse materials, as well. Reuse the blank side of scrap paper, print memos on used paper, try eco-friendly floppy disks.

Finally, you can recycle office mail, typing/computer paper, printer cartridges, cardboard, and drink containers.

In your break room, make sure to have bins for aluminum cans and plastics. Look up a service in your Yellow Pages under 'Recycling Services,' and arrange for recycling pickup.

ENVIRONMENTALLY FRIENDLY ACTIONS

- Use paper with recycled content www.greenlinepaper.com
- Install motion sensor lights and/or compact fluorescent bulbs.
- Use reusable versus disposable dishes.
- Place recycle bins in your break room and near workstations so that everyone has convenient access to them.
- Set all computer monitors on the energy-saving mode. Shut computers down at night.
- Sign your business up with Working Assets Long Distance. Call (800) 789-7022 or visit their website at: www.workingassets.com. (See the HOME chapter for more details.)
- Purchase Energy Star compliant office machines. Using the Energy Star website, you can compare different products to determine which ones use the least energy when in 'sleep' or 'off' mode. Visit the website at: www.energystar.gov, and check out the HOME chapter for more information on Energy Star. You can compare computers, monitors, fax machines, copiers, scanners, and more.

❑ Action: Value people over profits

If you employ or supervise other workers, make sure you take their concerns into account: don't overwork them, put their safety first, and try to give them the pay and benefits they deserve. Some of you may face the extremely difficult decision of whether or not to eliminate jobs to boost profits a bit more. Our economy trains us to separate our rational, business selves from our compassionate, humane selves, fostering the belief that we must do everything possible to increase shareholder profits. Do your best to place human concerns before profits.

❑ *Action: Work to make your company more socially and environmentally responsible*

The global economic system too often values profits over people. Too many businesses choose to maximize profits by instigating layoffs, pollution increases, production shortcuts, and the overworking of employees. This easy path to short-term profit has immense consequences for our communities and our environment.

Companies constantly change to meet the needs of their customers, employees, and the global marketplace. A single person often initiates changes that then catch on with others in the company. Be the person in your company that pushes for more investment in employees and your community, the efficient use of natural resources, and ethical business practices. In many cases, these kinds of changes have helped make companies more profitable, so don't be afraid to bring it up. Encourage your company to join a socially responsible professional organization, such as Businesses for Social Responsibility.

Businesses for Social Responsibility
☎ (415) 537-0888   🖥 www.bsr.org

FINDING GOOD WORK

Most of us will have several careers over our lifetime. Choosing those careers will be some of the most important decisions you will make in your life. We spend so much time and energy on our work that choosing a fulfilling job that benefits others has a huge effect on the world. Whether you choose a career that requires you to exploit people or to help them will have significant implications for your life and the lives of the people around you. We all have the opportunity to use our skills to make the world a better place. There are even many jobs available where the sole purpose is creating that world.

❑ *Action: Choose a fulfilling job*

When you work at an unfulfilling job, you're more likely to buy stuff you don't need, be in a foul mood even away from work, take out your frustrations on your friends and family, and generally have a negative outlook on the world. Our work means a lot to us. Therefore, when you choose a fulfilling job, it will transform your experience of life in general. Your fulfillment can't help but rub off on your surroundings, thereby making the world a better place.

Perhaps we're making this action sound easier than it is. You've got bills to pay, right? During your working years, you will face many important decisions: Should I take that promotion, which means more money but longer hours? Should I switch to a job that pays less but that I find more fulfilling? Should I accept the transfer to a new city while my kids are in school?

Many factors enter into our decisions about work. Just make sure your personal fulfillment and relationships and not money or status are at the top of your list. Keep in mind that working in a fulfilling job can also significantly decrease your living expenses when you no longer have to buy expensive cars, 'escape' vacations, or take-out meals every night to try to make up for your dreadful day at work.

❏ *Action: Use your current job skills to improve the world*

You have many opportunities to use your current skills to make the world a better place. If you're a nurse, consider volunteering or working at a low-income clinic. If construction is your trade, you might want to supervise a Habitat for Humanity building project. If you're good with computers, there are numerous non-profit organizations that could use your expertise. Accountants and other financial planners also have numerous skills to share. Think about the gifts your skills can bring to others and then take action.

❏ *Action: Work for justice*

For those of you searching for a career or looking to change careers, there are many opportunities to work with organizations whose sole purpose is to make the world a better place. In many cases, non-profit organizations need the exact same skills and experience you are now acquiring in your current job. They need computer programmers and promotions experts, administrative staff, and public relations folks. You can focus virtually any interest you have into a job that promotes justice.

SOCIALLY RESPONSIBLE PROFESSIONAL ORGANIZATIONS

Concerned individuals in many professions have formed affiliations where they can share information, offer concerns, and support one another's efforts towards social responsibility. There may be such an organization for your line of work. Contact your professional organization or search the Web to learn more. Here are a few examples:

Computer Professionals for Social Responsibility
☎ (650) 322-3778
🖳 www.cpsr.org

Physicians for Social Responsibility
☎ (202) 898-0150
🖳 www.psr.org

Businesses for Social Responsibility
☎ (415) 537-0888
🖳 www.bsr.org

Educators for Social Responsibility
🖳 www.esrnational.org

Social Investment Forum
☎ (202) 872-5319
🖳 www.socialinvest.org

RESOURCES

Resources to Help You Find Good Work

📖 Bolles, Richard Nelson. *What Color Is Your Parachute? 1999: A Practical Manual for Job-Hunters and Career-Changers.* Ten Speed Press, 1999. For 30 years *Parachute* has been a useful manual for job hunters and a guide for career changers. Helping people find fulfilling careers has made this book a bestseller. There is a new edition every year, and a regularly updated website at: 🖳 www.jobhuntersbible.com.

📖 Brophy, Paul C., and Alice Shabecoff. *A Guide to Careers in Community Development*. Island Press, 2000.
This guide introduces the field of community development — the economic, social, and physical revitalization of a community led by members of that community. Professionals, volunteers, and students will find useful information about getting directly involved with community organizing, financing housing, or redeveloping brownfields.

📖 Cowan, Jessica,ed. *Good Works: A Guide to Careers in Social Change*. Preface by Ralph Nader. Barricade Books, 1991.
Good Works offers both a website and a huge catalog of non-profit organizations. Their book gives detailed descriptions of over 100 organizations, including contacts and salaries. Order the book from your locally owned bookstore or from the website at:
🖳 www.essential.org/goodworks

📖 Everett, Melissa. *Making a Living While Making a Difference*. New Society Publishers, 1999.
This book is a cutting-edge guide to finding a career that reflects your values. It offers stories of people who have found meaningful careers and a ten-step program to help you begin or find a new career that you'll love.

📖 Hamilton, Leslie. *100 Best Non-profits to Work For*. IDG Books, 1998.
If you are looking to make a difference while maintaining your salary, benefits, advancement prospects, and job stability, then this is the book for you. Read about the pros and cons of working for some of the greatest non-profit companies on Earth.

📖 Lauber, Daniel. *Non-Profits and Education Job Finder*. Planning Communications, 1997.
This comprehensive book offers numerous resources to finding a job in a wide variety of fields. It directs you to newsletters, online resources, job directories, and job hotlines.

ACCESS: Networking in the Public Interest
Access posts job listings, offers career counseling, organizes non-profit career fairs, and helps you find meaningful work. They charge a fee for certain services.
☎ (202) 785-4233 🖳 www.accessjobs.org/

Charity Career Village (Canada)
Charity Career Village is a great place to look for jobs with Canadian non-profits.
☎ (800)610-8134
🖳 www.charityvillage.com/charityvillage/career.html

Community Career Center (CCC)

The CCC lists a variety of community jobs with not-for-profit employers. Search by region, career interests, salary, or job title.

☎ (702) 259-6570   💻 www.nonprofitjobs.org

Environmental Career Opportunities

Environmental Career Opportunities offers a variety of jobs in environmental fields. You can register to receive new job openings or subscribe to their publication.

☎ (800) 315-9777   💻 www.ecojobs.com

The Environmental Careers Organization (ECO)

The ECO helps people find paid internships in environmental fields.

☎ (617) 426-4375   💻 www.eco.org

Human Rights Internet Job Board

This site offers links to a variety of human rights-related jobs; organized into several categories, including government and non-government work.

💻 www.hri.ca/jobboard/joblinks.html

Idealist

Idealist posts jobs by state and jobs abroad. Learn useful tips and use their search engine to find numerous non-profit organizations.

☎ (212) 843-3973   💻 www.idealist.org

National Non-Profit Organization Classifieds

This comprehensive site features job posts and many links to more information.

☎ (800) 344-6627   💻 www.opportunitynocs.org/home.html

Non-Profit Career Network

This site lets you search for full- or part-time work by state. It also has a directory of non-profits around the country. You can submit your resume so that a non-profit can find *you*.

☎ (888) 844-4870   💻 www.nonprofitcareer.com/index.html

Non-Profit Times Online

This site is like a classified ad section for non-profits. It contains daily updates in a variety of jobs.

💻 www.nptimes.com/classified.html

Philanthropy News Network Online

The online version of *Philanthropy News Network* offers job searches by region of U.S. You can post your resume here.

☎ (919) 832-2325   🖥 www.pnnonline.org

Workplace Resources

📖 Employers Publications. *1999 Employers Reasonable Care Pack: Sexual Harassment Prevention in the Workplace.* Employers Publications, April 1999.
This booklet outlines an educational program for employees and managers. It also includes a poster defining sexual harassment. The poster is suitable for display in the workplace.

📖 McNaught, Brian. *Gay Issues in the Workplace.* Stonewall Inn Editions. St. Martin's Press, 1995.
In this well-written book, Brian McNaught discusses homophobia; what it means to be lesbian, gay, or bisexual; and what gay employees want. He also outlines a model workshop and answers common questions.

📖 Petrocelli, William, and Barbara Kate Repa. *Sexual Harassment on the Job: What It Is and How to Stop It.* 4th ed. Nolo Press, 1998.
This easy-to-read resource contains concrete strategies for confronting sexual harassment in the workplace, filing a complaint, and pursuing a lawsuit.

📖 Sonnenschein, William. *The Diversity Toolkit: How You Can Build and Benefit from a Diverse Workforce.* Preface by Arthur H. Bell. Contemporary Books, 1999.
A good beginning guide to creating and managing a diverse workplace.

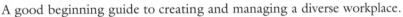

Helping Workers Resources

Jobs With Justice

Jobs With Justice creates worker coalitions and action campaigns to further workers rights. They offer concrete actions and a variety of educational materials to help you support your fellow workers.

☎ (202) 434-1106   🖥 www.jwj.org

National Whistleblower Center

This non-profit center is a strong advocate for people who report their employer's misdeeds. They provide educational resources, legal aid, and an attorney referral system.

☎ (202) 342-1902   🖥 www.whistleblowers.org

The 9 to 5 Job Survival Hotline

9 to 5, National Association of Working Women is a grassroots organization dedicated to helping women work for economic justice. They provide 'Action Packets' full of concrete steps anyone can take to close the gender pay gap, challenge sexual harassment, and contest unfair/illegal labor practices.
☎ (800) 522-0925 🖳 www.9to5.org

Socially Responsible Workplace

📖 Earthworks Group. *50 Simple Things Your Business Can Do to Save the Earth*. Earthworks Press, April 1991.

Written in the same format as the best selling 50 Simple Things You Can Do to Save the Earth, this book offers practical ideas for making your business more green.

📖 Nattrass, Brian, and Mary Altomare. *The Natural Step For Business: Wealth, Ecology, and The Evolutionary Corporation*. New Society Publishers, 1999.

Examines how four very successful corporations in Sweden and the United States have shown that a company does not have to choose between profitability and care for the environment.

MEDIA

Television
_____
Radio
_____
Magazines
_____
Newspapers
_____
Internet

GETTING QUALITY INFORMATION about the world is a vital first step to building a better one. What we allow children to see and do will shape their values and actions as they mature. The same principle is true for adults. The way we think and act in our daily lives is inextricably linked to the information we receive about the world. Unfortunately, many of us are awash in a sea of information about all the crime, war, and disasters in the world. Enough time spent absorbing these messages leaves us feeling frightened of the outside world and powerless to make changes.

Much of what we learn about the world is not from direct experience but from someone else's account of what is going on. Mass media fundamentally shape our perceptions of the world through the images, sounds, and information they deliver to us on a daily basis. The problem is that those who control the media do not necessarily have our best interests in mind when they decide what information is fit to transmit. Profit ultimately determines what we see and hear in the media. If you trust these media corporations as you trust your own mother, then you can skip this chapter. Otherwise, read on.

The media you choose to consult are important, not only because they shape how you think about the world but also because they determine what you are willing to do. You will live a very different life if you spend your free time thinking about how you can contribute to a better world than if you think all day about the lives of the rich and famous.

Here are some aspects of your life that you will gain power over once you more consciously choose your media:

✓   your mood
✓   what you think about when you are alone
✓   what you talk about at parties
✓   which social issues you consider most important
✓   what you demand from your political officials
✓   whether you feel apathetic or motivated
✓   which avenues you pursue to make the world better
✓   what solutions (if any) you see to the world's problems
✓   what stereotypes you have of people you have never met
✓   what you see as the 'good life'

This chapter addresses how the information we receive connects us to the outside world and, more importantly, how we can choose information sources that enrich our own lives and empower us to make a difference. We present alternative options for television, radio, magazines, newspapers, and the Internet that are geared toward social change and suggest actions to help you take responsibility for the media you use.

MAINSTREAM MEDIA

What events are newsworthy? Thousands of interesting and important events occur in the world every day. Which ones should make the news? Understanding how the media decide will help you understand the impact that the media have on our lives. One thing you can be sure of, the news is far from impartial. The values, culture, and economic interests of a news organization significantly influence which events will make it onto the front page or into a newscast.

How many newscasts have you seen that show a violent crime, then politics as usual, then a war, then a celebrity event, then the stock market, then the weather, then the sports, and then empty banter between the anchors? How many times do we have to learn the details of a gruesome murder? Why is a celebrity divorce worth putting on the local news? Why are urgent international issues presented without the necessary historical background? Why are so many shows full of needless violence? The reason is that these stories make money. Bringing in new viewers or readers increases advertising revenues. The most recent 'reality-based' show (or any other show for that matter) is on the air because it delivers a captive audience of a certain demographic (age, income, race) to corporations at commercial time.

The advertisements that urge us to buy more and more products are not just harmless, easily ignored messages. Advertising messages surround us and invade our public and private spaces so frequently that we often forget their presence and underestimate the power of their collective impact. For 24 hours a day, seven days a week, advertisers tell us that satisfying each of our fleeting desires is more important than contributing to the welfare of others — an extremely dangerous message, when you consider the ecological, social, and psychological challenges that we face as a global society.

> The average American is exposed to over 1500 ads every day.[1]

Unfortunately, the pressure to maximize profits often undermines the standards of quality journalism. Investigative reporting becomes a financial liability, as it is comparatively expensive to produce and leaves owners of the news organization open to possible lawsuits. This insatiable drive to produce cheap news has even led journalists to go directly to corporate and government spin-doctors to acquire their stories. In fact, the public relations industry (PR firms) in America creates as much as 40% to 70% of the news in today's media, mainly through press releases.[2]

Equally disturbing, corporate mergers are rapidly centralizing all aspects of global media production from newspapers to television and from books to movies. Today most of the information we consume on a daily basis comes from just nine major corporations.[3] Such a concentration of media power in the hands of a few runs contradictory to the democratic principles that are the foundations of an independent media system.

ALTERNATIVE MEDIA

Fortunately, concerned citizens all over the world have developed alternative media organizations to counter the lack of quality choices in the mainstream media. They produce alternative media to provide quality information about our governments, corporations, and communities so that we can live out the potential of a truly democratic society — a society where average people are well informed and actively involved in creating a better world.

Here are some differences in content between mainstream and alternative media that you are likely to find:

Mainstream Media	Alternative Media
Street Crime	Corporate Crime
Government and Corporate Sources	Independent Sources
U.S. Focus	Local and Global Focus
Tabloid News	Issues of Substance
Commercials	Consumer Protection
Entertainment	Education

How to Invest in the Market	How to Invest in Your Community
Partisan Politics	Effective Political Action
Corporate Mergers	Communities Working Together
Gas Prices	Alternative Energy
Dow Jones	Economic Inequality
Fads and Fashion	Voluntary Simplicity
Corporate Profits	Sweatshop Labor
Voices of the Powerful	Voices of the People
Encourages Passivity	Encourages Action
Military Solutions	Non-violent Alternatives

TELEVISION

The average American will spend almost one-quarter of their waking hours on this Earth watching TV.[4] Watching television has become almost as important as eating and sleeping in our daily rituals. The television has even become the electronic storyteller of our age. It provides us with our news, our entertainment, and increasingly, our link to the rest of humanity. In fact, TV spends more time raising the next generation than we do. The average child spends 900 hours at school and over 1000 hours in front of the TV each year.[5]

> By the age of 18, a child has witnessed 200,000 violent acts on TV.[6]

Plugging ourselves into the TV changes who we are and how we act as a people. We watch sitcoms instead of telling jokes. We watch romantic movies instead of taking romantic walks. We become friends with TV characters instead of with our neighbors. We watch sports instead of playing them. Many of us just turn on the TV to have some company and some kind of order to quiet our thoughts. Excessive TV watching keeps you from fully participating in life. It creates a world of watchers — not thinkers or doers but merely watchers.

CRITICAL TV VIEWER EXERCISES

- Watch a family member or friend watch TV for ten minutes. Notice their behavior.
- Turn the sound off and watch commercials for ten minutes. How are the advertisers appealing to your desires?
- Turn the TV off and watch the screen for ten minutes. How strong is your desire to turn it back on? As you notice your reflection on the screen, consider how we are a reflection of what we see on TV.

❏ *Action: Watch less TV*

If you are like most people, TV has had a bit of the upper hand for much of your life. In fact, millions of Americans are so addict-

> **3 hours, 46 minutes:**
> the amount of TV the average American watches each day.[7]

ed to watching television that they actually meet all the criteria of substance abusers!

It is time to renegotiate your relationship with television. For most people the benefits are enormous. Watching less TV will open up time for more constructive activities, such as spending quality time with friends and family, catching up on some reading, pursuing hobbies, volunteering, playing music, enjoying nature, exercising, playing with your dog, or just getting outside.

Tips for Taking Back Your Life from TV

Turn the TV off for one week. Turning off the TV for an entire week will give you enough time to evaluate the role of television in your life. Try it now. It's just one week. Keep your commitment, and you'll be surprised at what you find.

> National TV-Turnoff Week happens every year during the last week of April.
> (🖳: www.tvturnoff.org)

Set a daily limit on TV watching. A good way to start taking back your power is to actually log how much time you spend in front of the TV in any given week. Once you've done that, consider cutting your TV watching in half.

Choose what you watch (don't channel surf). Don't let the TV decide what you watch. You decide! Consult your TV listings to find programs that you want to watch instead of just flipping through all of the channels. You might even consider taping shows on your VCR so that you can watch them at your convenience and fastforward through the commercials. Don't get stuck watching programs that you don't really enjoy because 'there's nothing better to do.'

Turn off the sound during commercials. Have you ever noticed that the volume increases when the commer-cials come on? It's just another little trick to get you to buy something. Push the mute button. Then turn and talk to the person sitting next to you (or get up and do something).

> U.S. TV networks broadcast 50% more commercials in 1997 than in 1983.[8]

❏ *Action: Watch and support non-commercial television*

If there are alternative TV stations in your area, they are a wonderful asset to your community. They ensure that a major part of their programming will focus on quality public affairs and artistic productions that benefit your community (in a relatively ad-free environment). Be sure to support these stations financially because they do not rely heavily on corporate donations or advertising revenue to stay in business.

Public Access Television is television run by the citizens for the citizens. Community channels provide an electronic forum for the expression of social and political concerns, as well as the opportunity to share valuable information with friends and neighbors.

Find community and public access television stations around the world (and near you) at: 💻 www.openchannel.se.

Free Speech TV (FSTV)

Free Speech TV (FSTV) is available in over seven million American homes across the country, through public-access cable television.

FSTV works with progressive organizations to broadcast political, cultural, and environmental issues — all with a focus on social justice. Visit their website to watch programs online or to find out if they have a channel in your area. Call your cable provider and ask for FSTV.

☎ (303) 442-5693　💻 www.fstv.org

Public Broadcasting Service (PBS)

Public Television, despite criticism due to the corporate underwriting of some of its programs, still consistently produces the highest

quality TV in town. Be sure to keep up with what's new on public TV, because some of the most powerful, cutting-edge programs are shown on PBS stations.

💻 www.pbs.org

Look for these great shows on your local PBS station.

Frontline

A mainstay on PBS, "Frontline" is investigative journalism at its best. It gives 60 minutes of coverage to topics that often get

FRONTLINE

30 seconds on network news. "Frontline" tackles important topics, such as the Gulf War, campaign finance reform, hate crimes, nuclear waste, and terrorism.

💻 www.pbs.org/wgbh/pages/frontline (PBS Tuesdays — 10:00 pm)

The NewsHour with Jim Lehrer

Probably the best news show on television, "The NewsHour" covers current events in more depth with less sensationalism. Quality over hype.

💻 www.pbs.org/newshour (PBS Daily — 6 pm)

P.O.V.

"Point of View" shows independent documentaries on PBS, highlighting voices that are otherwise marginalized in our society. This show is a great way to catch what the cutting-edge non-fiction filmmakers are up to. "P.O.V." has won just about every major film and broadcasting award for its documentaries.
🖳 www.pbs.org/pov (Consult your local PBS listings for dates and times)

Livelyhood

Produced by San Francisco's KQED, "Livelyhood" is a show about how Americans are working to survive in the competitive global economy. "Livelyhood" has highlighted downsizing, temp work, the balance between work and family, and even an alternative currency system.
🖳 www.pbs.org/livelyhood (Consult your local PBS listings for dates and times)

America's Defense Monitor

Broadcast on 65 PBS stations across the country as well as on FSTV, the series presents critical information about the military's impact on our political system, the economy, the environment, and society as a whole. Other topics include foreign policy, international affairs, armed intervention, and nuclear and conventional weapons.
🖳 www.cdi.org/adm (Consult your local PBS listings for dates and times)

In The Life

This Emmy-nominated public newsmagazine that airs on over 120 public TV stations provides positive visibility and accurate reporting of both the history and contempory experiences of the gay and lesbian community.
🖳 www.inthelifetv.org (Consult your local PBS listings for dates and times)

The Awful Truth

Michael Moore's comedic examination of corporate power in the U.S. has just finished its second season on Bravo and will hopefully be back. Also look for re-runs of Moore's show "TV Nation" on Comedy Central, or rent them at your local video store.
🖳 www.theawfultruth.com (BRAVO Wednesdays — 10:30 pm}

RADIO

The Federal Communications Commission (FCC) is the governmental agency that manages our radio airwaves. Unfortunately it rents out our airwaves to radio stations for an amount small enough to be of little consequence for commercial radio stations but large enough to keep the majority of non-profit and public stations off the air. The result is a radio spectrum dominated by commercial stations.

Similar to commercial TV stations, the main purpose of commercial radio is to make a profit. This means that getting money from advertisers (by the means of expanding audience; for example Howard Stern) takes precedence over providing socially useful programming. Public radio stations, in contrast, have the meeting of public needs as part of their mission. Public radio exists on a continuum from no commercial presence to a large commercial presence. Most public stations will not air commercials, but many will accept corporate donations and sometimes even program sponsorship. Community radio stations are often the least commercial. They are a part of their communities, are run primarily by volunteers, and usually have the most true programming diversity on the air.

❏ Action: Listen to and support your community and public radio stations

Community and public radio stations tend to broadcast more public affairs programming and more programs that are of interest to progressive listeners. Frequencies between 87 and 92 mHz on the FM dial are almost always reserved for educational, community, and non-commercial use. Why not try browsing?

> 💻: Check out
> **www.gumbopages.com/other-radio.html**
> to find non-commercial radio stations
> across the world.

To find your local community radio station, look in your Yellow Pages under "Radio Stations."

❏ Action: Tune in to alternative radio programs

Public and community radio stations offer many of the following alternative radio programs. If your local stations don't offer these great programs, then give 'em a call and request them.

TUC Radio
Producing weekly interviews with some of the nation's most progressive thinkers, "TUC Radio" focuses particularly well on the impacts of big corporations on society.

☎ (415) 861-6962 💻 www.tucradio.org

Democracy Now!
A half-hour show from Pacifica Radio, "Democracy Now" deals with hard-hitting political topics you won't hear anywhere else. It features discussions with leading writers, scholars, and activists.

☎ (202) 588-0999 💻 www.pacifica.org

Alternative Radio

Produced by David Barsamian, "Alternative Radio" offers taped speeches and interviews of many of the most well-known progressive intellectuals and activists in the U.S.

☎ (800) 444-1977 ▉ www.alternativeradio.org

The Pacifica News Network

"Pacifica" brings you what's happening in the world every day, including issues and viewpoints that the mainstream media just won't cover.

☎ (202) 588-0999 ▉ www.pacifica.org

Radio Nation

Created by the same people who bring us *The Nation* magazine, "Radio Nation" is a weekly offering of news and opinion from activists, with commentary by Marc Cooper.

☎ (212) 209-5447

▉ www.nationinstitute.org/radionation

CounterSpin

Produced weekly by Fairness and Accuracy in Reporting (FAIR), "CounterSpin" uses criti-

cal media analysis and well-researched reporting to expose the influence those in power have over mainstream news.

☎ (212) 633-6700 ▉ www.fair.org/counterspin

National Public Radio (NPR)

NPR's public affairs programming is available across the U.S. on public radio stations. Take a look at their website to learn about NPR programming, and listen to any show in their radio archive on your computer with free Real Audio Software.

☎ (202) 414-2000 ▉ www.npr.org

All Things Considered

NPR's respected daily news program provides in-depth stories on a wide variety of interesting political, social, and cultural issues. They provide a state-by-state searchable website to help you find NPR's programs in your area.

☎ (202) 414-2000 ▉ www.npr.org/programs/atc

New Dimensions Radio (NDR)

NDR focuses on bringing the public intimate interviews on a weekly basis with some of the wisest, most creative, innovative figures of our age. NDR is dedicated to empowering people to live a life more connected with themselves, their families, their communities, their spirituality, and the planet. Call for a list of stations that carry New Dimensions worldwide.

☎ (707) 468-5215   💻 www.newdimensions.org

E Town

An hour-long show of diverse, live music, mixed in with interviews of policymakers, authors, and cutting-edge thinkers, includes a short weekly talk with an 'E-Chievement Award'winner — an individual who is hon- ored for making a positive contribution in his or her community.

💻 www.etown.org

MAGAZINES

One of the easiest ways to expand your awareness of current social justice and environmental issues is by reading progressive magazines on a regular basis. We have put together a list of what we think are the best alternative magazines available. Most of them have low-cost subscriptions, but you can also find many of them on the Internet, in your local library, or in nearby independent bookstores. By consciously choosing what kind of news you read, you reclaim control of the thoughts, feelings, and values that the mainstream media marginalizes. It's a great way to keep yourself motivated and focused on making a difference.

❏ *Action: Read alternative magazines*

Where, besides in alternative magazines, are you going to find stories about sweatshop labor, inequality, corporate crime, and actions that allow you to stand up and fight these problems? Many alternative magazines also make it a point to focus on the positive work others are doing around the globe and on progress we're making in those areas.

If you find that you can't afford to subscribe, consider sharing a subscription with a like-minded friend. Be sure to share your alternative magazines with others. Take them to work (especially if there is a waiting room), give them to a friend, or donate them to your local public library.

For a comprehensive list of just about every alternative magazine in existence, check out the Alternative Press Index at your local library or online; search it alphabetically or by subject.

💻 www.altpress.org

General

Title:	*Mother Jones*
Issues:	6 per year
Cost:	$18/yr
Phone:	(800) 438-6656
Website:	www.motherjones.com

Mother Jones provides hard-hitting stories in a beautiful layout — what more could you ask for? *Mother Jones* is known for its investigative reporting and its photo essays on arms dealing, exploitation, inequality, and social change activism. It is one of the most engaging magazines on the newsstand. A bonus for Web surfers, it is one of the few magazines that publishes its own full Web version, so you don't have to miss a story even if you missed the issue.

Title:	*YES!*
Issues:	6 per year
Cost:	$24/yr
Phone:	(800) 937-4451
Website:	www.yesmagazine.org

yes!
A Journal of Positive Futures

YES! A Journal of Positive Futures "supports people's active engagement in creating a just, sustainable, and compassionate future." *YES!* provides real-world solutions that are being implemented in communities around the globe and in individual lives. Holistic analysis of the world's condition leads this magazine to consider the environmental, economic, political, and spiritual problems and solutions that are before us as a global society. *YES!* will inspire you into action.

Title:	*The Nation*
Issues:	50 per year
Cost:	$52/yr
Phone:	(800) 333-8536
Website:	www.thenation.com

The Nation.

One of the oldest, most respected weeklies for progressives, *The Nation* is full of cutting-edge social criticism, intelligently written articles, and political commentary. *The Nation* is considered the mainstay of the Left for political news that is lacking in the corporate media. Art, film, and book reviews round out the magazine. How about trading in your *Time* and *Newsweek* for some progressive reporting on Washington politics?

Title: *The Progressive*
Issues: 12 per year
Cost: $32/yr
Phone: (800) 827-0555
Website: www.progressive.org

Lively political and cultural commentary, congressional transcripts, and monthly interviews with the most respective figures on the Left make *The Progressive* an informative and engaging read (it's also been around for 90 years). Writers include: Howard Zinn, Molly Ivins, and humorists Will Durst and Kate Clinton. It is a great choice for those looking to keep their finger on the pulse of progressives in America. If you like Paul Wellstone, you'll like this magazine.

Title: *Z Magazine*
Issues: 11 per year
Cost: $30/yr
Phone: (508) 548-9063
Website: www.zmag.org

Z is full of commentaries that unveil the oppression of the masses by the hands of the powerful. In each issue, you will find biting analysis of politics, economics, culture, and foreign policy with acidic cartoon humor interspersed throughout. Imperialist policymakers, tyrannical governments, and corporate headhunters do not want you to read *Z*, but Noam Chomsky does.

Title: *The Progressive Populist*
Issues: 22 per year
Cost: $30/yr
Phone: (800) 732-4992
Website: www.populist.com

The Progressive Populist: a Journal from America's Heartland, is an employee-owned newspaper that addresses issues dealing with workers, small business owners, and family farmers. It often uses articles from people like Jim Hightower, Jessie Jackson, and Molly Ivins to challenge fatcats and a government that doesn't work for the average citizen. *The Populist* is full of straight-talking progressives who advocate universal health care, living wages, and corporate accountability.

Title: *In These Times*
Issues: 24 per year
Cost: $36.95/yr
Phone: (800) 827-0270
Website: www.inthesetimes.com

The biweekly *In These Times* is always winning awards for its top-level journalism, frequently making Project Censored's list of Top Ten under-reported stories of the year. Military cover ups, organizing workers, despotic foreign governments, civil rights issues, editorials, and movie reviews — *In These Times* has it all.

Title:	*Utne Reader*	**UTNE⊛READER**
Issues:	6 per year	
Cost:	$20/yr	
Phone:	(612) 338-5040	
Website:	www.utne.com	

A kind of New Age *Reader's Digest* for progressives, the *Utne Reader* collects articles from the alternative media and creates a very readable bimonthly magazine. The full enjoyment of life, spirituality, ecology, community, and alternative health are common topics. The *Utne Reader* appeals to a wide variety of tastes in an eye-catching format.

Animal Rights

Title:	*The Animals' Agenda*	
Issues:	6 per year	
Cost:	$24/yr	
Phone:	(410) 675-4566	
Website:	www.animalsagenda.org	

Perhaps the premier animal rights magazines in circulation, *The Animals' Agenda* covers everything from poaching to cosmetics, medical experiments to veganism. You'll find a good mix of personal stories, well-documented research, gripping photography, and opportunities to join the struggle.

Economics

Title:	*Co-op America Quarterly*	Co-op America
Issues:	4 per year	**CO⊕P AMERICA**
Cost:	free with $25 membership	**QUARTERLY**
Phone:	(800) 58-GREEN	
Website:	www.coopamerica.org	

Co-op America Quarterly focuses on how you can use your buying and investing power to create a socially and environmentally responsible economy. Easy-to-take steps are provided to help end sweatshops, nurture locally owned businesses, and promote community investment. *Co-op*

America Quarterly is only one of the excellent publications of Co-op America. With a membership, you also receive the *Financial Planning Handbook* and the *Greenpages* directory of socially and environmentally responsible businesses.

Title: *Dollars and Sense*
Issues: 6 per year
Cost: $23/yr
Phone: (617) 628-8411
Website: www.igc.apc.org/dollars

For over 25 years, *Dollars and Sense* years has provided some of the best Left perspectives on current economic affairs, printing articles by journalists and scholars on topics ranging from poverty, inequality, social security, and the labor movement to winners and losers in the global economy. *Dollars and Sense* provides an alternative to the mainstream economic news that treats corporate mergers like celebrity events.

Environment

Title: *E: The Environmental Magazine*
Issues: 6 per year
Cost: $20/yr
Phone: (203) 854-5559
Website: www.emagazine.com

Every issue of *E* highlights articles that show how the natural environment is linked to our health, lifestyles, homes, and economy. The feature stories give great overviews to important topics such as environmental racism, 'green' taxes, overconsumption, and population growth. In addition, *E* provides many resources for linking with environmental organizations in the field — all in an engaging and eye-catching format.

Title: *Earth Island Journal*
Issues: 4 per year
Cost: $25/yr
Phone: (202) 452-1999
Website: www.earthisland.org

Earth Island Journal

A publication of the late environmentalist David Brower's Earth Island Institute, this magazine addresses issues affecting the conservation, preservation, and restoration of the global environment. It analyzes how the actions of governments, corporations and individual citizens affect the sustainability of our planet.

Title: *World Watch*
Issues: 6 per year
Cost: $20/yr
Phone: (800) 555-2028
Website: www.worldwatch.org/mag

World Watch magazine is a product of the highly respected World Watch Institute (which publishes *State of the World* yearly reports). Its issues usually focus on one or two environmental themes presented in highly researched articles, useful for both policymakers and informed citizens. Common topics are natural resource use, water and air quality, climate change, and human health issues.

Title: *Sierra*
Issues: 6 per year
Cost: $15/yr
Phone: (415) 977-5653
Website: www.sierraclub.org/sierra

Sierra, the official magazine of the Sierra Club, educates and informs readers about the latest wildland conservation issues, environmental legislation, and hidden dangers facing our ecosystems as well as engaging personal essays on experiencing the beauty of nature. Clearly written and filled with beautiful photography, *Sierra* is perfect for anyone who loves the outdoors.

Feminist

Title: *Ms.*
Issues: 6 per year
Cost: $45/yr
Phone: (800) 234-4486
Website: www.msmagazine.com

The major feminist magazine of our day, *Ms.* is one of the few periodicals that you can find on the newsstand without any ads. Every issue has commentary on women's health, work, and the arts. Almost 100 pages of hard-hitting stories address everything from Norplant to working mothers to sweatshops.

Title: *Sojourner*
Issues: 12 per year
Cost: $21/yr
Phone: (888) 475-5996
Website: www.sojourner.org

Sojourner: The Women's Forum is an activist, community-based, feminist newspaper. Reproductive rights, single motherhood, images of women in the media, and women's economic struggles are common topics of commentary. Issues of racial and economic inequality help fill out the range of topics so that it represents the interests of a multitude of women. Each issue also includes a list of feminist events around the country. For 25 years, *Sojourner* has committed to fueling a powerful and effective women's movement.

Gay and Lesbian

Title:	*The Advocate*
Issues:	26 per year
Cost:	$40/yr
Phone:	(800) 827-0561
Website:	www.advocate.org

The Advocate is the premiere national news magazine for gays and lesbians. Every issue has commentary on politics, culture, and the arts for the lesbian and gay community. Topics include civil unions, adoption, workplace discrimination and legal protection, and interviews with leading activists and politicians. *The Advocate* is a great resource for keeping informed on the successes and challenges facing the movement for lesbian and gay equality in the U.S.

International

Title:	*Cultural Survival Quarterly*
Issues:	4 per year
Cost:	free with $45 membership
Phone:	(617) 441-5400
Website:	www.cs.org

Cultural Survival Quarterly networks with indigenous groups and researchers to provide you with in-depth articles on the human rights and struggles of endangered cultures around the globe. Each issue focuses on how industrial development, subsistence agriculture, and other factors impact indigenous cultures and ways of life. Cultural and economic globalization is creating an intense need for the protection of global diversity. *Cultural Survival Quarterly* will inform you and inspire you to act for this cause.

Title:	*The New Internationalist*
Issues:	11 per year
Cost:	$36/yr
Phone:	(800) 661-8700
Website:	www.oneworld.org/ni

The New Internationalist brings you what's happening around the globe, focusing on such issues as economic inequality, pollution, the status of women, globalization, and war — especially detailing the condition of the poorest countries. Extremely readable and full of oversized beautiful pictures, this monthly magazine keeps you informed and aware of what's going on from Albania to Zimbabwe.

Title:	*Third World Resurgence*
Issues:	12 per year
Cost:	$30/yr
Phone:	none
Website:	www.twnside.org.sg/twr.htm

Third World Resurgence, published by the Third World Network, is a monthly magazine on development, ecology, economics, health alternatives and South-North relations. A team of Third World journalists and researchers have been assembled to contribute to *Third World Resurgence*.

Title:	*Multinational Monitor*
Issues:	10 per year
Cost:	$25/yr
Phone:	(202) 387-8030
Website:	www.essential.org/monitor

The Multinational Monitor "tracks corporate activity, especially in the Third World, focusing on the export of hazardous substances, worker health and safety, labor union issues and the environment." It is *the* magazine for keeping an eye on some of the most powerful (and destructive) entities on the planet — multinational corporations from McDonald's to Mitsubishi. Each December brings the issue 'The Ten Worst Corporations of the Year.'

Media

Title:	*Adbusters*
Issues:	4 per year
Cost:	$20/yr
Phone:	(800) 663-1243
Website:	www.adbusters.org

The Adbusters Media Foundation is a non-profit group of 'Culture Jammers' working to counter the interests of big business that have created our out-of-control consumer culture. *Adbusters* creates 'subvertising' and 'counter-commercials' that combat the never-ending stream of corporate advertising. The advertisements and articles cleverly combine slick production with a biting social message. This is a fun magazine to read.

Title:	*Extra!*
Issues:	6 per year
Cost:	$19/yr
Phone:	(212) 633-6700
Website:	www.fair.org

Fairness and Accuracy in Reporting (FAIR) is one of the nation's largest media watchdog organizations and the publisher of *Extra!* Fighting for diversity in media content, *Extra!* combats censorship and media bias with some of the hardest-hitting stories in print. Find out how the stories of the day are often covered in a misleading manner by the corporate media. (Also, listen in to FAIR's weekly radio show on your local public radio station).

Race

Title:	*Color Lines*
Issues:	4 per year
Cost:	$16/yr
Phone:	(510) 653-3415
Website:	www.colorlines.com

Color Lines is possibly the best magazine in the country dealing with the politics and issues important to communities of color. Each issue includes commentary on organizing; an in-depth look at diversity in the arts; and creative, insightful analysis of such complex issues as prisons, welfare, educational inequality, and environmental justice.

Religious

Title:	*Sojourners*
Issues:	6 per year
Cost:	$30/yr
Phone:	(800) 714-7474
Website:	www.sojourners.com

SOJOURNERSmagazine

A Christian social justice magazine, *Sojourners* focuses on progressive social issues using the wisdom of the gospels. The authors refuse to separate "personal faith from social justice, prayer from peacemaking, contemplation from action, or spirituality from politics." The religious right is not the only group of Christians who have something to say. Compassion for the poor, persistence for justice, and hope for the future makes *Sojourners* a powerful magazine.

Title:	*Tikkun*
Issues:	6 per year
Cost:	$29/yr
Phone:	(800) 395-7753
Website:	www.tikkun.org

Tikkun magazine is based on the Jewish principle of *tikkun olam* — the obligation to be involved in healing and transforming the world. This social justice magazine is deeply rooted in the wisdom of Judaism, while also emphasizing the connectedness of all human beings on the planet regardless of faith. It focuses on creating a world that is ethical, caring, just, and ecologically sound. Michael Lerner, a well-known author and rabbi, is the editor.

CANADIAN MAGAZINES

General

Title:	*Briarpatch*
Issues:	10 per year
Cost:	Can$24.61
Phone:	(306) 525-2949
Website:	www.briarpatchmagazine.com

Title:	*Canadian Dimension*
Issues:	6 per year
Cost:	Can$24.50 Students and unemployed folks pay only Can$18
Phone:	(204) 957-1519
Website:	www.canadiandimension.mb.ca/frame.htm

Title:	*THIS MAGAZINE*
Issues:	6 per year
Cost:	Can$23.99
Phone:	(416) 979-9429
Email:	thismag@web.net
Website:	www.thismag.org

Environment

Title: *Alternatives Journal*
Issues: 4 per year
Cost: Student: Can$21.35
             Individual: Can$26.75
Phone: (519) 888-4442
Website: www.fes.uwaterloo.ca/alternatives

Title: *Encompass*
Issues: 5 per year
Cost: Can$25.68
Phone: (800) 884-3515
Website: www.encompass.org

Peace

Title: *Peace Magazine*
Issues: 4 per year
Cost: Can$17.50
Phone: (416) 533-7581
Email: office@peacemagazine.org
Website: www.peacemagazine.org

NEWSPAPERS

Newspapers are a mainstay on many North Americans' morning tables. They can be a great way to keep up on current events. Unfortunately with any commercial periodical, advertising eats up a considerable portion of the total space. In fact, advertising demands 60% of the space in the average newspaper.[9]

❑ *Action: Read and recycle your local newspaper*

Your local newspaper is a great source for finding out about community events and local issues. Local celebrations, concerts, protests, and other get-togethers are easy to miss if you don't have an updated community calendar. Keep your eyes open for an alternative local weekly paper. They often contain a listing of community events and more alternative reporting, and they are usually available next to newspaper vending machines for free. Consider only subscribing to the Sunday edition of your paper or reading the news online if you would like to save a tree or two.

Title: *The Christian Science Monitor (CSM)*
Issues: 260 per year (Mon — Fri)
Cost: $96/yr, $8/mo
Phone: (800) 456-2220
Website: www.csmonitor.com

If you're looking for an alternative to the typical newspaper you receive every day on your doorstep, the *Christian Science Monitor* may be for you. Except for one religious article in every edition, the paper focuses exclusively on regular news coverage from a refreshingly independent point of view. Compared to most papers, *CSM* tends to have much less advertising, less sensational headlines, and a more positive focus on daily happenings in the world and at home. It has won numerous journalistic awards for its insightful reporting and even guarantees your money back if you are for any reason unsatisfied.

❑ Action: Write a letter to the editor

Be sure to make your opinions known. The opinion section of the local newspaper is one of the last bastions for public discourse in a world where the average Joe doesn't have much of a voice. Take advantage of it. A lot of people read this part of the paper. Your letter is more likely to be published if it is concise, well thought out, and relates to a recent article or editorial in that newspaper. Most papers accept emails as well as typed letters.

INTERNET

With the advent of the Internet, we can communicate with others around the globe in a fraction of a second. The Internet has provided progressives the opportunity to get their message out about the environment, labor struggles, indigenous people's rights, and movements for democracy. This type of communication can inform you about the actions and ideas of others around the world and inspire you to act in your community to produce social justice.

❑ Action: Get connected to progressive websites

General News

NEWS FOR CHANGE (www.workingfor- change.com) is a unique daily news site that focuses specifically on stories of interest to those interested in a better world. Sponsored by Working Assets, this site also makes a point of linking every story to an action that you can take to make a difference around the issue you've just finished reading about.

STRAIGHTGOODS (www.straightgoods.com) is "Canada's independent online source of news you can use." A neat website, with loads of great information on a variety of topics.

COMMON DREAMS (www.common-dreams.org) is the most comprehensive news site on the Web, covering issues of interest to  progressives. They even provide an extensive list of direct links to related websites of newspapers, magazines, and radio and TV stations.

Activist News

THE INDEPENDENT MEDIA CENTER (www.indymedia.org) was founded by a number of independent and alternative media  organizations. They dedicated themselves to reporting those stories that may not otherwise be told about grassroots issues of fundamental social change and the activists that are working to make it happen. They offer news from seven Canadian cities in addition to many in the U.S.

Radio News

WEBACTIVE (www.webactive.com) is an excellent place to access alternative, on-demand radio broadcasts over the Internet. From *Counterspin* to Jim Hightower, Webactive links you to the most current broadcast, as well as all of their radio archives.

Environmental News

ENVIROLINK (www.envirolink.org) is perhaps the best starting point for finding environmental resources on the Web. This site has everything you can imagine, from the latest environmental news headlines and a comprehensive list of eco-organizations to a powerful search engine for finding all things green.

THE ENVIRONMENTAL NEWS NETWORK (www.enn.com) is not only a great source of up-to-date news on pressing envi- ronmental issues, but it includes in-depth explanations of important environmental topics (alternative energy, global warming) and an engaging format.

Political News

SPEAKOUT.COM (www.speakout.com) was started to provide people with quality information about a number of important political issues and to provide avenues for people to speak out about how they feel. In one site, it gives you everything you need to get involved.

ELECTRONIC POLICY NETWORK (www.epn.org), a project of *American Prospect* magazine, provides in-depth information for progressives on a broad array of topics, ranging from campaign finance reform to criminal justice and poverty.

❑ Action: Subscribe to some alternative newsgroups

Subscribing to alternative newsgroups is a free and convenient way for you to keep up on some of the latest news, discussions, ideas, and events around the globe that concern people trying to make the world a better place. You can read the latest messages, post your own, or even ask some very basic questions of the newsgroup participants that you can't seem to get answers to anywhere else. Alternative newsgroups are often filled with friendly folks who are more than willing to share their knowledge with others.

To access these newsgroups, just use your favorite email program or Browser (Outlook, Netscape, etc.) and click on the newsgroup option. Then type in the names of the newsgroups you'd like to take a look at.

Here are some newsgroups you should check out:

- 💻 Alt.activism
- 💻 Misc.activism.progressive
- 💻 Alt.politics.greens
- 💻 Alt.save.the.earth
- 💻 Rec.food.veg
- 💻 soc.feminism
- 💻 Talk.environment
- 💻 Talk.politics.animal

❑ Action: Join an action alert email list

A number of active organizations have email lists set up specifically for those times when your actions will have their most powerful impact. You will receive an email telling you what the issue is, its importance, and what action you can take to really make a difference. This is a great way to stay involved even if you're otherwise very busy.

To sign up, just go to the website and fill in your email address in the appropriate box. You should receive your first message almost immediately.

Here are some sites that offer email lists to check out:

Amnesty International   www.amnesty.org
Center For A New American Dream   www.newdream.org
Earth Island Institute   www.earthisland.org
Greenpeace   www.greenpeace.org
Human Rights Campaign   www.hrc.org
National Organization for Women   www.now.org
Peace Brigades International   www.igc.apc.org/pbi/
The Humane Society   www.hsus.org
Working Assets   www.workingassets.com

MEDIA RESOURCES

Adbusters Media Foundation
1243d West 7th Avenue,
Vancouver, British Columbia, Canada, V6H 1B7
☎ (604) 736-9401   🖳 www.adbusters.org

Adbusters is on the cutting edge of 'jamming' corporate culture. You have got to see their 'uncommericals' on their website. You can even work to get their 'uncommericals' on your local TV stations! The 'uncommercials' use the master's tools (TV) to take apart the master's house (consumerism) by criticizing the over-watching of TV, ecological destruction, and eating disorders. They also sponsor "Buy Nothing Day," which is an annual event on the Friday after Thanksgiving, to publicize the effects of overconsumption on our culture and the planet.

Center for Media Literacy
4727 Wilshire Boulevard, Suite 403,
Los Angeles, CA 90010, U.S.A.
☎ (323) 931-4177   🖳 www.medialit.org

Media literacy education teaches critical and analytical viewing skills to people of all ages so they can better understand and navigate our media culture. Print literacy (the ability to read and write) is no longer enough. Media literacy teaches people to ask the right questions: Who created this message? Why? How and why did they choose what to include and what to leave out of this message? How is it intended to influence me?

Fairness and Accuracy in Reporting (FAIR)
130 W. 25th Street,
New York, NY 10001, U.S.A.
☎ (212) 633-6700   🖳 www.fair.org

FAIR is the highly respected national media watch group that offers well-doc-umented criticism of media bias and censorship. FAIR criticizes media practices that marginalize public interest, minority, and dissenting viewpoints. Their magazine *Extra* is the most respected periodical on media criticism.

📖 Hazen, Don, and Julie Winokur, eds. *We the Media*. New Press, 1997.
Hazen and Winokur's book uses an engaging format (and excerpts from the most eloquent media critics) to discuss the issues of corporate ownership of the media, media literacy, and the numerous alternative sources of information on TV, radio, and the Web.

📖 Just about anything by Bill Moyers
Bill Moyers is perhaps one of the most profound and influential journalists of our time. He has won more than 30 Emmy Awards for his work making thought-provoking documentaries. He is a prolific writer, and his interviewees include some of our most prominent figures, as well as average people dealing with everyday problems. Whether it's a book, film, or television program, it's hard to go wrong if Bill Moyers is involved in its creation.

📖 Phillips, Peter, and Project Censored. *Censored 2001: 25 Years of Censored News and the Top Censored Stories of the Year*. Seven Stories Press, 2001.
Project Censored is an annual collection of the Top-25 important news stories that were largely neglected by the mainstream media. Examples of past censored stories are: (1) the secret negotiations of the Multilateral Agreement on Investment (MAI), which threatened to restrict a government's ability to stand up to multinational corporations, (2) that the U.S. supplied Iraq with microorganisms that were used in biological and chemical weapons, and (3) that the World Bank and multinational corporations seek to privatize water.
💻 www.projectcensored.org

POLITICS

Voting

Getting Involved

The Top Issues List

MANY OF US IN THE U.S. are frustrated with politics, and we have some good reasons to be. Misleading campaign ads fill the airwaves. Dubious campaign donations find their way into both parties' coffers. Washington lobbyists, representing everyone but the average American, convince our elected officials to pass legislation in the lobbyists' interest rather than ours. The 2000 election fiasco turned even more of us off to the political process. As people's votes were counted and miscounted in Florida, depending on the political party of obscure officials, we saw how popular and electoral votes can point to completely different results. We also saw how the political makeup of the Supreme Court ultimately decided the outcome. It's no wonder so many of us have stopped participating in politics altogether. When we feel that rich and powerful interests drown out our voices, there isn't much incentive to speak up. Half of all eligible American citizens don't even vote for their president! That's not much of a democracy.

The current state of politics has also created the best opportunity for us to become involved. Americans understand that the system we have isn't working anymore. Stepping up to this challenge, we are beginning to produce long-term political change. Third parties are making unprecedented inroads into a system once considered the exclusive domain of the two major parties. Bills promoting campaign finance reform are showing up in Congress every year. The average person's political power is actually increasing. In a world where most people are content to remain silent, even the smallest of voices becomes a roar. If the 2000 election proved anything, it's that every vote counts (just 537 votes determined who became president). Our engagement in the political process is now more important than ever.

In this chapter, you will learn how our political system actually works; how to inform yourself and vote effectively; how to get involved and make a powerful difference in city, state, and national politics; and you will understand the top political issues we face at the turn of the century. When you understand and participate in your government, it will help you feel more engaged and connected to a number of ways in which you can help the world. Ultimately, by taking this on, you can shift the balance of power back to the people, where it belongs.

VOTING

Many people assume that their time to participate in politics comes every four years, in November. In fact, state and national elections happen every two years (during even-numbered years), and local elections for smaller offices can happen in any year. At a minimum, it is important to remember to vote every two years during major elections, the first Tuesday in November.

WHO GETS ON THE BALLOT?

Every other year between January and June, every state holds either a primary or a set of caucuses, where members of the Republican and Democratic parties select their respective party's presidential and congressional candidates. You must be a member of the party to vote at your local primary or caucus, but in most cases you can sign up at the door. For third parties, the candidate selection process often occurs at the party's state convention. Each state's results are tallied to determine the parties' presidential candidate. To find out when your primary or caucus meets, call toll free (800) 424-9530 or visit www.fec.gov/. Then go to your local primary or caucus and help determine who your party nominates.

❏ *Action: Register to vote*

To be eligible to vote in most states, you must register to vote (at your current address) at least 30 days prior to an election. This means that every time you change addresses you have to re-register — even if you only move across the street. You can register to vote at your local Department of Motor Vehicles (DMV) or drivers' licensing office, county elections office, or many City/County office buildings. At the DMV, you can register to vote instantly just by getting your new driver's license! Many states also offer registration opportunities at public libraries, post offices, and public high schools and universities.

To get a copy of the National Mail Voter Registration Form, which most states accept, go to the Federal Election Commission's website at:

💻 www.fec.gov/votregis/vr.htm.

WHERE'S MY POLLING PLACE?

If you are registered to vote, you should receive notification in the mail of the location of your polling place. You may also contact your county election official to find out where you can vote. Look in the 'Government' section of the phone book for the 'County/Municipal Clerk,' 'Supervisor of Elections,' or 'Board/Commission of Elections.'

To find out about voting in Canada, go to Elections Canada (www.elections.ca), where you'll find party information, election results, registration information, and more.

☐ *Action: Seek out good information before each election*

Every couple of years as we close in on the month of November, campaign strategists barrage us with information, trying to influence how we vote. It comes in the mail, on our doorstep, over the telephone and through the TV. Ninety-nine percent of this information is worse than useless. It's advertising disguised as valid information, but instead of trying to sell us used cars, they are trying to sell us candidates. As citizens in a democracy, it is essential that we fully inform ourselves about the issues and candidates through channels we can trust.

Looking for a good starting point to get a handle on major political issues that includes easy-to-read summaries, how the issues are being framed, graphs, and facts? Check out the nonpartisan group Public Agenda Online at: www.publicagenda.org. You won't be disappointed. It is *the* best site for a nonpartisan exploration of the issues.

It's not only important to understand where the candidates stand on the issues, but also the other measures on the ballot that may even be more important than who gets elected. We often decide on important issues concerning school funding, abortion, gun control, and campaign finance in the voting booth.

Step 1: Contact Vote Smart

A bipartisan group of people started Vote Smart because they were tired of the poor quality of information available to voters. Their excellent website (www.vote-smart.org) offers election information that is as well researched and unbiased as you can find anywhere. You can also call them toll free at (888) VOTE-SMART. They can provide you with information on specific candidates, from state legislators up to the president. Or they can just point you in the right direction on basic questions about being an effective voter, the electoral process, or campaign financing.

When you contact them, be sure to order *The Voter's Self-Defense Manual* and *The U.S. Government Owners Manual* (both are free).

BAD INFORMATION

Unsolicited Mail

TV Ads

Unsolicited Calls

SO-SO INFORMATION

Government Mailed Information

TV Debates

Calls from Groups

GOOD INFORMATION

Vote Smart's research

League of Women Voters material

Information from organizations you respect

Cross-checked research in local newspapers

Step 2: Get in Touch with the Local League of Women Voters

The League of Women Voters is a nonpartisan educational organization that seeks to create informed citizens for a more powerful democracy. Every state and many counties have League of Women Voters chapters that can provide you with information on state and local candidates as well as on ballot issues. They also have a comprehensive website (www.lwv.org) that includes a section for looking up the chapter nearest you.

Step 3: Ask Organizations That You Respect for Information

Be sure to seek out organizations that you know are doing good work in the world, and ask them to send you information on issues and candidates. Almost every organization will have some carefully reasoned positions for you to consider. You don't have to be a member to request this kind of information. Also keep your eyes open for guides put out by organizations you trust that evaluate the candidates' voting records and current stands on the issues. Here are some examples to get you started:

- AFL-CIO: www.afl-cio.org/vrecord
- League of Conservation Voters: www.lcv.org
- Peace Action: www.peace-action.org
- Human Rights Campaign: www.hrc.org

Step 4: Survey Local Newspapers for Election-Related Material

As the elections near, begin collecting information from your local and statewide newspapers about issues and candidates. Pay special attention on the weekend before election day, which is when many newspapers set aside a large section to deal with the upcoming election. Often newspapers will interview candidates about where they stand on a number of issues, as well as provide arguments for and against upcoming ballot measures. The key is to collect your information from the widest variety of newspaper sources available so that you can truly make informed decisions come election time.

❏ *Action: Create your own voting strategy*

Most Republicans vote for Republicans. Most Democrats vote for Democrats. Most Greens vote for Greens. Break out of this robotic behavior and open yourself up to choosing the best candidates based on the issues. Voting usually involves imperfect information, limited choices, and striking a balance between being true to your values and being effective. It is important to come up with a voting strategy that you can feel good about. The following strategies can get you thinking:

- Vote for a major party candidate if the race looks close; otherwise vote for a candidate that more closely matches your values.

- Don't vote on anything or anyone about which you couldn't find information beforehand. Make a note to yourself for next election.

- Cast no vote for a particular office if you feel you have to choose the lesser of two evils.

- Vote for third-party candidates in smaller elections where you think they have a better chance of winning.

- Remember, you can abstain from voting on any particular position or issue and your ballot will still count.

What's the Electoral College?

The way the electoral college system works in presidential elections mystifies many Americans. Here is a brief explanation.

Every state in the U.S. is worth a certain number of points, based on the number of national legislators that state has in the U.S. Congress. This means that a state is worth 2 points (for its 2 senators), plus 1 point for however many representatives it sends to the U.S. House of Representatives. How many representatives a state has is based on that state's population. So, for example, while California is worth 54 points as of this writing, Colorado is only worth 8 points. Points change every ten years, based on national census information, and that state is allotted more or fewer house representatives accordingly.

When people in a given state cast their votes on election day, all of the votes are tallied, and the presidential candidate with the most votes gets all the electoral points for that state. In the end, the candidate that receives the most points wins.

Why do we use the electoral college system instead of just tallying up the whole nation's votes and awarding the presidency to the candidate with the greatest number of votes? Good question. The answer most commonly given answer is that the electoral college system provides more power to less populated states that could otherwise be completely ignored by presidential candidates. The thinking goes that if candidates only needed the popular vote, then they would spend all of their time campaigning in only the most populated parts of the U.S. (California, New York, Texas, etc.).

The flaw in the system is, of course, that it's possible for a candidate to win the popular vote and still lose the electoral vote, and thus the election. Except for three times in the 1800s and in the 2000 election, the winning presidential candidate has always had the most popular votes, as well a majority of the electoral points.

Over the years, many have debated the pros and cons of the electoral college system. To learn more about them and how the system works, go to the following websites:

🖥 www.nara.gov/fedreg/elctcoll   🖥 www.fec.gov/pages/ecmenu2.htm

☐ *Action: Vote*

After you have researched all the referenda, initiatives, and candidates, write down your choices before you go to the polls. That way you don't have to stand there reading the complex wording on the ballots or deciding between city council candidates you don't know much about.

Be sure to take the opportunity to vote in every election — school board, county, state, and federal. It's easy to forget about local and state elections and pay attention only to the heavily funded and widely publicized federal races. Actually, local and state elections may have more impact on your life. Local candidates decide how to run your schools, how to 'reform' welfare, and whether to build bike paths or more roads. Voting is one of the many perks and responsibilities of living in a democracy. It is the first important step in having a say in how your government works.

VOTE FROM HOME

Many people don't realize that you no longer have to even show up to a voting booth on election day to vote. Millions of people every year vote from the comfort of their own homes weeks before election day arrives, using an absentee ballot. Most political parties encourage as many people as possible to vote absentee, as the overall convenience has led to higher turnout rates. Why should you apply for a permanent or ongoing absentee ballot?

✓ You can vote from home.
✓ You can vote on a day and time that work best for you.
✓ You can take time to really consider your choices.
✓ You are more likely to vote in every election.

There should be a form for an absentee ballot at the same government offices that keep copies of voter registration forms.

GETTING INVOLVED

Voting is only the first step in getting involved in politics. The real work comes between elections in organizing, building coalitions, and educating the public on issues you care about. There are a lot of great ways to get more involved in politics. You can:

- Talk to friends and family about important community issues.
- Write a letter to the editors of your local newspapers.
- Call or write your elected officials.
- Distribute some literature in your area around election time.
- Register people to vote.
- Assist at the polls.
- Become directly involved in campaigns for people that you believe in.
- Go to a city council meeting and state your desires or concerns.

❑ Action: Join a party that reflects your values

Joining a political party is a great way for you to band together with like-minded people to increase your collective voice within our political system. Joining a political party does not mean that you are pledging your unwavering support for every single piece of a party's platform or giving your unquestioning loyalty to each and every candidate they sponsor. It just indicates that you agree with a majority of the issues that the party stands for.

When considering which party to join, you come to a fundamental dilemma. Is it better to change the system from the inside or the outside?

Becoming a member of the Republicans or Democrats allows you to work inside the system. It gives you access to more power to make change, but this power usually comes at the cost of having to compromise some of your values. These parties seek to attract such broad coalitions of voters that they may water down issues you care about. You also run the risk of becoming so focused on winning that you lose sight of your values altogether.

Joining a smaller party allows you the ability to work from the outside. Working outside the system lets you hold firmly to your values, but this often comes at the expense of gaining access to the power necessary to change the system. On top of that, there is a danger of spending so much time outside the mainstream that you lose your ability to relate to anyone who is working on the inside. Smaller parties have played an important historical role in U.S. politics, though. Many smaller parties focus on one or two issues that both mainstream parties currently neglect. When the small party gains enough popular support, the Democrats or Republicans usually take on the issue to attract voters back to their party. Smaller parties are also useful for re-energizing disaffected voters.

Democratic Party

The Democratic Party has long been the traditional party of the Left in the U.S., forming coalitions with labor unions, environmentalists, women's rights groups, and communities of color — although in recent years that position has come into question. There are many who say the Democrats and the Republicans are looking more and more like each other as both parties take in large campaign donations from corporations and other wealthy interest groups, whose interests they are then obliged to serve. Others would argue that the Democratic Party is the only realistic option and that we must work to bring it back into line with its more traditional progressive values.

☎ (202) 863-8000   🖥 www.democrats.org

Republican Party

The Republican Party is committed to a limited role for federal government, a strong military, school vouchers, tax cuts, and traditional family values. Unfortunately the Republicans' economic policies tend to disproportionately benefit wealthy individuals and corporations. The Republican Party also has historically advocated ending legalized abortion and has been hostile toward equality for lesbian and gay Americans. Some signs of hope are the Log Cabin Republicans (lesbian/gay rights) and Republicans for Choice (abortion rights) who are working to change the social conservatism of the party.

☎ (800) 200-1294   🖥 www.rnc.org

Green Party

The Green Party is perhaps the most exciting third party on the political map. As one of the few parties with global support, the Green Party is well established in Europe but also has a presence in Africa, Asia, Canada, and South

America. The Green Party is based on ten key values: ecological wisdom, social justice, grassroots democracy, nonviolence, decentralization, community-based economics, feminism, respect for diversity, personal and global responsibility, and future sustainability. In the U.S., local and state Green parties form the backbone of this political party, as volunteers build the party from the grassroots level up. In 2000, the Greens had local parties in 24 states. More than 200 candidates ran for office, including presidential ticket Ralph Nader and Winona La Duke, who received almost three million votes (for third place), and 33 local candidates who were elected to office.
☎ (303) 543-0672   💻 www.greenparties.org

Labor Party
A relatively new, up-and-coming political party, the Labor Party was originally founded by a small group of labor unions discouraged with both major parties' constant coddling of corporations at the expense of working people. The ever-widening gap between the haves and the have-nots in America is unconscionable in their eyes, and they are willing to stand up to powerful interests in order to change it. The Labor Party values a society focused on working people, their families, and local communities. They demand a living wage, universal health care, quality housing, non-discrimination, quality affordable public education, environmental responsibility, and fair retirement benefits.
☎ (202) 234-5190   💻 www.igc.apc.org/lpa

New Party
The New Party primarily runs candidates in local elections, and they've been extremely effective at getting them elected. In fact, in the past five years they have won 200 out of their first 300 races! They sit out races that they know they can't win and endorse candidates from other parties that carry similar values. In this way, they never take away votes from other progressive candidates — a strategy that has served them well. The New Party is working to reinvigorate our democracy by bringing the power back into the hands of the people, where it belongs. Their priorities include campaign finance and other electoral reform, education, public safety, environmentally sustainable economic development, and living wages.
☎ (800) 200-1294   💻 www.newparty.org

Natural Law Party
Founded in 1992, The Natural Law Party ran hundreds of candidates at the local, state, and national level for the 2000 elections. Their platform focuses on crime prevention, education that maximizes student potential, preventative health care, mandatory labeling of genetically engineered foods, transition to clean renewable energy sources, increased drug treatment programs, and getting big money out of politics. They argue that if we get beyond partisan bickering, we can solve many of our social problems by implementing

programs already proven effective. For the 2000 election, the Natural Law presidential candidate John Hagelin forged a promising alliance with some parts of the Reform Party.

☎ (800) 200-1294 💻 www.natural-law.org

Reform Party

The Reform Party presents us with a political mixed bag. On the one hand, they are the largest and one of the most successful third parties in U.S. history. The popularity of Ross Perot and his presidential candidacy in 1992 and 1996 created the party. The Reform Party is committed to fundamental changes in how our political system works, and wants to eliminate the power of interest groups, reestablish government accountability, and bring politics back to the people. On the other hand, when some Reform candidates won offices, it became apparent that they carried with them conservative agendas to turn the clock back in a number of important areas, while campaign finance reform (a tougher issue to fight for) sat on the back burner. The Reform Party currently is split and is at a political crossroads that will determine its future.

☎ (972) 450-8800 💻 www.reformparty.org

Libertarian Party

The Libertarian Party is committed to shrinking the role of government down to the protection of individual rights and national defense. They advocate for the protection of civil liberties, such as privacy rights and an end to the drug war that has imprisoned hundreds of thousands of non-violent drug offenders. Unfortunately the Libertarians also call for the elimination of many social services and the social safety net. They oppose any form of government assistance to the poor; social security; public schools; and laws to protect workers, consumers, and the environment. Inequality is not of great concern to them under their economic policies, which put their trust completely in the corporate-run free market to create a better world.

☎ (800) 200-1294 💻 www.lp.org

Democratic Socialists of America (DSA)

DSA is the only U.S.-based socialist organization that has official ties with the major socialist parties in Europe, such as the Labour Party in the U.K. It is a political organization, not a party, so DSA doesn't nominate candidates to run in elections. Rather, they act as a kind of educational and grassroots activist organization that seeks non-violent political change outside of the electoral process. Their values include "a humane international social order based both on democratic planning and market mechanisms to achieve equitable distribution of resources, meaningful work, a healthy environment, sustainable growth, gender and racial equality, and non-oppressive relationships." Your local chapter should offer a number of social justice campaigns that you can get involved in.

☎ (202) 726-0745 💻 www.dsausa.org

❏ *Action: Contact your representatives*

Legislators hear very little from their constituents on many issues. Thus they may take your letter, call, or email as representative of the view of hundreds or even thousands of voters. Don't ever think that your voice doesn't count — it does. Especially at the local and state level, policymakers pay attention to comments from the public. Legislators often change their minds and votes when even a moderate number of citizens contact them. Remember, it is just as important to support your legislators when they are doing things right as it is to urge them to change when they are headed in the wrong direction. It is best to contact them when they are considering a bill you care about.

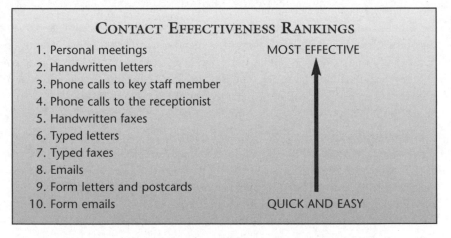

CONTACT EFFECTIVENESS RANKINGS

1. Personal meetings   MOST EFFECTIVE
2. Handwritten letters
3. Phone calls to key staff member
4. Phone calls to the receptionist
5. Handwritten faxes
6. Typed letters
7. Typed faxes
8. Emails
9. Form letters and postcards
10. Form emails   QUICK AND EASY

Here are some general tips for contacting your representatives:

• If you are concerned with a particular piece of legislation, refer to the legislative bill by both number and title. For example, "I am writing to urge you to support the 'Family Leave Act' (HR.2384, sponsored by Representative Henry Jones), the most important legislation supporting the American family in years."

• Don't worry about not being an expert on an issue. You don't have to be. Your opinion still makes a difference.

• Be courteous and reasonable. Show respect for the policymakers you contact, even when you disagree with them; otherwise they may disregard your message.

• Contact your legislator even if you don't know where they stand on an issue. If you do know that a legislator is doing something right, commend them. If they are doing something wrong, firmly but politely ask them to change their position on the issue.

Use these addresses to write your Senators and Representatives at the national level:

Your Representative
U.S. House of Representatives
House Office Building,
Washington, DC 20510, U.S.A.

Your Senator
U.S. Senate
Senate Office Building,
Washington, DC 20510, U.S.A.

Check out Vote Smart (www.vote-smart.org) and type in your zip code to find out contact information for your local, state, and national govern-ment representatives.

In Canada, look at Democracy Watch's website (www.dwatch.ca), type in your postal code, and find your MP's contact information.

Tips for Writing Your Representatives

✓   It's best to be brief, clear, and specific. Do not write more than one page.

✓   State your opinion and your specific request within the first few sen-tences. Give reasons to back up your opinion in your own words.

✓   Hand-write your letter if possible. That is the only way your represen-tative knows that it truly comes from an individual. If you must type the letter, add a P.S. that is handwritten.

✓   Make the letter as personal as possible, using your own words.

✓   At the end of your letter, make a specific request and ask the policy-maker to state her or his position on a specific issue.

✓   If you want to get noticed, have your letter read by the top people and receive an original reply. Then ask a question that is too specific to be covered by a general response in any form letter. If you do at first receive a form letter that does not respond to your particular question, call or write again and ask politely that they do so.

EXAMPLE LETTER

Representative Mark Udall
U.S. House of Representatives,
Washington, DC 20510, U.S.A.

Dear Representative Udall:

There is a bill moving through Congress, called the "2001 Taxpayer Relief Act" (HR 1725, sponsored by Representative Sam Smith), which is completely misguided in its approach.
Taxpayers do not need an extra few hundred dollars when the U.S. has such a large deficit, social security is running out, and our schools are some of the least developed in the industrialized world.
I am writing to strongly encourage you to vote against this destructive piece of legislation. The money could be better spent on improving education, a top priority for most Americans, including myself.
Please send a written reply explaining your position.
I look forward to your response. Thank you.
Sincerely,

(Signature)
Jane Smith
123 W Elm Street,
Boulder, CO 80305, U.S.A.

Remember, at the state and federal level the representative will most likely not read your letter. One of his/her staff people will read it, tabulate your letter, and tell the representative that X number of his/her constituents feel this way about Issue Y.

Tips for Calling Your Representatives

- Begin your call with something like, "Hi. This is Bob Carlson from Little Rock, Arkansas, and I'm calling about X." In this way you let the person know exactly what you're calling about. You also make it clear that you are a constituent.
- Most people who call will only be able to talk to a receptionist. Ask to speak with the staff member in charge of your particular issue. If you have to, leave a message with your name and phone number as well as what you are calling about.
- Before ending any phone call, make sure to ask for a written response.
- It is usually quite difficult to get to talk to your legislator personally on the phone (although you'll have more luck with your state legislators

than national). If you feel very strongly about an issue, be persistent in your efforts. Make it clear that you wish to speak with your legislator personally and that you are willing to call back for as long as it takes. When you finally get to speak to your legislator, it is important to be quick and to the point about your issue.

You can call the U.S. Capitol switchboard, (202)224-3121, and the operator will connect you directly to your Senator's or Representative's office. To contact your state legislators, check out: www.piperinfo.com.

If you want to go straight to the top with your opinions, leave a message on the White House comment line, from 9 a.m. to 5 p.m. EST, seven days a week, at (202) 456-1111. The President is given a summary every day of how many people called in about each issue. Only about 2,000 people call in on any given day![1]

Having trouble getting started? 20/20 Vision provides its members with monthly action notices, full of facts about a pressing environmental or peace issue and tips for contacting an elected official. Their  timely action notices guarantee that your voice is heard at the most pressing moment in the legislative process. Your energy goes directly where it will have the most impact. Call them at (800) 669-1782, or look up their website at: www.2020vision.org

Actforchange.com is another amazing site that allows you to instantly send your representatives your opinion on a variety of issues. If you want to make your voice heard, but feel that you need to know more about the issues first, this is the site for you. Visit them at: www.actforchange.com.

Tips for Meeting with Your Representative

A personal meeting with your legislators shows both that an issue is very important to you and that you are very politically active (someone they would prefer to have on their side rather than against them). Although it may take more time and effort than any other option, it is also the most effective of your contact options.

- Call to schedule an appointment with your legislator. If s/he is not able to meet with you, plan a meeting with the key staff member or legislative assistant in charge of the type of issue you are concerned about.
- Pick one issue. Be prepared to talk about why this issue is important to you and everyone. You don't need to be an expert, just somewhat informed and very concerned.
- Find out what your legislator's stand is on your issue so that you understand how much you are asking him or her to move from it.

- If you have time, consider creating a packet of materials that you can hand your legislator that provides more information about the issue. This could include newspaper clippings, fact sheets, editorials, and your own contact information.
- Tell the legislator what you would like him/her to do and give your reasons why. Be specific in your request. Do you want him/her to vote for a bill, co-sponsor it, or take a public leadership role on the issue?
- Before leaving, thank the legislator for his/her time and patience.

THE SEVEN THINGS YOU SHOULD KNOW ABOUT MONEY AND POLITICS

1. Both the Republicans and the Democrats seem to agree on more and more issues, most of which financially benefit people in positions of power at the expense of the average citizen. In fact, many people are having a difficult time distinguishing between the two parties.

2. Corporations and wealthy interest groups have made both parties dependent on their help, and thus they have a powerful influence on how our political representatives behave.

3. Political parties need corporations and wealthy interest groups, because there is no other way to get the large amounts of money needed to win an election.

4. Politicians need large amounts of money, because running political ad campaigns is incredibly expensive — especially television ads, which are the most effective at influencing voters.

5. There is such a powerful correlation between how much a candidate spends on advertising and how many votes s/he gets, it is almost impossible to win without big money.

6. Campaign contributions are like drugs: corporations and wealthy interest groups are like the dealers and our political representatives like the addicts. The average citizen cannot come up with enough drugs to get the addict high, and thus has little influence on the addict.

7. Some people blame the addicts (our representatives) for the problem, when the real issue is how to curb the addiction.

THE TOP TEN NATIONAL ISSUES LIST

ONE: Campaign Finance Reform

In recent years, we have seen huge increases in 'soft money': those unlimited donations to political parties that are given largely by corporations and wealthy individuals, earmarked for specific election candidates. Big-money lobbyists also follow up their campaign contributions with increased access to our leaders. Each year, candidates break campaign contribution records, and each year our government representatives become more beholden to the people who fund them than to those who vote for them. Campaign spending exceeded $3 billion for the 2000 federal elections.[2] In fact, many elite donors give to both the Democrats and Republicans in the same races so that they can ensure that no matter who wins, they always win. This big-money stranglehold on our government far too often sabotages our efforts to make government work effectively for the people. It is time to take our government back!

To educate yourself and take action on this issue, contact:

Public Campaign

☎ (202) 293-0222   💻 www.publicampaign.org

TWO: Global Trade Agreements

Corporate interests have dominated trade negotiations thus far, so corporate profits have always taken precedence over labor standards, environmental protection, and any other social considerations. As the protests at the 1999 World Trade Organization meeting in Seattle indicated, however, corporate leaders and government officials no longer monopolize interest in global trade. Trade agreements will increasingly become battlegrounds for labor unions, environmentalists, and advocates for local sovereignty and indigenous peoples. And whenever the public gets a chance to hear what's going on, they tend to prevail. The preliminary drafts of the MAI (Multilateral Agreement on Investment) — commonly called 'the corporations' Bill of Rights' or 'NAFTA on steroids' — were leaked to the public and summarily squashed by a public outcry across the globe in 1998. But keep your eyes peeled, because big business leaders are a crafty bunch.

To educate yourself and take action on this issue, contact:

Public Citizen's Global Trade Watch

☎ (202) 588-1000   💻 www.citizen.org

THREE: Prisons

The U.S. incarcerates a higher percentage of its citizens than any other country in the world. In 2000, over two million people called U.S. prisons 'home.'[3] Prison construction is one of the fastest-growing industries in the U.S., and increasingly prison laborers provide many common goods and services (blue jeans, airline reservations, etc.) without the knowledge of the consumer. This trend places a downward pressure on wages for other workers in similar industries. Further, the increase in profit-driven corporate prisons threatens our values of fair and humane treatment of prisoners.

Despite widely acknowledged statistics showing that the national crime rate (including violent crime) has been going down for years, politicians continue to be rewarded for appearing tough on crime. Since few dollars end up focused on reintegration and rehabilitation, the prison system has become merely a place to lock up our societal problems and hope they go away. Collectively, we have the opportunity to create a safer and more humane society by limiting the growth of the prison industry and by implementing effective crime prevention and treatment programs.

To educate yourself and take action on this issue, contact:
The Center on Juvenile and Criminal Justice
☎ (415) 621-5661   🖳 www.cjcj.org

FOUR: Reproductive Health

Reproductive health is essential to the economic, political, and social empowerment of women around the globe. The ability to be physically healthy and to exercise control over one's fertility is an essential component of individual freedom. Unfortunately, access to family planning methods, sexual health information, and abortion services can be quite scarce and/or too expensive for much of the world's population. Even in the U.S., many health insurance plans do not cover the costs of birth control. With concerted effort, we can empower the world's women by helping to ensure healthy, planned pregnancies and quality sexual and prenatal health.

To educate yourself and take action on this issue, contact:
NARAL (National Abortion and Reproductive Rights Action League)
☎ (877) 968-3324   🖳 www.naral.org

FIVE: Global Warming

Human-caused warming of the planet threatens our future. As the temperature of our atmosphere increases, changes in climate have a significant impact on agricultural yields, habitat integrity, and vulnerable coastal populations around the globe. To effectively address the challenges of global warming and climate change, the nations of the world must act collectively and cooperatively. As a global society, we must overcome the conflicts between rich and poor countries of the world and choose to take responsibility for the quality of our future. Unfortunately, many powerful constituencies, including the automobile and oil industries, oppose a decisive global transition from fossil fuels to cleaner sources of energy. This very serious threat to humanity may yet lead to the creation of a more healthy and sustainable society, where factories, transit systems, and communities function in balance with the natural environment — if we are up to the challenge.

To educate yourself and take action on this issue, contact:

Union of Concerned Scientists

☎ (617) 547-5552   🖥 www.ucsusa.org

SIX: Racial Inequality

Despite the historical advances made in providing equal opportunities for minorities, our society still faces the challenge of overwhelming racial inequality. The impacts of historical racism live on in our schools, neighborhoods, churches, and workplaces. A de facto segregation, added to current discrimination, creates significant inequalities that affect income, education, home ownership, treatment by the police and courts, entry to corporate America, and access to the halls of government for people of color. We need to demand a more inclusive society where each and every person, regardless of their race or ethnicity, has educational and occupational opportunities.

To educate yourself and take action on this issue, contact:

National Association for the Advancement of Colored People (NAACP)

☎ (410) 602-6969   🖥 www.naacp.org

SEVEN: Health Care

The U.S. is the only industrialized country in the world that does not have universal health insurance. The existence of over 40 million uninsured people, combined with excessive costs of our health care system led the World Health Organization to rank the U.S. health care system as the 37th Best in the world.[4]

The increasing administrative pressure to generate profits in the health care system is squeezing both patients and doctors. Medicare HMOs routinely kick seniors off their plans. Denial of treatment and fights with insurance companies have become commonplace for many Americans. In the richest country in the world, doctors should not have to choose between the health of their patients and the pressure to cut costs. And patients should not have to choose between paying their skyrocketing health insurance premiums or paying their rent. It is high time that the U.S. public demanded health care as a basic component of living.

To educate yourself and take action on this issue, contact:

Physicians for a National Health Program

☎ (312) 554-0382   🖥 www.pnhp.org

EIGHT: Militarism

In a time when the U.S. claims to be the only superpower left standing, we behave as if the whole world is on the brink of starting a war against us. If you include our close allies, we will spend five times more on the military than our officially identified 'potential enemies' combined: China, Russia, Iraq, Iran,

Syria, Sudan, Cuba, North Korea, and Libya.[5] It is time that we start to build bridges globally with all nations, instead of constantly preparing for war. A peaceful world will not come about through fearing each other. It will only come as citizens around the world stand up to their governments and demand alternatives to militarism. The enormous economic savings of a peace-based economy would also create the opportunity for us to fight disease and poverty, and to bring justice to millions around the world.

To educate yourself and take action on this issue, contact:

Center for Defense Information
☎ (202) 332-0600   🖳 www.cdi.org

NINE: Lesbian and Gay Rights

Lesbians, gays, bisexuals, and transgendered people are perhaps the last remaining minority group that it is still acceptable to ridicule. Could you imagine a prominent U.S. leader comparing Asians to kleptomaniacs? Senator Trent Lott had no problem comparing homosexuals to compulsive thieves, however. Important political issues in the years to come will revolve around eliminating these last vestiges of discrimination.

In the corporate world, more and more companies are allowing employees to share benefits with their same-sex partners; however, the vast majority still does not. In 2000, only 11 states had laws banning discrimination on the basis of sexual orientation.[6] Hate-motivated crimes against gays and lesbians are far too common in the U.S. and abroad. As a global society, we now have the opportunity to stand up and support equal rights and to nurture all loving relationships.

To educate yourself and take action on this issue, contact:

National Gay and Lesbian Task Force
☎ (202) 332-6483   🖳 www.ngltf.org

TEN: Economic Inequality and Tax Reform

Slick methods of tax avoidance among the wealthy have increased economic inequality in the U.S. For too long, corporations have used campaign contributions and threats of leaving the country to get millions of dollars in handouts from all levels of government. We bet you didn't vote on that decision! The conservative Cato Institute estimates that U.S. taxpayers dole out almost $135 billion each year in federal corporate welfare to U.S. businesses.[7] These special tax breaks and subsidies usually come with no strings attached (as states play a high stakes bidding war to attract corporate jobs). From the 1940s to the 1990s, corporations' share of federal tax revenues fell from 33% to 15%.[8] It's no wonder that the U.S. Treasury Department says the problem of corporate tax evasion is "unacceptable and growing".[9]

Beware of proposals to 'flatten' or 'simplify' the tax structure. Although they may look very appealing at first, they are often just tools to decrease the share that the wealthy have to pay! The most recent boondoggle of the American public is the drive to repeal the estate tax. Only the richest 2% of American estates are affected at all by this tax.[10] A grassroots movement is needed to create a fair tax structure that encourages investment in inner cities, wealth creation among the poor, and renewable energy development.

To educate yourself and take action on this issue, contact:

United for a Fair Economy

☎ (202) 588-1000 💻 www.ufenet.org

TRANSPORTATION

Walking

Bicycling

Public Transport

Automobiles

R OAD RAGE AND TRAFFIC JAMS have become routine experiences for millions of us as we join countless commuters in a daily ritual of bumper
to bumper mayhem. North Americans love their cars and are stuck in
the habit of always driving, whether they are traveling 1/2 mile or 2,000
miles. Even when bicycling might get us to our destination just as fast as driving, we hop in the car. Our dependence upon the internal combustion engine
is a major cause of global warming, air pollution, oil spills, traffic congestion,
high taxes for road construction and maintenance, accidents, and international conflicts to secure oil resources. It also contributes to the exploitation
of impoverished communities, such as those in Nigeria and Burma, during the
extraction of petroleum. The key to becoming transportation 'literate' is to be
fluent with all forms of transportation so that you can choose at any given
time which one is best for you, your family, your community, and the world.

In this chapter, you will learn about transportation options that can maximize your personal well-being while minimizing your environmental impact.

❏ *Action: Use the slowest form of transportation that is practical*

Using slow transportation goes against much of what our society stands for —
efficiency, speed, and the notion that time is money. We seem to be in a hurry
even in our leisure time. Unfortunately our focus on maximizing the quantity of
our daily experiences has led us to lose focus on the quality of our experiences.

The slower your form of transportation, the more connected you feel to your surroundings. You have time to more fully appreciate the beauty of your environment and your community — the character of architecture, the uniqueness of local people, the smell of flowers, the mischievous nature of a squirrel. You live in the present, ready to fully experience whatever happens. When you are moving too fast, you can't even register individual human faces.

WALKING

❏ *Action: Go on a daily walk*

A walk is a wonderful way to take a breather from your fast-paced life and get to know your community. It's ironic that we hop in the car to travel six blocks, then go home and exercise on the stairmaster for an hour. Walking is free, healthy, and produces no pollution. You will learn more about your local businesses, find shortcuts through wooded areas or interesting neighborhoods, and stop and talk with people that you know. Walking is also a great form of meditation. It can create a serene place for you to think about your day and to consider what's important to you. Any errands that take you within a mile of your home afford a perfect opportunity for you to use your walking shoes and give the atmosphere a break. Consider picking up litter along the way!

How many of us walk to work:[1]
1960 . . . . 10%
1980 . . . . 5.6%
1997 . . . . 4%

BICYCLING

Biking is an exciting way to get around town and to get some exercise. Free parking, no fuel costs, low maintenance costs, no pollution, the wind blowing through your hair — what more could you ask for? Quick parking and easy shortcuts can also make biking more versatile than driving. Trips of less than three miles (5 kilometers) are a great opportunity for you to get out on your bike, because it will probably take 15 or 20 minutes at most.

❏ *Action: Use your bike for commuting and errands*

Biking is a great way to get to work and do errands, especially if you live within a few miles of your destination. In high traffic areas, bike paths often allow cyclists to move faster than car traffic. Just put a backpack on and you're set.

> Bicyclists around the globe are taking back the streets from cars, in organized 'critical mass' rides. To find out more, check out:
> 🖳 www.critical-mass.org

> In some Dutch cities, one-half of all the trips people make are by bicycle.[2]

You may even want to transform your bicycle into a sport utility vehicle by purchasing a bike rack, some panniers, and a cargo cart that you can pull behind you. Biking to work once a week would be a great start.

Make some time to find out if your community has any designated bike paths. This is a great way to bike — it's safer, has less pollution, and no stop lights! Contact your city government or local bicycle shop to see what resources they have for bikers. Some cities even publish a map of designated bike paths, as well as the safest streets that have bike lanes.

ELECTRIC BICYCLES

Electric bicycles are normal bikes that have a small electric motor hooked up to the back tire. The motor can give you that extra push up the hill during your commute, and that by itself may get you out of your car for good. Bicycle motors can propel you 10 to18 miles per hour (16 to 29 kilometers per hour) under normal conditions (but you can peddle to move even faster). You can either buy a bike with the system installed or install it yourself on your current bike. Ask for details at your local bike store.

The Electric Bikes Page
⌨ www.electric-bikes.com
This website includes the benefits of electric bicycles and a variety of electric bike manufacturers and products (including ZAP bikes, U.S. Pro Drive, Schwinn, and Charger). Prices start around $350 for a system that you can install on your bike.

PUBLIC TRANSIT

Our sprawling highway system has taken its toll on the number of people who use public transit. In 1960, 13% of Americans took public transit to work. By 1990, that number had dropped to 5%.[3] However, public transit is making a comeback in some American cities. Subways, cross-town buses, and light rail lines are great ways to get around town. It's also a great way to experience the diversity of our American cities, while knowing that you are doing your part to clean up the environment.

❏ Action: Use public transit for commuting and errands

Taking public transit to work in the morning can be a wonderful experience. You can take a nap, read, or talk with a friend without worrying about traffic. You also save wear and tear on your car and money for gas and parking. Make sure to talk with your employer about discounts on bus fares. Some cities encourage businesses to give incentives to workers who use public transportation because they are doing good for their communities. To learn more about public transit and to find which routes are convenient for you, contact your local transit authority — look in your phone book under 'Transportation' in the 'Government' pages.

❏ *Action: Take a bus*

A bus is like a carpool for up to 80 people. What a great way to save gasoline and cut pollution! The next time you have to travel to the next city, consider taking the bus instead of driving your car by yourself. It is also one of the cheapest ways to travel. Greyhound serves over 2,600 destinations in the U.S. as well as areas of Canada and Mexico.

☎ (800) 231-2222   ⌨ www.greyhound.com

❏ *Action: Take a train*

Join the train enthusiasts by taking Amtrak the next time you are traveling cross-country. Trains have big comfy seats suitable for long trips, and they are a great way to experience the beauty of our country while avoiding crazy airports. Observation cars allow you to spread out and enjoy the views.

If you ride coach, you can create a nice community in your car. It's even better to travel with a group of family and friends, because there are plenty of opportunities to walk around, play cards, and talk! The trip itself becomes an enjoyable part of your vacation.

☎ (800) USA-RAIL   ⌨ www.amtrak.com

SOCIALLY RESPONSIBLE AIRLINES

Flying is the least environmentally friendly mode of travel, but many of us want or need to fly occasionally. Consider flying with those airlines that have better social and environmental responsibility records than others.

GOOD: Southwest, American, (United)

FAIR: Delta, TWA, (Continental), (Northwest)

POOR: USAir

Note that all airlines listed in parentheses are at the bottom of their rating category. See the SHOPPING chapter for data sources.

AUTOMOBILES

North Americans sure love their cars. We spend an average of one hour every day in our cars. Although driving is incredibly polluting, cars are extremely convenient when you are hauling large loads or making several quick stops. (You can only fit so many bags of groceries on your handlebars.) Since few of us will give up our cars completely, the goal is to become a responsible user of

> Automobiles continue to be the largest source of urban air pollution.[4]

our automobiles — using them only when other modes of transport just won't do, and then driving them in a manner that reduces their environmental impact.

AUTOMOTIVE DESTRUCTION

According to the Union of Concerned Scientists, "personal use of cars and light trucks (including pickups and SUVs) is the single most damaging consumer behavior."[5] Automobile driving is a major cause of:

1. **global warming.** Carbon dioxide emissions from autos are the largest contributor to global warming.

2. **air pollution.** Automobiles produce nitrogen oxides, sulfur dioxide, hydrocarbons, carbon monoxide, and particulate matter that contribute to smog and respiratory illnesses.

3. **water pollution.** Automobile manufacturing; gas and oil production; road runoff of fuel, oil, and antifreeze; underground gasoline storage tanks; and marine oil spills all pollute our water.

4. **habitat destruction.** Oil drilling, metals mining, and road construction all damage wildlife habitat.

5. **international conflict.** Nations compete over oil reserves. The U.S. currently imports 48% of its oil — the highest levels ever.[6] Many people tie this oil dependency to the $61 billion we spent on the Persian Gulf War.[7]

Driving Your Car

❑ *Action: Set concrete goals for reducing driving*

Every gallon of gas that you conserve means less oil that has to be extracted and refined, fewer oil spills, and less air and water pollution. Take account of your odometer so that you can monitor how much you drive. Set a goal to reduce your driving. If you drive an average of 200 miles (320 kilometers) per week, cut it by 25% to 150 miles (240 kilometers).

> The U.S. has 4% of the world's population and uses 40% of the world's gasoline.[8]

> In 1998, U.S. passenger cars drove 1,549,577,000 miles (2,493,269,393 kilometers).[9]

Consider combining trips so that you save gasoline. Since you're already out on the roads, why not stop by the grocery store for your groceries and the hardware store for your garden tools? It's important to limit the number of car trips you take, because cars pollute the most during the first couple minutes when they are cold.

❑ *Action: Be a considerate driver*

Don't give in to road rage. Not only is it safer to be a considerate driver, it also results in less stress and gives you the opportunity to brighten someone's day when you let them change lanes or pull in ahead of you. Also, be sure to watch out for pedestrians and cyclists when you're out on the streets. They are the real troopers out there using sustainable transportation, so treat them with respect and share the road.

Put Some Bumper Stickers on Your Car

Especially in rush-hour traffic, bumper stickers are a great opportunity to get people to think about what's important to you. They often spark good conversations between drivers and passengers. If you can't find any good ones locally, just call *Northern Sun* or *Donnelly/Colt* and request a free catalog of progressive T-shirts, bumper stickers, buttons, posters, and more.

Northern Sun
☎ (800) 258-8579
💻 www.northernsun.com

Donnelly/Colt
☎ (860) 455-9621
💻 www.donnellycolt.com

❑ *Action: Maintain your car in good running condition*

A poorly maintained car uses more gas, emits more pollutants, and costs you big money in repairs. Check your owner's manual for maintenance specifics. You should also keep track of any maintenance or repair work that is done on your car in a logbook.

> Do-it-yourselfers pour 400 million gallons (1.8 billion liters) of highly toxic used oil into drains every year.[10]

1. **Check your oil weekly.** Depending on how new your car is, you may have to do this less often. You will greatly extend the life of your car greatly by keeping the right amount of oil in it.

2. **Check your air pressure monthly.** It can cost you 5-10% in fuel efficiency if your tires are even 5 pounds (34 kiloPascals) under-inflated.[11] (Don't forget to pump up your spare tire, too.)

3. **Get your oil changed about two to four times per year.** According to *Consumer Reports*, you should change your oil every six months or 5,000 miles (8000 kilometers).[12] Make sure your service station recycles the used oil.

4. **Check your fluid levels two to four times per year.** Check your radiator coolant, automatic transmission, and power steering fluid levels at every oil change.

5. **Get your tires rotated twice yearly.** It will even out the wear and extend the life of your tires.

6. **Get a tune-up every one to five years.** Tune-ups can save you up to10% on fuel efficiency.[13] Check your owner's manual for an exact maintenance schedule. Older models need tune-ups more often.

7. **Change your air filter yearly.** If you can't see light through your filter, it's time to replace it.

8. **Log your gas mileage on long trips.** Any dramatic decreases in fuel mileage may indicate engine problems.

❏ *Action: Drive moderately*

Driving like a bat out of hell is not only a public nuisance but is bad for the environment. Rabbit starts and brake slamming waste gas and are hard on many car parts. Accelerate gradually and anticipate stops instead.

Cars run most efficiently at around 45 miles per hour (70 kilometers per hour), so the faster you drive, the lower your fuel efficiency. Driving at 70 miles per hour (110 kilometers per hour) uses 20% more gas than driving at 55 miles per hour (90 kilometers per hour).[14]

❏ *Action: Carpool*

A carpool is a great way to help protect the environment. Whether you are driving to work or driving to a football game, carpooling is more fun, saves money on parking, and makes you feel like you are using your car responsibly.

Some cities have carpooling services that will send you a list of people in your area who are commuting to a similar location. Vanpooling services charge a monthly fee to pick up a group of people and take them to work (a kind of personalized form of public transit). Call your city government for more information.

Some communities are even instituting car-sharing programs, where a group of people will share a fleet of cars for a monthly fee. If you don't drive very much, this is a great way to save money on insurance and depreciation.

Percentage of people who carpool to work:[15]

1980: 20%	1990: 13%	1999: 9%

Percentage of people who drive alone to work:[16]

1980: 64%	1990: 73%	1999: 78%

❏ *Action: Fuel up responsibly*

When you are at the pump remember three main rules:

1. **Don't top off the gas tank.** When the gas pump automatically shuts off, don't keep pumping. If you top off the gas tank, you allow more fumes to escape and often spill some on the ground. Then as you drive, gasoline expands and spills out on the road, which causes ground level ozone (leading to smog).

2. **Buy the lowest octane that your owner's manual recommends.** The higher the octane the more oil is necessary to produce the gasoline (and you don't get any better mileage).[17]

3. **Buy gas from a socially and environmentally responsible gas station.** Oil companies are, in general, not the most socially conscious corporations on the planet. Their drilling, processing, refining, and transportation are usually very environmentally destructive. Many have been implicated by human rights groups as being closely involved with exceptionally repressive Third World governments. It's important not to reward the worst oil companies with your dollars. Use the following list to help you choose better stations to gas up at.

GASOLINE STATIONS

BETTER:	Sunoco
FAIR:	BP, Amoco, Arco
WORSE:	Citgo, 7 Eleven, Diamond Shamrock, Total, (76), (Circle K), (Shell), (Unocal), (Conoco)
WORST:	Phillips 66, Chevron, Texaco, (Exxon), (Mobil)

Note that all gas stations listed in parentheses are at the bottom of their rating category. See the SHOPPING chapter for data sources.

Choosing a Car

For most North Americans, aside from our homes, our car is the most expensive purchase we will make. We consider many factors when buying a car, including size, model, color and make. We also need to consider the impact our car will have on the world over its lifetime.

❑ *Action: Buy a used car*

Buying a used car allows you to reuse a car (preserving resources necessary to build a new car), and it saves you significant amounts of money. Remember that a car loses a significant portion of its value immediately after you drive it off the lot. Also, the more expensive the car, the bigger your loan and the more you will pay in interest to the bank. A five-year $20,000 loan at 9% will cost you almost $5,000 in interest.[18]

Reliability is an important environmental issue. The more parts that break, the more parts are thrown into landfills, requiring the manufacture of new cars. Also cars that are not running at full capacity have a lower than average fuel efficiency.

Consider checking out the *Consumer Reports Used Car Guide* at your local library for guidelines on how to find a reliable used car. (See www.consumerreports.org.)

DON'T BUY MORE CAR THAN YOU NEED

Big vehicles are currently in vogue. In 1980, only 17% of new auto purchases were light trucks (SUVs, vans, and pickups). By 2000, over 50% of new car buys were these monster vehicles.[19] The bigger the car, the more it will pollute, and the more it will cost in gas and repairs. The average light truck (SUVs, vans, and pick-ups) gets 21 miles per gallon (34 kilometers per liter) as compared to 29 miles per gallon (47 kilometers per liter) for the average car.[20] That's almost 40% lower fuel efficiency! Unfortunately, light trucks not only burn more fuel, they also have less stringent emission standards. And extras such as automatic transmission, power windows and doors, and turbo-charged engines lead to lower fuel efficiency and additional repair costs. Consider getting the smallest engine available in the model that you want, with a manual transmission and cruise control. All of these features will increase your car's fuel efficiency.

❑ Action: Choose a low emission, fuel-efficient car

The car you buy is one of the most important environmental choices that you will ever make — partly because of the environmentally destructive nature of the automobile but also because it will have an impact on the environment for as long as you drive it.

There are two main factors to consider when assessing the environmental impact of an automobile: (1) tailpipe emissions, (2) fuel efficiency.

Tailpipe Emissions

Automobile emissions are one of the primary causes of global warming and air pollution. Carbon dioxide, a primary greenhouse gas, is a common byproduct of internal combustion engines. Also, as you drive, your tailpipe spews out sulfur oxides and nitrous oxides, which cause acid rain. Since California implemented strict emission standards, there have been immense improvements in tailpipe emissions, but many of these car models are only available in California. A number of states have begun to adopt similarly strict standards. New cars sold in many areas of the country will now carry emissions standards labels.

Diesel engines often significantly surpass gasoline engines for fuel efficiency. Unfortunately, that's not the whole story. Many diesel cars sold today have nitrous oxide certification levels over twice the gasoline car values, and some test at more than 10 times the amount.[21] Recent data indicate that diesels emit at least 10 and perhaps as much as 300 times more particulate matter mass than properly operating modern gasoline vehicles, so avoid buying them.[22]

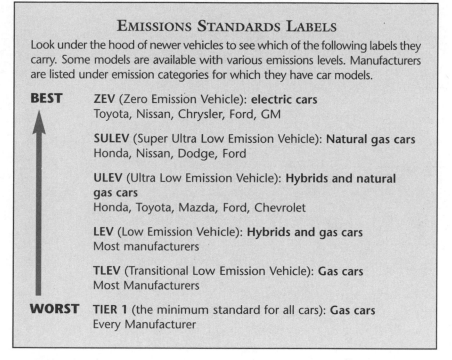

EMISSIONS STANDARDS LABELS

Look under the hood of newer vehicles to see which of the following labels they carry. Some models are available with various emissions levels. Manufacturers are listed under emission categories for which they have car models.

BEST   **ZEV** (Zero Emission Vehicle): **electric cars**
Toyota, Nissan, Chrysler, Ford, GM

SULEV (Super Ultra Low Emission Vehicle): **Natural gas cars**
Honda, Nissan, Dodge, Ford

ULEV (Ultra Low Emission Vehicle): **Hybrids and natural gas cars**
Honda, Toyota, Mazda, Ford, Chevrolet

LEV (Low Emission Vehicle): **Hybrids and gas cars**
Most manufacturers

TLEV (Transitional Low Emission Vehicle): **Gas cars**
Most Manufacturers

WORST   **TIER 1** (the minimum standard for all cars): **Gas cars**
Every Manufacturer

Fuel Efficiency

It is important to drive a car that gets at least 30 miles per gallon (48 kilometers per liter). Each 0.1 mile per gallon (0.2 kilometer per liter) improvement in the U.S. car fleet saves 12 million gallons (55 million liters) of gas annually.[23] Gas mileage largely correlates with the size of a vehicle. Subcompacts and compacts always get better gas mileage than do sport utility vehicles and minivans. If you do choose a larger vehicle, make sure that you get the model with the best fuel efficiency in its class.

Green Cars

The internal combustion engine is a technological dinosaur. It is inefficient, highly polluting, and loud. It will still be around long enough for you to say your farewells, but there are now many more environmentally friendly technologies that are being used to power automobiles:

Compressed natural gas vehicles emit 80% fewer hydrocarbons, 90% less carbon dioxide, and 22% less nitrous oxides than gasoline engines.[24] Most qualify as Ultra Low Emission Vehicles (ULEV). The Honda Civic GX and Toyota Camry CNG run on compressed natural gas and are available in many parts of the U.S.

Electric vehicles are considered Zero Emission Vehicles (ZEV), which means that there are no tailpipe emissions (they don't even have a tailpipe!). If they recharge with electricity generated from solar or wind power, your car is using completely renewable energy! Even recharging your electric vehicle with coal-generated electricity dramatically cuts pollution by as much as 90%.[25] By increasing the aerodynamic nature of the body and using regenerative braking which recharges the battery, electric vehicles are able to squeeze 55 to 130 miles (90 to 210 kilometers) out of each charge.

Electric vehicles are also virtually maintenance free because they have no plugs, no valves, no muffler, no air or fuel filter, no hoses, no radiator, no transmission, and need no tune-ups or oil changes. Electric vehicles on the market now include: GM EV-1, Ford Ranger, Toyota RAV-4, Chrysler EPIC, and Nissan Altra.

As little energy as it takes to power a TV for six hours can recharge an electric car.[26]

Hybrid vehicles combine a highly efficient gasoline engine with a battery powered electric motor (that never needs to be recharged!!) to propel the car. These vehicles cut CO2 emissions in half and other pollutants by as much as 90%, when compared to standard gasoline engines.[27] They have the potential to get 70 to 80 miles per gallon (110 to 130 kilometers per liter) of gasoline, without the range limitations of standard electric vehicles. Hybrid vehicles available now include the Honda Insight and the Toyota Prius.

Remember that no matter how 'green' your car is, it won't lessen traffic congestion or urban sprawl.

Fuel cell vehicles use hydrogen, methanol, or natural gas to produce electricity in your car and an electric motor to propel it. Upcoming fuel cell technology may have as much impact on our society as the advent of the light bulb.[28] The fuel cell vehicle of the future promises to be 98% to 100% percent cleaner than today's cars. When running on renewable fuels, fuel cell vehicles reduce emissions of greenhouse gases by 85% to 100% percent. Even when their fuels are produced from natural gas, fuel cells reduce these emissions by 60% to 70%.[29] Daimler-Chrysler plans to have a fuel cell vehicle (Necar 4) in limited production by 2004. Toyota and Honda are also in the prototype stage.

WHAT KIND OF CAR SHOULD I BUY?

Ultimately, you have to make a decision that combines your values with your specific needs and budget. We can, however, provide some good recommendations — above and beyond what we've already mentioned — that you should consider when buying your car.

The first list combines a rating of the overall social consciousness of the corporation that manufactured the car, with the reliability ratings of the average vehicle they produce. Listings in parentheses are at the bottom of their rating category. The second list contains all the current car models that get 30 miles per gallon (50 kilometers per liter) or better. It is divided into sections, based on their rankings in the first list. Especially reliable models are marked with an asterisk.

RELIABLE, SOCIALLY CONSCIOUS CAR COMPANIES

GOOD   Toyota, Lexus, (Honda), (Acura)

FAIR   Nissan, Infiniti, Mercedes, Dodge, Jeep, Chrysler, Isuzu, (Mazda), (Ford), (Volvo), (Lincoln), (Mercury), (Jaguar)

POOR   Saturn, Geo, Chevrolet, Pontiac, Saab, GMC, Buick, Cadillac, Oldsmobile, (Mitsubishi)

CAR MODELS THAT GET 30+ MPG (50+ KM/L)

Toyota	Corolla*, Celica, Echo, Paseo, Prius, Tercel
Honda	Civic*, Insight
Nissan	Sentra/200SX
Dodge/Plymouth	Neon
Mazda	Protégé
Mercury	Tracer
Ford	Escort, Focus
Volkswagen	Beetle, Golf, Jetta
Suzuki	Esteem, Swift
Hyundai	Accent
Daewoo	Lanos
Chevrolet	Metro, Prizm*
Saturn	SC, SL, SW
Mitsubishi	Mirage

* especially reliable models

BICYCLES RESOURCES

League of American Bicyclists
The League of American Bicyclists (LAB) is working on improving conditions for cycling throughout the country by influencing transportation policy and legislation, identifying and designating Bicycle Friendly Communities, and sponsoring National Bike Month and Bike-to-Work Day.

☎ (202) 822-1333   💻 www.bikeleague.org

Rails-to-Trails Conservancy (RTC)
Since 1996, RTC has converted over 7,000 miles (11,200 kilometers) of abandoned railroad track corridors to pedestrian and bicycle paths. Contact them for information about how to accomplish this in your community.
☎ (202) 797-5400   💻 www.railtrails.org

AUTOMOBILE RESOURCES

📖 Decicco, John, ed., Jim Kliesch, and Martin Thomas. *ACEEE's Green Book: The Environmental Guide to Cars and Trucks.* American Council for an Energy Efficient Economy. [Published annually.]
Put out yearly by the American Council for an Energy Efficient Economy, this book gives a 'green' rating from 1 to100 for every new model car, based on emissions and fuel economy. It includes listings for alternative fuel cars as well.   💻 www.aceee.org

📖 Alvord, Katie. *Divorce Your Car: Ending the Love Affair with the Automobile.* New Society Publishers, 2000.
This insightful book tells the story of the advent of car culture, the social and environmental consequences in an automobile addicted society, and myriad reasons and methods to escape your car.

📖 *Consumer Reports New Car Buying Guide 2001, Used Car Buying Guide 2001.*
Put out by the editors of *Consumer Reports* magazine, these books give the highest quality information available on what you should know for purchasing a car that meets your exact needs. Best known for their reliability ratings for every model of car by year, Consumers Union gives us an island of reason and common sense in a sea of advertising.

TRANSPORTATION RESOURCES

Alliance for a Paving Moratorium
Launched in 1990, the non-profit Alliance for a Paving Moratorium's goal is to halt the tremendous environmental, social, and economic damage caused by endless road building. The Alliance assists road fighters all over the world, and publishes *Road Fighters' Alerts* and the quarterly *Auto-Free Times* magazine.
☎ (707) 826-7775   💻 www.tidepool.com/alliance

TRAVEL

Where to Go

Where to Stay

What to Do

Extraordinary Travel

P EOPLE TRAVEL A LOT. Tourism has become a major part of the global economy and an especially important source of income for many developing countries. In fact, it is one of the largest industries in the world, employing 204 million people and producing 10.2% of the world's gross national product![1] Many Americans travel to take a breather from our stressed-out, fast-paced world and to enjoy life a little more fully. There are many other great reasons to travel throughout the U.S. and around the world, as well:

- to better understand and appreciate other cultures and people
- to experience the amazing diversity of geography and wildlife
- to spend time with your loved ones
- to take time to reconsider your priorities in life
- to recharge your batteries

There is no better way to build understanding across cultures and communities than to actually experience other people's way of life. Traveling can be an intense learning experience about how people outside of your own community live. And breaking down barriers goes a long way towards making the world a better place!

It is important to remember that our travels have huge effects both on other people and on our natural environment. Whether you are interested in exploring the Himalayas, the Amazonian rainforest, or your local state park, there are easy steps you can take to ensure that your travels have a positive impact on you, the people you meet, and the natural environment.

In this chapter, you will learn about opportunities for exciting and educational travel that supports the cultures, economies, and environments that you experience. Tips on where to go, where to stay, what to do, and how to make your trip extraordinary will help your travels reflect your values. When you add concern about the environment and other human beings to your traveling, it can transform your vacation into an adventure far beyond what you've come to expect.

BEFORE YOU LEAVE ON YOUR TRIP DON'T FORGET TO:
- stop your newspaper delivery
- ask a neighbor to collect your mail and water your houseplants
- turn down your water heater, furnace, and air conditioner
- tell friends or loved ones how to contact you in an emergency

---

WHERE TO GO

We all know the common destinations for American travelers: Disneyland, Disney World, Las Vegas, or a shopping spree in the nearest big city. Put some extra thought into choosing your travel destination, instead of accepting the pre-packaged vacation experiences that often drain your pocketbook and leave you exhausted. Think about what you want from a vacation: a sense of relaxation and calm, connection with nature, beautiful vistas, excitement, action, quality time with loved ones, an experience of new cultures, or new learning opportunities. Consider how your next vacation might better reflect your most deeply held values.

❑ Action: Explore your own backyard

It's easy to forget that in every community, including your own, there are many cultural landmarks and natural settings that you can explore and enjoy. Staying close to home will not only save money, gasoline, and vacation time, it will make you feel closer to your community and your natural environment. State parks, museums, and local celebrations and fairs provide great opportunities for you to get away and have some fun. Buy a travel book that includes your local area for interesting ideas on nearby destinations, and pay attention to event announcements in your local paper. What you've overlooked or forgotten about may surprise you.

❑ Action: Experience nature

Vacation time is a great time to connect with the living environment all around us. Hiking within the serenity of wilderness, feeling the crashing of ocean waves, or observing playful wildlife are great alternatives to the frantic overly scheduled vacations that have become common for most Americans. You will actually return rested and ready to take on new challenges back home, while having enhanced your appreciation of the natural environment.

Hiking and camping are great ways to relax and enjoy the outdoors. Inexpensive or used camping gear is easy to find. You can even rent gear if you just want to give it a try. Without the conveniences of home — such as a microwave and television — you will focus more on enjoying the scenery and your loved ones.

When you are hiking or camping, consider these easy tips to protect the habitats you encounter:

- Stay on established and designated trails.
- Never touch, harass, or disturb wildlife.
- Whenever possible, use existing campsites
- Choose a durable campsite (not on delicate wildflowers).
- Take only pictures; leave only footprints (take all litter with you; leave rocks and plants where they are).

❑ Action: Visit state and national parks

The 378 state and national parks that we have here in the U.S. provide wonderful educational, cultural, and recreational opportunities for people of all ages (often at an inexpensive price). Beautiful ecological reserves, ancient Native American artifacts, and local historical landmarks make up one of the most extraordinary park systems in the world. Go out and experience it for yourself.

National Park Service
☎ (202) 208-6843   💻 www.nps.gov

HUMBOLDT REDWOODS STATE PARK (HUMBOLDT, CA)

Ancient redwoods and Sequoias are the oldest living creatures on the planet, some reaching up to 2000 years old. They are also the tallest, some having grown over 360 feet (110 meters) tall (taller than the Statue of Liberty!). The Redwoods State Park in Humboldt County is the largest old-growth redwood preserve in the world. The awe you will experience at being in the presence of these majestic creatures is indescribable. Admission is free in most of the park's areas. There are fees for camping.

☎ (707) 946-2409
💻 www.humboldtredwoods.org

FIVE POWERFUL MUSEUMS

U.S. Holocaust Memorial Museum (Washington, DC)
The Holocaust Memorial Museum in Washington, DC provides us with a meaningful education on the Nazi Holocaust. It is a powerful call to remember those who suffered and inspires us to contemplate the moral implications of our choices and responsibilities as citizens. The museum offers exhibitions for adults and children and includes the designated national memorial to victims of the Holocaust. Admission is free, but assigned times are required to space out visits.
☎ (202) 488-0400   💻 www.ushmm.org

National Civil Rights Museum (NCRM) (Memphis, TN)
The NCRM houses the first and only comprehensive overview of the civil rights movement in exhibit form. Its mission is to provide an understanding of the civil rights movement and its impact on human rights movements worldwide. Located in the Lorraine Motel, the site of Martin Luther King's assassination, a visit to this museum may well be one of the most moving experiences you could have on a vacation.
☎ (901) 521-9699   💻 www.civilrightsmuseum.org

Smithsonian Institution Museums (Washington, DC)
The Smithsonian Institution maintains a collection of 16 incredible museums and galleries most of which are located on or near the National Mall in Washington, DC. Museums include the National Museum of African Art, the National Air and Space Museum, and the National Museum of Natural History. Admission is free to most of the museums.
☎ (202) 357-2700   💻 www.si.edu

National Museum of the American Indian (New York)
The National Museum of the American Indian works with indigenous Western peoples to protect, foster, and share their unique cultures with the rest of the world. It gives us the opportunity to educate ourselves about Native life and history in interesting and creative ways. There will be an additional branch of the museum opening on the National Mall in Washington, DC in 2002. Admission is free.
☎ (212) 668-6624   💻 www.si.edu/nmai

National Women's Hall of Fame (Seneca Falls, NY)
Long considered the birthplace of women's rights, Seneca Falls is now home to the National Women's Hall of Fame as well as the Women's Rights National Historical Park. The Hall is a tribute to some of the greatest women in American history, including Jane Addams, Harriet Tubman, and Rachel Carson. Admission runs $2-$3 per person.
☎ (315) 568-8060   💻 www.greatwomen.org

❏ *Action: Travel off-season and to unknown places*

Some of our most famous parks, such as Yellowstone and Rocky Mountain National Parks, receive millions of visitors every year. If you can, schedule your travel outside of the peak travel times (which differ, depending on the country or area of the U.S.). If you travel during the off-season, it lessens the social and environmental impacts a region must endure at one time. You will also encounter fewer crowds, have less stress, and pay cheaper prices during your visit. Contact your destination beforehand to find out when their visitor traffic is low. Avoiding the most common destinations is also a great strategy for an incredible vacation. Many lesser-known sites around the world are just as beautiful and enjoyable as the famous ones.

WHERE TO STAY

Whether you are traveling abroad or staying near home, there are a lot of great alternatives to the high-rise hotel with sterile hallways and free cable. Think about where you could stay on your trip that would have a positive impact on the local economy and create the most meaningful experience for you.

❏ *Action: Stay with the locals*

One great way to get to know an area is to stay with the people who live there. They are a great source of knowledge and provide the best way to learn about the local culture. By staying at a local host's home or at a Bed and Breakfast you will experience unforgettable hospitality.

Bed and Breakfasts

The B and B experience is the polar opposite of staying in a big chain hotel. Each B and B is unique and is usually run by a local family in a large, old home with an interesting history. Often you will wake up to a home-cooked breakfast and a chance to meet a few fellow travelers, as well as learn about the area from your knowledgeable hosts. Best of all, your money stays in the hands of the locals and promotes a more meaningful, human travel experience. Check out these resources to find a B and B in the areas you're interested in visiting.

BBOnline

☎ (615) 868-1946   🖳 www.bbonline.com

Bed and Breakfast.com

🖳 www.bedandbreakfast.com

SERVAS International

SERVAS works to build understanding, tolerance, and world peace through a network of hosts around the world who are prepared to open their doors to travelers for a two-to-three-day stay. Good for both domestic and international travel. It costs $65 per year to register as a traveler.

☎ (212) 267-0252   🖳 www.servas.org

❑ *Action: Exchange your home*

Do what?! Yes, you read right. You can trade houses with someone in another country. Hotels can be expensive, both for folks traveling here and for us when we go abroad. They can also prevent us from really experiencing our destination. If you want to get a feel for the local way of life, living in a neighborhood through home exchange might be for you. You can cook your own meals, sightsee at your leisure, and feel more at home. In the meantime, foreign travelers will enjoy your home while you're gone.

HOME EXCHANGE RESOURCES

📖 Barbour, Bill, and Mary Barbour. *Home Exchange Vacationing: Your Guide to Free Accommodations.* Rutledge Hill Press, 1996.
 The authors gather firsthand stories from home exchangers to supplement practical tips on achieving a successful home exchange vacation. From avoiding common pitfalls to handling problems and enjoying exchanges, this guide provides all the basics.
 The following websites include both a wide variety of countries to choose from and detailed information on each home and family.
 💻 www.homeexchange.com 💻 www.homexchange.com

❑ *Action: Stay in a hostel*

When you're on a tight budget, finding cheap lodging is a must. Prices usually don't get much cheaper than a hostel. Hostels come in all shapes and sizes and are scattered around almost every country imaginable (including the U.S.). Most offer clean, dormitory-style rooms (some even have a few private rooms), a shower, and possibly some food. Best of all, people from all over the world stay in hostels, giving you a great opportunity to make a variety of friends who share your passion for traveling.

Hostelling International
☎ (202) 783-6161
💻 www.hiayh.org

Hostels.com
💻 www.hostels.com

HOSTELLING
INTERNATIONAL®

WHAT TO DO

Socially responsible travel is more meaningful, because it combines your passion for travel with your interest in preserving the environment, supporting local cultures, and nurturing local economies. A number of actions can ensure that your trip is both rewarding for you and helpful to your host community. Bon voyage!

Tips

✓ **Consider not working the day before and after your trip.** You will more fully enjoy your vacation and adjust easier to being home.

✓ **Slow down and be flexible.** Many Americans lead such hurried daily lives that they schedule their vacations as if it were a three-day business meeting. Make sure to leave flexibility in your schedule so that you can enjoy unexpected events.

❏ Action: Connect with the local people

You may have noticed that no matter what incredible sights you see, what museums you visit, or what entertainment you take in while on vacation, your best memories are often of the people you meet. Having a discussion with someone from a different place and being open to what they have to teach can be a great learning experience, and it's a way of appreciating the people who opened up their community for your enjoyment. You may even consider studying up on the local history and culture (and even the language) as a show of respect. These connections that we make with people from different backgrounds help us build bridges across our differences and ultimately create a more humane world.

Here are some other tips for connecting with the locals:

• Walk around town instead of driving.

• Visit local neighborhoods.

• Seek out unique experiences that reflect the local culture, instead of just hitting the normal tourist sites and eating at McDonald's.

> When traveling abroad, be sure to avoid buying products made from endangered plants and animals. Also avoid genuine local artifacts, such as relics from archeological digs.

❏ Action: Limit your vacation trinkets

Many of us get overwhelmed on vacation and buy carloads of T-shirts, stuffed animals, mugs, and other assorted souvenirs (Brett has an ugly Seaworld drinking glass at home that is over ten years old and has never been used). The workers who produce our cheap vacation trinkets often work in poor conditions. Consider the usefulness of a souvenir before you buy it. Often pictures are the best souvenirs for capturing the essence of our travel experiences.

❏ Action: Support local economies

Tourism has given a significant boost to the economies of many struggling communities and developing nations. Even though tourism brings millions of dollars to impoverished countries, corporate hotels and resorts siphon off much of the wealth in such a way that the host community actually gains little wealth. To keep your tourism dollars in the hands of those who need them and to avoid feeding the corporate beast, buy from local merchants whenever you can. The principle of supporting local economies applies whether you are driving through Nebraska or canoeing in the Amazon.

> **Ross:** While traveling in the American Southwest, I wanted to purchase a small Navajo rug. I had the opportunity to buy one from many tourist shops that buy from local people, raise the prices, and sell the rugs for a profit. However, wanting to support the native people, I waited to buy a beautiful rug straight from a Navajo woman on the reservation. My money went directly to their economy (which needed it) rather than to the hands of a dealer. With this choice, I was able to make a small contribution to the Navajo traditional way, as well as bring home a cherished reminder of my journey.

When we're traveling, it's easy to stop for meals at fast food chains and to shop at large corporate retailers that exist in every town. They're familiar, convenient, and cheap. However, we can do more to support local economies by seeking out local diners and stores — the food and service are generally better, and we're helping Mom and Pop stay in business. For a real treat, find out which locally grown fruits and vegetables are in season and purchase them directly from the growers at roadside stands or farmers' markets.

PREVENT WESTERN 'PARADISE' FROM DESTROYING LOCAL CULTURE

You've probably noticed travel advertisements that show a beautiful couple frolicking on a white sand beach with their five star, state of the art resort behind them. The exotic images seem to suggest that although the resort is in a Third World country, guests will have all the comforts of home and more — a virtual paradise. Developing countries often cater to what they believe Western tourists want. Corporations from industrialized countries attempt to create a paradise for Westerners, often at the expense of local businesses, culture, and the environment. Before you schedule a cruise or take a pre-packaged resort vacation, consider the impact that our demands for paradise have on local workers, the environment, and indigenous culture.

If you need someone to show you around, particularly in a foreign country, find a local guide. You will not only be contributing to the economic well-being of the community, but you will have an opportunity to learn directly about the area and culture from a local.

❏ *Action: Use alternative transportation*

Get out of the car on your vacation! It is definitely worth your time to learn about the transit options in the areas where you are traveling. Many places in the U.S. and around the world have excellent rail, subway, and bus systems that may make the automobile obsolete. Walking around town is also a much better way to get to know the geography and the people firsthand while avoiding the traffic and parking hassles that come with the automobile. Above all, it is only courteous to reduce the amount of pollution you leave behind at the place that treated you to a wonderful vacation.

EXTRAORDINARY TRAVEL

Traveling can be so much more than getting away from it all. Imagine going on a spiritual retreat, backpacking through extraordinary wilderness areas, taking an educational trip to learn about social injustice, or volunteering in another country. If you want a traveling experience that will really expand your mind, you must begin to reshape your fundamental ideas about travel itself. We have detailed five amazing opportunities for the traveler who is ready for the experience of a lifetime: (1) study abroad (2) reality tours, (3) eco-journeys, (4) volunteer travel, and (5) personal growth vacations.

❏ *Action: Study abroad*

One of most exciting and least expensive ways to travel is to study abroad. Picture visiting Mexico City's greatest museums as part of your art class or curling up with a good book near an ancient Buddhist temple in Thailand. When you study abroad, it is a wonderful opportunity to learn about another part of the globe while earning course credit. Here are some of the leading programs:

Council on International Educational Exchange (CIEE)

Council *International Study Programs*
CIEE: Council on International Educational Exchange

CIEE is a non-profit group that provides college and high school level educational programs for both students and teachers. CIEE offers work exchange and voluntary service programs, as well as discount travel services for students, teachers, and young people. CIEE puts out a good magazine called *Student Travels,* available on most college campuses or directly from CIEE.
☎ (888) COUNCIL 💻 www.ciee.org

American Field Service (AFS)

AFS is a non-profit exchange organization that sends people to over 55 countries. It focuses more on high school students, teachers and administrators than do other international exchange programs, claiming to "help people develop the knowledge, skills, and understanding needed to create a more just and peaceful world." Its emphasis on diversity, tolerance, and global citizenship make it an excellent choice.

☎ (800) AFS-INFO 💻 www.afs.org

National Student Exchange (NSE)

NSE is a great program for college students who want to participate in an exchange but aren't interested in leaving the States. U.S. universities from all parts of the country participate in a national exchange, where students can attend another university for a semester or year while paying their home university's tuition. It's fun, relatively cheap, and you get to live in another part of the country.

☎ (800) 735-1989 💻 www.buffalostate.edu/~nse

❑ Action: Take a reality tour

A 'reality tour' is an opportunity to travel across the planet and learn first-hand about war, poverty, globalization, sustainable agriculture, and other forces that are shaping our future. Reality tours are a great way to move beyond the mainstream media's portrayal of global issues and experience them for yourself. Another advantage of reality tours is that you will be able to travel with others who are committed to social justice and environmental sustainability.

Global Exchange

Now you have an opportunity to visit and GLOBAL ⟨⟩ EXCHANGE learn about the another country's history and current situation from the people themselves. You may choose to meet with community leaders in Cuba, Haiti, South Africa, or Ireland and learn about military atrocities, sustainable farming, or exciting breakthroughs in the fair trade movement. Global Exchange's Reality Tours take groups abroad to visit people and places you would never encounter during your normal travels.

☎ (800) 497-1994 💻 www.globalexchange.org/tours

Witness For Peace

For almost 20 years, Witness for Peace has been **Witness for Peace** sending groups of average U.S. citizens to Mexico, Central America, and the Caribbean to see firsthand the impacts of uncontrolled globalization on Third World people. In addition, participants experience what it's like to work for justice abroad at the grassroots level. The trips typically last one to two weeks and are offered throughout the year.

☎ (202) 588-1471 💻 www.witnessforpeace.org

❑ *Action: Take an eco-journey*

Many of us like to spend our vacations exploring the wonders of our natural world: crystalline caves, old-growth forests, rugged badlands, or painted deserts — we love them all. Generally, tourism affects nature less than other types of development, such as logging, mining, or real estate; however, poorly managed tourism can result in long-term ecological damage.

Eco-journeys, also called eco-tourism, work on the assumption that traveling should contribute to the long-term preservation of entire ecosystems in the communities. Governments and business people are realizing that tourists love visiting wilderness areas, so by supporting eco-tourism, you are stating that wilderness areas here and around the world deserve protection and are valuable beyond their uses as raw materials. Your vacation may become an adventure that raises your awareness about our fragile environment.

By supporting environmentally responsible tourism, you are:

✓ **Encouraging** local landowners to develop tourist facilities with less environmental impact.

✓ **Promoting** environmental awareness, education, and the protection of natural resources.

✓ **Spending** money that supports local projects in agriculture, water supplies, tree farms, and others.

✓ **Providing** economic incentive to stop wildlife poaching and protect natural areas.

Sierra Club Outings

Sierra Club volunteers lead outings that contribute to the overall conservation and environmental goals of the club. Most of their trips are wilderness trips. They expect participants to help with chores and other necessary work. Sierra Club outings are also a great way to learn about eco-friendly travel and camping tips.

☎ (415) 977-5630   🖥 www.sierraclub.org/outings

World Wildlife Fund (WWF)

WWF's tours like to feature the wondrous wildlife that surrounds us all. Visits to WWF-funded conservation projects are also a part of many of their trips. On most trips, a WWF staff member accompanies you throughout, while local guides, guest speakers, and other experts complement the staff.

☎ (888) 993-8687   🖥 www.worldwildlife.org

> ### WARNING
>
> A word of caution: eco-tourism has become so popular that some places may falsely claim eco-friendly tourism. It's best to ask a lot of questions and try to check a company's references before signing on. Some important questions include:
>
> ✓ How long has the company been in business? Often businesses that have been around for a while have earned the necessary customer support by living up to their claims.
>
> ✓ Does the company offer locally owned businesses such as hotels, restaurants, and guided tours?
>
> ✓ How has the company affected the locals' lives?
>
> ✓ Does the company contribute directly to conservation efforts?

ECO-JOURNEYS RESOURCES

📖 *Eco-Traveler Magazine.* A good resource for adventure travelers with an environmental conscience. ☎ (800) 334-8152.

📖 Foehr, Stephen. *Eco-Journeys.* The Noble Press, 1993.
   Just a great all-around eco-travel resource, this book has descriptions of over 100 eco-friendly tours. ☎ (800) 486-7737

📖 Grotta, Daniel, and Sally Wiener Grotta. *The Green Travel Sourcebook.* John Wiley and Sons, 1992.
   Possibly the most comprehensive guide to the various kinds of responsible travel this book also provides information about 80 different green travel organizations.

The Eco-tourism Society
   This non-profit organization works to promote eco-tourism through education and networking. They publish fact sheets, books, and newsletters, educating the public about the benefits of eco-travel.
   ☎ 802-447-2121   🖥 www.ecotourism.org

❑ *Action: Combine service and travel*

Have you ever considered volunteering during your travels? What? Work while on vacation? Imagine the best vacation you've ever taken. It might have been relaxing, adventurous, or just new and exciting. Now imagine a time when you really helped someone out, someone you may not have even known, expecting nothing in return. Picture their appreciation and how you made a difference in their lives. You can create these feelings for yourself and others on a regular basis! Today, there are many opportunities for you to combine the fun of traveling with the powerful experience of satisfaction that you get from volunteering. Traveling is a privilege and a luxury for most in the world. By using your vacation time to volunteer you make incredible connections with people and help them out with your labor or expertise.

Volunteer experiences help build understanding, compassion, and hope — important keys to creating a more humane world. When you serve, in the U.S. or abroad, you expose yourself to other ways of life. Perhaps more importantly, you eventually come home and share your experiences with others. Volunteering can create tremendous changes within you; through your experiences, you can also create tremendous change in others.

Short-Term Volunteering

Many organizations lead volunteer travel excursions around the globe for periods of time as short as one week. These short-term volunteer trips can be a great way to travel abroad, get to know the locals, and make a difference in other people's lives.

> **Ross:** Working with children at an orphanage in the forests of Guatemala transformed my life. Experiencing first hand the problems of the Third World made me reflect on my life and my role in helping to make the world a better place.

Global Citizens Network (GCN)

Global Citizens Network offers a variety of service trips around the world, where volunteers immerse themselves in the daily life of the community. Trips last one, two, or three weeks, depending on the site, and a trained

Global Citizens Network

GCN team leader leads each team. The team works on projects initiated by people in the local community. Such projects could include setting up a library, teaching business skills, building a health clinic, or planting trees to reforest a village.

☎ (800) 644-9292
🖥 www.globalcitizens.org

Global Volunteers

Global Volunteers offers you the chance to help people out both inside and outside the U.S. Trips last anywhere from two to four

weeks. You volunteer and live in the local community, work during the weekday and have evenings and weekends open for adventures of your own making. Participants come from all kinds of backgrounds and ages. Besides the U.S., you can serve in countries such as Costa Rica, Ireland, and Vietnam. Depending on your interests and skills, you could be teaching English, repairing buildings, encouraging business development, or providing health care.

☎ (800) 487-1074
🖥 www.globalvolunteers.org

Habitat for Humanity International

Habitat is an ecumenical Christian organiza- **Habitat for Humanity®**
tion composed of volunteers that help families **International**
build affordable housing — don't worry, extensive construction skills are not
required. One- to three-week trips to U.S. or international destinations will
teach you about the local culture, poverty, and social empowerment in ways
that you will never forget.

☎ (912) 924-6935 💻 www.habitat.org

Long-Term Volunteering

If you are really looking for the best way to experience another culture, you
need to live with its people for an extended period of time. Ever since
President Kennedy helped initiate the Peace Corps, it and many other organizations have sent people around the world to help people in developing
countries. There are many opportunities for longer-term commitments
abroad and at home, so that you can find the group that best suits your needs
and interests. Many churches also provide the opportunity for long-term
global service.

> **Ellis:** In 1993 I joined the Peace Corps. I signed up right out of college,
> feeling as if I needed to get my hands dirty and make a difference in the
> world after reading so many books that just talked about it. They placed
> me in the Environmental Education Program in the southern region of
> Panama, despite my having no knowledge of Spanish. I ended up teach-
> ing, making movies, organizing environmental groups, putting on
> conferences, writing a book, editing a newsletter, speaking on national
> television (all in Spanish, mind you) — things I never dreamed I'd do.
> More importantly, though, the people there were so kind that I learned a
> real generosity of spirit. It seems that as much as I had to teach, the peo-
> ple always had twice as much to teach me.

The Peace Corps

Founded in 1961, the Peace Corps has sent
over 160,000 Americans to other countries to
fight "hunger, disease, illiteracy, poverty, and
lack of opportunity." Volunteers from agriculture, business, education, health, engineering,
urban planning, environmental education,

and other fields help Third World countries face the challenges of development. The Peace Corps offers 77 possible destinations, including countries in
Africa, Asia, the Pacific, Central and South America, the Caribbean, Central
and Eastern Europe and the former Soviet Union. Volunteers sign on for a

two-year stay, receive a monthly stipend to cover living expenses, and take up to two weeks vacation per year.

☎ (800) 424-8580 🖥 www.peacecorps.gov

Voluntary Service Overseas (VSO)

Sharing skills • Changing lives

VSO is Canada's version of the Peace Corps. They send volunteers for two-year stays in developing countries around the world. They need people from a variety of professions, including teachers, health workers, computer technicians, business people, natural resource development workers, and more. Volunteers work in a variety of programs, including health, poverty, and AIDS projects. VSO pays a small stipend for living expenses, travel expenses, health and medical coverage, and a 'resettling' grant when you return home.

☎ (888) 876-2911 🖥 www.vsocan.com/

Americorps

Each year, more than 40,000 members serve with Americorps programs in every state in the nation. You can tutor kids, build new homes, restore parks and coastlines, help communities hit by natural disasters, and take on many other challenges, either in your community or far away from home. For your service, you will garner valuable skills, a living allowance, an education award to help pay for college, and the satisfaction of having made a difference.

☎ (800) 942-2677 🖥 www.americorps.org

VOLUNTEER TRAVEL RESOURCES

📖 Giese, Filomena, and Marilyn Borchardt, eds. *Alternatives to the Peace Corps: A Directory of Third World and U.S. Volunteer Opportunities.* Food First Books, 1999.
A small book, offering information on voluntary service organizations, technical service programs, work brigades, study tours, and alternative travel in the Third World. It also includes a reference section, resources about jobs in development, and a brief critique of the Peace Corps.

📖 McMillon, Bill. *Volunteer Vacations: Short-term Adventures That Will Benefit You and Others.* Chicago Review Press, 1999.
A fantastic source for journeys in the U.S. and abroad. The book details many different adventures, indexing them by cost, length, location, season, and project type. It also lists many other resources including agencies, directories, and periodicals.

❑ *Action: Take a personal growth vacation*

Most vacations help us relax and get away from it all, but some end up being life-changing experiences. Have you ever taken a vacation or been on a retreat that left you feeling exhilarated, emotionally uplifted, or ready to take on the world? We all need time to recharge our batteries, particularly when we're committed to making the world a better place. If you want to supercharge your batteries, consider the following possibilities:

- Yoga Retreats
- Women's Groups
- Zen Meditation Weekends
- Outward Bound Programs
- Spiritual Workshops
- Catholic Monasteries

PERSONAL GROWTH VACATIONS RESOURCES

📖 Lederman, Ellen. *Vacations That Can Change Your Life: Adventures, Retreats and Workshops for the Mind, Body and Spirit.* Sourcebooks Trade, 1998.
Ellen Lederman details several types of vacations, including holistic, spiritual, healing and health, self-improvement, and learning vacations. She includes cost ranges and contact information for each program.

TRAVEL RESOURCES

📖 Lonely Planet Guidebooks. Lonely Planet guidebooks have been a great resource for travelers for over 20 years. They have a book for almost any destination you can imagine, in the U.S. or abroad. Each tells you everything you need to know, including background information, transportation options, medical concerns, lodging possibilities, maps, common phrases, and the best sites. They also publish walking guides and phrasebooks. Their authors are generally sensitive to the concerns of travelers who are socially and environmentally responsible. Look for these guides at your local library or bookstore.
☎ (800) 275-8555   🖥 www.lonelyplanet.com

📖 *Transitions Abroad* Magazine. *Transitions Abroad* is full of practical information on affordable alternatives to mass tourism: living, working, studying, or vacationing alongside the people of the host country.
☎ (800) 293-0373   🖥 www.TransitionsAbroad.com

ORGANIZATIONS

Getting Involved

Giving

Finding Organizations

Amazing Organizations

The Best of the Rest

H<small>AVE YOU EVER FELT ALONE</small> in your desire to make the world a better place? Ever wonder if what you do really makes a difference? Have no fear. You don't have to do it all by yourself. There are literally millions of people working all over the globe to bring peace and justice to this world. Groups of organized, forward-looking people with a deep-seated desire for justice and equality have always been the most important catalysts for bringing about a better world.

✓ The labor movement fought for and won the eight-hour workday, safer working conditions, and paid vacations.

✓ The populist movement demanded and won the right to public education and instituted the progressive income tax to fight historic levels of economic inequality.

✓ The suffrage movement helped gain the right to vote for women.

✓ The civil rights movement helped dismantle the legalized segregation of blacks on buses, at lunch counters, and in schools.

✓ Lesbian and gay activists have fought for cultural acceptance and legal equality and have transformed Americans' views on sexual orientation.

✓ Community activists in Convent, Louisiana successfully fought to keep a highly toxic industrial facility out of their already heavily polluted community.

By joining together with our neighbors and other like-minded citizens, we create the potential for significant positive social change in our communities and around the world. Successful acts of cooperation and solidarity create momentum that empowers our communities and propels our vision of justice into the future.

It's inspiring to see the number of organizations that work for a better world on a daily basis. Some are even creating a truly global vision of social justice and are building solidarity between all people. In November 1999, more than 50,000 people from around the globe joined together in Seattle, Washington to protest the meeting of the World Trade Organization (WTO). The protests educated millions of people about the economic and environmental injustices of the global economy and the non-democratic nature of the WTO. The protesters shut down the meetings and kick-started the fair trade and global justice movements.

As one woman said of her experiences in Seattle, "I came unprepared for the beautiful and unconditional solidarity between people. As I experienced the outpouring of love, concern, food, and support from thousands of strangers, I felt as if I was experiencing true community for the first time....We are powerful people and we have the ability to take the beautiful solidarity we created in the streets of Seattle and bring it into our daily lives."[1]

> There's no greater antidote to powerlessness than joining with others in common cause.
> — Paul Loeb, (Soul of a Citizen)

Every day, people like you confront injustice, sometimes very publicly and other times very much behind the scenes. While working in concert with others, the individual and the group can nurture and inspire each other. With this synergy, we increase the possibility for more profound and long lasting social change. Your single voice becomes a deafening roar, and your single action becomes part of a social movement when you join with others to build a better world.

This chapter will help you to support and get involved with causes you believe in and to identify specific local, national, and international organizations that are working to transform your ideals into reality. Now is our time to stand up and make a difference.

GETTING INVOLVED

There are many ways to get involved with organizations that you care about. Each level of involvement is crucial to a group's success. Consider, for a moment, how creating an effective social justice organization requires many of the same elements that go into a good theatrical play. A collaboration of everyone from the set designers to the lighting crew and actors makes a fantastic play. Likewise, everyone from the people who send in a check to those who carry picket signs to folks who talk with government officials make a social change organization run.

Many of us participate by becoming a donating member of an organization. If you want to give more, consider any special talents, skills, or interests that you have and figure out how you could be useful to an organization you care about. Are you good at promotions? Are you media savvy? Have you done research on a specific issue? Do you perform music? Do you know how to raise money? Can you design eye-catching posters? Do you like speaking in public? Perhaps you are simply very passionate about your cause. There is always a place for you — regardless of the amount of time or money you have!

❏ Action: Join an organization you care about

When you join an organization, you become the committed audience for the social change 'actors.' Without the audience to purchase tickets and appreciate what's being created, the play would not survive. The audience not only helps financially support the production of the play but it generates word of mouth interest for other prospective audience members and helps to inspire the actors in their work.

The easiest way to support an organization is to become a member. This usually involves sending a small donation and keeping informed of the group's work. Members often wait in the wings to become involved when the organization most needs their efforts.

❏ Action: Participate in an organization you care about

Consider getting out and showing your support for the organizations you care about. Just by attending a lecture, meeting, or fundraiser or by participating in a demonstration, you can really lift the spirits of the more involved members of that organization. Your participation is a quick, easy, and fulfilling way to show your appreciation for what the group does. And it helps educate your community about issues you care about. Ask the organization to keep you informed of any events in your area. And if it's a demonstration, don't forget your picket sign.

PROTEST NET (znet.protest.net) is the Web's most comprehensive listing of protests (and other activist events) around the world. You can search by region, date, and topic or just about anything else. Essential for making your presence known.

❏ Action: Volunteer for an organization you care about

Many of us would like to support the great work of organizations that reflect our values — if we just had enough time. Getting involved in an organization may seem like an overwhelming commitment, but remember that involvement is not an all or nothing endeavor. Figure out how much commitment is sustainable for you and then just go get involved — even if it's only a few hours a month! You may think that the last thing you need is another commitment — that if you just had more free time and fewer obligations you would be happier. Ironically, we're often happiest and most fulfilled when we're helping someone else out. Becoming involved can enrich your life as you get to know other like-minded people and spend your time contributing to a better world.

A play is not possible without the efforts of the people behind the scenes. Time spent preparing the set, costumes, and programs is necessary for a successful performance. The supporting cast of an organization attends events and meetings and puts in the sustained effort that keeps a group going by answering the phones, passing out literature, and fundraising. The work of the supporting cast and stage crew set up the groundwork for the organization to be successful on a daily basis. Don't worry, you don't have to spend 20 hours a week volunteering. Donate whatever amount of time works for you.

ORGANIZING RESOURCES

📖 Bobo, Kim, Jackie Kendall, and Steve Max. *Organizing for Social Change: A Manual for Activists in the 1990s.* Seven Locks Press, 1996.
A great sourcebook for the fundamentals of social change: planning and facilitating meetings, recruiting, fundraising, using the media, public speaking, and networking with unions and religious organizations.

📖 The War Resisters League. *Handbook for Non-violent Action.* War Resisters League, 339 Lafayette Street, New York, NY 10012, U.S.A.
Available for $3. This classic guide offers simple, straightforward guidelines for organizing a campaign. It discusses the philosophy of non-violence and suggests further resources.

📖 Kaner, Sam. *Facilitator's Guide to Participatory Decision-Making.* New Society Publishers, 1996.
This book explains how to create a group where everyone feels involved and committed by encouraging full participation, promoting full understanding, and building inclusive, sustainable agreements within your group.

🖥 Ruckus Society Manuals [online]. For online media, action planning, and other manuals, check out the Ruckus website. Their brief manuals give practical organizing tips, and you can download them for free.
🖥 www.ruckus.org/man

📖 *The Activist Cookbook: Creative Actions for a Fair Economy* by United for a Fair Economy. United for a Fair Economy, 1997.

A hands-on manual for activists and artists who want to find new ways to spice up their messages. Full of inspiring examples and creative action ideas to liven up any event. Available for $15 from UFE.

☎ (616) 423-2148   💻 www.ufenet.org

TIPS FOR MAKING AN ORGANIZATION MORE EFFECTIVE

• **Make new people feel welcome.** Make sure you introduce a new person to everyone in your group. Nametags are a great way to help new folks fit in. Asking everyone "What compels you to be here?" is often a great way for members to share their passions.

• **Have fun and build community.** One of the biggest myths about social change is that it's all work and no play. Be sure to take time to build strong relationships by having fun and even scheduling recreational time outside of your organizational work.

• **Make everyone feel involved and important.** One of the best ways to keep members involved is to make sure that they feel they're making a contribution to the group. Rotate meeting facilitators, share responsibilities, and make sure everyone has concrete tasks.

• **Start and end gatherings in an inspiring way.** Too many long meetings end with members feeling drained and overwhelmed. Use your creativity to send people off inspired to fulfill their commitments to your organization. Start gatherings with a ritual, end meetings with a cheer, and tie social change to personal growth.

• **Set concrete, attainable goals.** When you begin recognizing and challenging injustice it's easy to want to take on the whole world at once. Trying to change everything overnight only produces frustration. Set short-term, attainable goals in addition to your long-term vision.

• **Be open to setbacks; learn from mistakes.** No one ever said social change was easy. If you commit to living out your passions, you're bound to make mistakes and encounter setbacks. Make time periodically to review your accomplishments and discuss setbacks. Build reflection time into your organization and create concrete ways to improve.

• **Celebrate your successes.** After your organization makes progress, it's easy to just jump right into pursuing your next goal. If you take time to acknowledge your hard work and celebrate your successes, then you will ensure that members stick around for the next campaign.

• **Form coalitions with like-minded groups.** Don't be afraid to call upon potential allies when your group needs help. Often different organizations' goals overlap enough that pooling resources and supporting one another makes complete sense.

• **Be creative.** Creativity is the soul of social change. For any issue that comes up, you can ask your group How can we be creative about this? Fundraising, recruiting, demonstrations, and community education all require creativity. If you have the intention to be creative, your group will be dynamic and effective.

GIVING

A contribution to social change organizations is a great way for you to create positive change with your money. In our society we tend to think negatively of money's power — an 'Everyone has their price' way of thinking. Donating some of your money to amazing organizations is one way you can control the power of money.

❑ **Action: Donate money based on your values**

Take one, two, five, or ten percent of all the money you make and give it away. When you donate money to something that you believe in, you are helping to make your values real in the world. Your donation becomes an investment in positive social change. For example, if you give some of your earnings to Amnesty International, the time you spend at work suddenly becomes time working for human rights, regardless of your job. Don't worry if you don't have much money — every dollar counts. You can even automatically deposit a certain percentage of your income into a separate 'giving account' if that will inspire you to reach your giving goals.

❑ **Action: Set up a giving budget**

2001 GIVING BUDGET			
VALUES/GROUPS	**$$$ BUDGETED**	**DATE TO GIVE**	**ACTUAL**
Environment			
Sierra Club	$25	April	
Local enviro group	$30	Feb	Feb 3rd $30
Assisting the Poor			
Habitat for Humanity	$50	Jan	Jan 25th $60
Local Homeless Shelter	$25	Mar	
Social Justice			
National Gay and Lesbian Task Force	$45	Sept	
NAACP	$35	Jun	
Faith/Religious Group			
Church, Mosque, Temple, etc.	$40	monthly	
Sustainable Culture			
Center for a New American Dream	$50	Dec	
Public Media			
PBS Ch.12	$20	Oct	

Many people consider creating a monthly spending budget, but very few consider that their charitable contributions are worth budgeting. On January 1st every year, make up a list of your values. Then find organizations that are working to make those values real in the world. Don't let your giving be dictated by who sends you a request in the mail, either. Do some research to find the best organizations and the ones that best represent your ideals. The last step is to set up dates and the dollar amounts that you plan to send to those organizations. A giving budget keeps your charitable giving at the forefront of your mind throughout the year so that it doesn't take a back seat to all of the other ways you want to spend your money.

❑ *Action: Put an organization in your will*

A gift that you make to an organization through your will is a great way to keep supporting great causes into the future. Your vision for a better world can live on even after you have passed. Just contact an organization that you care about and ask them for more information.

GIVING RESOURCES

Give for Change boasts the BEST list of the top organizations that are working for a better **giveforchange.com** world. You can learn about organizations under topic categories or search for your favorite. You register with the site for free, and then whenever you feel like giving to a particular organization, just specify the amount and your credit card is instantly billed. It's one of the easiest way to give. As an added bonus for people who want to give to organizations but do not want to receive mail from them or other organizations, it is also possible to donate anonymously to the organization(s) of your choice.
🖥 www.giveforchange.com

Guide Star

Guide Star is an online searchable database of non-profits that allows you to find and compare organizations to which you are considering donating time or money. It provides a wealth of information on just about every non-profit you can think of, including mission statements, programs, financial reports, goals and accomplishments, areas served, and contact information.
☎ (757) 229-4631   🖥 www.guidestar.org

The Funding Exchange

The Funding Exchange is a network of 15 progressive community foundations that fund local environmental justice, gay rights, economic justice, and many other exceptional groups. They currently distribute about $12 million in grants for social and economic justice. This is a great opportunity for someone who wants to help support progressive social change but doesn't have the time to research which projects are the best. Local community activists are involved at all levels of the granting process.

☎ (212) 529-5300   ☐ www.fex.org

☐ Collins, Chuck and Pam Rogers, with Joan P. Gardner. *Robin Hood Was Right: A Guide to Giving Your Money for Social Change.* W.W. Norton, 2001. This book argues that traditional charity often reinforces the dynamics of dependency and control. The book focuses on the ethic of giving to address the root causes of social problems instead of just the symptoms. With numerous detailed listings and hundreds of helpful suggestions, *Robin Hood Was Right* is a great guide for the socially conscious giver, whether you have $50 or $5 million.

FINDING ORGANIZATIONS

There is at least one organization committed to fighting for almost any issue that you can imagine (and it may even be right in your own community). With just a little research, you will find the organizations that best fit your values and desire for involvement.

Are you interested in an organization that:

✓ has a local, state, national, or global focus?
✓ has a lot of opportunities for direct involvement from members?
✓ is focused on legal, political, or social issues?
✓ works with children, adults, or the elderly?

Be sure to seek out organizations that address the root causes of social and environmental problems, as well as your community's immediate needs. For example, although giving money to your local homeless shelter has an immediate impact on people's lives, giving to the National Low Income Housing Coalition will help eliminate the need for homeless shelters. Other groups creating long-lasting social change focus on sustainable economic growth, nonviolent conflict resolution, community development and empowerment, local businesses, and getting money out of politics.

HOW TO FIND AN ORGANIZATION FOR YOU

- Rotate subscriptions to organizational newsletters.
- Visit organizational websites or request information by phone.
- Attend an organizational meeting or event.
- Talk with members.

☐ *Action: Support local organizations*

Although supporting national and global social justice organizations is important, there is simply no substitute for helping out groups in your own community. When you support local organizations, you have the opportunity to more tangibly experience the positive results of the money you donate and the time you volunteer. Also when you get involved locally, you become part of a tight community of people who share your values and commitment, which can make your experience even more fulfilling.

RESOURCES

The Nonviolence Web is a great resource for issues and organizations built around non-violence, direct action, and peace. Members include many of the religiously based peace groups that established the peace movement.
🖥 www.nonviolence.org

IGC is the largest community of progressive activist organizations on the Internet. IGC's four subgroups (PeaceNet, EcoNet, WomensNet, and Anti-RacismNet) provide everything from job listings and headline news to events calendars and extensive listings of social change organizations.
🖥 www.igc.org

AMAZING ORGANIZATIONS

We've compiled a short list and briefly described some of the most powerful social change organizations in the world. We have selected organizations that are both accessible to a wide number of people and doing good work in a number of very important areas. You can find a more comprehensive list, 'The Best of the Rest,' directly after.

Animal Rights

Humane Society of the United States (HSUS)
2100 L Street, NW,
Washington, DC 20037, U.S.A.
☎ (202) 452-1100 🖥 www.hsus.org

THE HUMANE SOCIETY OF THE UNITED STATES

Working primarily through legislation and education, HSUS is a massive animal protection organization with a variety of programs. Pet overpopulation, animal sheltering, circus cruelty, dissection, fur, animal research, factory farming, and wildlife are just some of their concerns. HSUS continually monitors legislation at the state and federal levels, including the Endangered Species Act. They also work closely with animal shelters to provide healthy environments for animals.

People for the Ethical Treatment of Animals (PETA)
501 Front Street, Norfolk, VA 23510, U.S.A.
☎ (757) 622-PETA 🖥 www.peta.org

PeTA

With over 700,000 members, PETA is the world's largest animal rights group. Founded in 1980, PETA is dedicated to establishing and protecting the rights of all animals. PETA operates under the simple philosophy that animals are not ours to eat, wear, experiment on, or use for entertainment. Using non-violent direct action, research, education, legislation, investigation, animal rescue, and celebrity supporters, PETA focuses its efforts on factory farms, the fur trade, laboratories, and the entertainment industry. Members receive an informative newsletter, *Animal Times*, which includes actions and campaign updates.

Community

Association of Community Organizations for Reform Now (ACORN)

88 Third Avenue,
Brooklyn, NY 11217, U.S.A.
☎ (718) 246-7900   🖳 www.acorn.org

Formed by a group of welfare mothers, ACORN is a coalition of community groups dedicated to standing up for the poor and powerless. Living wages, jobs, affordable housing, better schools, and environmental justice are among ACORN's many struggles. Community members lead this grassroots group in filing lawsuits, lobbying, organizing petitions and nonviolent direct actions such as sit-ins and marches.

Big Brothers Big Sisters of America (BBBSA)

230 North 13th Street,
Philadelphia, PA 19107, U.S.A.
☎ (215) 567-7000   🖳 www.bbbsa.org

Since 1904, BBBSA has created powerful relationships between millions of kids and positive adults. This unique mentoring program links 'Littles' one on one with 'Bigs.' Bigs and Littles usually get together several times each month for sporting events, a trip to the park, visiting a museum, or just to hang out and talk. Research shows that BBBSA's programs are one of the most effective at reducing delinquency, drug use, school absence, and violence. Indeed, there is perhaps no better way to positively affect a child's life than through individual mentorship.

Boys & Girls Clubs of America

1230 W. Peachtree Street, NW,
Atlanta, GA 30309, U.S.A.
☎ (404) 815-5700   🖳 www.bgca.org

Boys & Girls Clubs have provided a safe, empowering place for more than three million kids to spend their free time. Clubs encourage kids to develop their athletic, artistic, and scholastic abilities to their full potential. Gang prevention, alcohol/drug prevention, health education, and leadership development are just a few of the amazing programs clubs offer. *The Chronicle of Philanthropy* ranked B&GCA the number one youth organization five years in a row. The clubs serve many inner city youth from low income and single parent households, making them an excellent investment in these kids' futures.

Habitat for Humanity International
121 Habitat Street,
Americus, GA 31709, U.S.A.

☎ (912) 924-6935   💻 www.habitat.org

Habitat for Humanity® International

Since 1976, Habitat volunteers have built more than 100,000 houses for families around the world. Habitat is a non-profit ecumenical Christian organization that brings together families in need, volunteer labor, and donated materials to eliminate homelessness and poverty housing. The receiving families help build their homes and then buy them with no-interest, affordable financing. To find your local affiliate, check their website or give them a call.

Economic Justice

Co-op America
1612 K Street NW, Suite 600,
Washington, DC 20006, U.S.A.
☎ (800) 58-GREEN
💻 www.coopamerica.org

Co-op America
COOP AMERICA QUARTERLY

Co-op America offers a wide range of phenomenal services and information for businesses and individuals who want their money to make the world a better place. Co-op America helps you support local environmentally friendly businesses, invest in socially responsible companies, and make informed decisions on how you save and spend your money. Membership includes the *Co-op America Quarterly* magazine, *National Green Pages,* and a financial planning handbook. Learn how to live sustainably!

United for a Fair Economy (UFE)
37 Temple Place, 2nd Floor,
Boston, MA 02111, U.S.A.
☎ (617) 423-2148   💻 www.ufenet.org

United for a Fair Economy works to narrow the growing gap between the rich and the rest of us. They report that the wealthiest 1% of the population controls more wealth than the bottom 95%. Through education and policy campaigns, UFE hopes to create a fairer economy where families need not struggle just to get by. UFE can teach you how to educate and organize your community about both local and global economic disparity. Their publications and workshops will rock your world.

Environment

Greenpeace
702 H Street NW,
Washington, DC 20001, U.S.A.

☎ (800) 326-0959

💻 www.greenpeaceusa.org

Greenpeace uses a variety of nonviolent direct action tactics to raise awareness and protect the environment, including blocking ships filled with genetically engineered corn, observing whaling vessels, and hanging protest banners on toxic refineries. Greenpeace is an independent organization that refuses donations from governments, companies, and political parties. Instead it relies completely on donations from its 2.5 million supporters. Toxic waste, genetic engineering, climate issues, and forests are among the many issues Greenpeace takes on.

Rainforest Action Network(RAN)
221 Pine Street,
San Francisco, CA 94104, U.S.A.

☎ (415) 398-4404 💻 www.ran.org

Rainforest Action Network "works to protect the Earth's rainforests and support the rights of their inhabitants through education, grassroots organizing, and nonviolent direct action." Since their founding in 1985, RAN has helped indigenous groups secure protection of their native rainforest lands, convinced a large segment of the retail lumber industry to stop purchasing wood taken from old-growth forests, and built a national network of college student groups that are committed to taking action to preserve forests and the people who inhabit them worldwide.

Sierra Club
85 Second Street, Second Floor,
San Francisco CA, 94105-3441, U.S.A.

☎ (415) 977-5500

💻 www.sierraclub.org

For over 100 years, Sierra Club has lobbied at the local, state, and national levels for environmental reform and wilderness protection. In 2000, Sierra Club challenged factory farm pollution, urban sprawl, logging in national forests, and wildland destruction. Chapters in every state promote local issues and involvement; members can even attend locally sponsored Sierra Club

Outings, retreats, hikes, and other events. Members also receive the superb *Sierra* magazine.

World Wildlife Fund (WWF)
1250 Twenty-fourth Street, NW,
Washington, DC 20090-7180, U.S.A.
☎ (800) CALL-WWF
🖥 www.worldwildlife.org

World Wildlife Fund is the largest independent conservation organization in the world with almost five million members in 100 countries. WWF works with governments, corporations, landowners, and local citizens to preserve wildlife habitat and endangered species; and to address global threats such as climate change, forest destruction, and ocean degradation.

Gay and Lesbian

Human Rights Campaign (HRC)
919 18th Street, NW,
Washington, DC 20006, U.S.A.
☎ (202) 628-4160
🖥 www.hrc.org

Human Rights Campaign's fundamental mission is equal rights and safety for gays and lesbians. Their full-time lobbying team is the largest working for gay and lesbian issues, such as eliminating workplace discrimination, demanding protection under federal hate crime laws, fighting for AIDS-related and other health issues, blocking anti-gay legislation, and electing open-minded politicians. HRC lobbies, educates the public, recruits and organizes volunteers, takes part in elections, and conducts training and out-reach at the local level.

National Gay and Lesbian Task Force (NGLTF)
1700 Kalorama Road NW,
Washington, DC 20009-2624, U.S.A.
☎ (202) 332-6483
🖥 www.ngltf.org

Since 1973, NGLTF has struggled for lesbian, bisexual, transgender, and gay rights at the local state, and national levels. It provides vital information, funding, and resources for grassroots organizations. Key NGLTF issues include fighting Radical Right anti-gay legislation, ending job discrimination, and demanding improved government action on the AIDS crisis. They also create publications and organizing materials.

Human Rights

Amnesty International (AI)
304 Pennsylvania Avenue SE,
Washington DC 20003, U.S.A.
☎ (202) 544 0200 ▦ www.amnesty.org

The world's largest human rights organization, Amnesty International puts pressure on countries to abide by the Universal Declaration of Human Rights. AI works to free prisoners of conscience; ensure fair and prompt trials for political prisoners; abolish the death penalty, torture, and other degrading treatment; and end 'disappearances' and extrajudicial executions. They use a variety of tactics, including 'Urgent Actions,' or letter campaigns on behalf of political prisoners; lobbying, investigating and exposing human rights violations; and promoting youth activism.

Human Rights Watch
350 Fifth Avenue, 34th Floor
New York, NY 10118-3299, U.S.A.
☎ (212) 290-4700 ▦ www.hrw.org

Human Rights Watch exposes government abuses and human rights violators in the international community. Using the influence of the U.S. government, World Bank, United Nations, Tokyo, and the European Union, HRW pressures countries to abide by international human rights law. They interview victims and witnesses directly and meet with a variety of government, church, labor, and local human rights leaders. By publishing reports and holding perpetrators accountable, HRW creates a more humane world.

International

Global Exchange (GX)
2017 Mission Street #303,
San Francisco, California 94110, U.S.A.
☎ (415) 255-7296
▦ www.globalexchange.org

Global Exchange is "a non-profit research, education, and action center dedicated to promoting people-to-people ties around the world." They educate Americans to injustices, urging governments to support humane, fair, and sustainable development; and promote Reality Tours, a program that takes people to struggling countries. GX craft stores and online shopping are part of a growing international fair trade movement, offering goods created under fair labor standards. Their books, videos, and speakers educate grassroots organizations about political and economic rights.

Oxfam

26 West Street,
Boston MA 02111 1206, U.S.A.
☎ (617) 482-1211
💻 www.oxfamamerica.org

Oxfam builds partnerships with poor communities around the world, helping them become self-sufficient for the long term. Oxfam works to alleviate the root causes of poverty and hunger, end social injustice, and improve health programs. They also support community activism, encourage governments to adopt long-term development plans, and promote education around social justice issues. Their 11 branches worldwide have earned enormous respect for helping local grassroots groups help their people rather than dictating programs.

United Nations Children Fund (UNICEF)

3 United Nations Plaza,
New York, NY 10017, U.S.A.
☎ (212) 326-7000   💻 www.unicef.org

UNICEF struggles for the protection of children's rights and basic needs and tries to expand kids' opportunities to reach their full potential. As the only UN organization exclusively focused on children, it helps fund health care, education, safe water, and sanitary sewage conditions through programs in 161 countries. UNICEF advocates raising the minimum military age, eliminating child sex trafficking, and increasing child immunization.

Peace

Peace Action

1819 H Street, NW, #420,
Washington, DC 20006, U.S.A.
☎ (202) 862-9740   💻 www.peace-action.org

Formerly SANE/FREEZE, Peace Action is the nation's largest grassroots peace and justice organization, with a membership of 55,000, 27 state affiliates, and over 100 local chapters. Through national and grassroots citizens' action they promote global nuclear disarmament, significant military budget reductions, and the ending of the international arms trade. Peace Action also produces voter guides to educate the public on candidates' voting history and current stands on peace and human rights. They also promote campus organizing through the Student Peace Action Network.

War Resisters League (WRL)

339 Lafayette Street,
New York, NY 10012, U.S.A.
☎ (212) 228-0450   💻 www.warresisters.org

Beginning in 1923, members of the War Resistors League have insisted that war is a crime against all humanity, and thus a top priority for making the world better. WRL uses education, lobbying, nonviolent direct action, and demonstrations to "work for peace within a framework of social justice." They support war tax resistance, publish *Nonviolent Activist* magazine, and use their Youthpeace program to create a culture of peace by resisting war toys and military recruiting.

Witness for Peace (WFP)
1229 15th Street, NW,
Washington, DC 20005, U.S.A.
☎ (202) 588-1471 🖳 www.witnessforpeace.org

Witness For Peace is a politically independent, grassroots organization that raises awareness about injustice in the Americas through letter writing campaigns, publications, non-violent direct actions, and speaking tours. WFP has sent over 7,000 U.S. citizens to Central and South America, Cuba, Mexico, and Haiti. The delegations' goals include education, exposure to alternative economies and cultures, and creating momentum for advocacy campaigns at home. Their current 'Stop the War Against the Poor' campaign challenges U.S.-sponsored terrorism and economic exploitation in the Americas and the Caribbean.

Women's International League for
Peace and Freedom (WILPF)
1213 Race Street,
Philadelphia, PA 19107, U.S.A.
☎ (215) 563-7110 🖳 www.wilpf.org

Women's International League for Peace and Freedom's broad agenda includes world disarmament, women's rights, racial and economic justice, and challenging corporate power. They advocate lesbian and gay rights, freeing political prisoners, and shifting defense spending to social campaigns. Through demonstrations, education, lobbying, writing resolutions, organizing, and media, WILPF peacefully promotes its agenda at the local, national, and international levels. Groups in 44 countries share resources and information, making this a powerful feminist organization.

Political Action

20/20 Vision
1828 Jefferson Place, NW,
Washington, DC 20036, U.S.A.
☎ (800) 669-1782 🖳 www.2020vision.org

20/20 Vision's mission is to make grassroots political action easy for busy people who care about peace and environmental issues. Members receive information each month on how they can make the most difference in 20 minutes. 20/20 provides up-to-date research and timely action notices for contacting your legislators. They campaign on issues of air and water pollution, military waste, campaign finance reform, and arms control. 20/20 offers you a unique way to stay informed and politically active from month to month. Voice your opinion!

Public Interest

Public Citizen
1600 20th Street NW,
Washington, DC 20009, U.S.A.
☎ (202) 588-1000   💻 www.citizen.org

Public Citizen is the ultimate Washington watchdog, working on consumers' behalf. Since Ralph Nader founded the organization in 1971, they have fought for safer drugs and medical products, fair trade, a cleaner environment, and a more democratic government. The Congress Watch branch lobbies and monitors lawmakers to protect public safety and end corporate welfare. The Global Trade Watch branch works for government and corporate accountability. PC helps you protect your own rights as a citizen.

Public Interest Research Groups (PIRG)
[your state] PIRG, c/o state PIRGs
29 Temple Place,
Boston, MA 02111-1350, U.S.A.
☎ Varies by state   💻 www.pirg.org

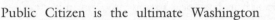

The State PIRGs

State PIRGs work in 26 states to protect their citizens' interests. They fight for greater democracy, the environment, and consumer safety. The PIRG website offers a Congressional scorecard system, where you can evaluate your lawmakers' voting records on public interest issues. They also have action alerts explaining simple actions you can take to make a difference. Visit their website to learn how your safety, rights, and your own backyard are threatened in your own state. Then take action!

Race and Ethnicity

National Association for the Advancement of Colored People (NAACP)
4805 Mt. Hope Drive,
Baltimore, MD 21215, U.S.A.
☎ (410) 602-6969   💻 www.naacp.org

The NAACP's main goal is "to ensure the political, educational, social, and economic equality of minority group citizens of the United States." Over 2,200 branches of the NAACP press for change, using non-violent strategies including petitions, court struggles, voter organizing, demonstrations, and press releases. As the largest U.S. civil rights organization, the NAACP uses its resources to create stay-in-school programs, economic development, and health care outreach.

National Council on La Raza (NCLR)
1111 19th, NW Suite 1000,
Washington, DC 20036, U.S.A.
🖥 www.nclr.org

National Council on La Raza seeks to eliminate poverty and discrimination and provide opportunities to Hispanic Americans. Their research and advocacy branch provides Hispanics a powerful voice in national policy decisions. Their community support branch assists local groups in economic development, local governance, and resource management. Health care, immigration, housing, education, and welfare are just a few of NCLR's many issues. Their blend of national policy goals and local development is especially crucial as the number of Hispanic working poor grows.

Native American Rights Fund (NARF)
1506 Broadway,
Boulder, CO 80302, U.S.A.
☎ (303) 447-8760 🖥 www.narf.org

Native American Rights Fund provides "legal representation and technical assistance to Indian tribes, organizations, and individuals nationwide." Their goals include protecting human rights, tribal resources, and tribal existence. By educating Native Americans and the public about Indian rights, NARF seeks to hold the government accountable for its actions. NARF monitors court cases, legislative action, and activist campaigns, sending updates to concerned individuals and issuing press releases to inform the public.

Religious

American Friends Service Committee
1501 Cherry Street,
Philadelphia, PA 19102, U.S.A.
☎ (215) 241-7000 🖥 www.afsc.org

American Friends Service Committee is a Quaker organization working for social and economic justice around the world. Members belong to a variety of faiths, but all believe in the fundamental worth of every human being. Through relief work, funding, education, and lobbying, AFSC pushes to create a new culture based on peace and justice rather than war and exploitation. They are involved in almost any progressive cause you can name. AFSC has a vibrant youth program that brings young people of different nationalities together for service work.

Christian Peacemaker Teams (CPT)
P.O. Box 6508,
Chicago, IL 60680, U.S.A.
☎ (312) 455-1199
🖳 www.prairienet.org/cpt

Faith compels members of Christian Peacemakers Teams to put their bodies on the line for peace and justice and to mobilize their communities when they return home. CPT is a faith-based group supported by the Mennonite Churches, Church of the Brethren, and Friends United Meeting. Local groups send trained delegates to be a peaceful presence in hot spots such as Gaza, Haiti, Hebron, Bosnia, and Chechnya. CPT accepts invitations from non-violent grassroots organizations for longer stays as well, providing delegates committed to a three-year service term to emergency situations such as the Israel/Palestine conflict.

The Fellowship of Reconciliation (FOR)
P.O. Box 271,
Nyack, NY 10960, U.S.A.
☎ (914) 358-4601   🖳 www.forusa.org

The Fellowship of Reconciliation is the largest and oldest interfaith organization dedicated to peace and justice. FOR not only pushes for an end to war, it seeks to create a just and loving world. Members appreciate all forms of diversity and use nonviolent means to challenge racism, sexism, homophobia, and religious persecution. Programs include demilitarization, peacemaker training, education, the lifting of sanctions on Iraq, monitoring human rights abuses in Latin America, and much more. FOR tactics include nonviolent demonstrations and direct actions, sending delegations to distress areas, and pressuring political leaders.

Simplicity

Center for a New American Dream (CNAD)
6930 Carroll Ave., Suite 900,
Takoma Park, MD 20912, U.S.A.
☎ (877) 683-7326   🖳 www.newdream.org

The motto "More fun, less stuff" reflects CNAD's dedication to "reduce and shift consumption to enhance quality of life and protect the environment." Debt, bankruptcy, overworking, neglected relationships, and environmental degradation are all consequences of our insatiable desire to buy more and more stuff. CNAD's educational campaigns, such as 'Kids and Commercialism' and 'Simplify the Holidays,' have reached millions of people overwhelmed by materialism. Their newsletter *Enough!* provides you with amazing information about what you can do to create a culture of simplicity.

Violence

**The Brady Campaign to Prevent
Gun Violence (TBC)**
1225 Eye Street NW, Suite 1100,
Washington, DC 20005, U.S.A.
☎ (202) 898-0792   🖳 www.handguncontrol.org

Brady Campaign

To Prevent Gun Violence

The Brady Campaign pushes for more sensible gun laws at every level of government. Thanks to their hard work, legislators have passed an assault weapon ban, child access prevention laws, and waiting periods and background checks on handgun purchases. TBC also monitors enforcement of current laws and resists making concealed weapon permits easier to obtain. The Center to Prevent Handgun Violence is the educational and research branch of TBC, where a variety of professional researchers work against the spread of gun violence in the U.S.

Women's Rights

National Abortion and Reproductive Rights Action League (NARAL)
1156 15th Street, NW Suite 700,
Washington, DC 20005, U.S.A.
☎ (202) 973-3000   🖳 www.naral.org

NARAL's mission is "Securing and Protecting Safe, Legal Abortion and Making Abortion Less Necessary — Not More Difficult or Dangerous." Although the majority of Americans are pro-choice, a very vocal minority continues the fight to eliminate a woman's right to choose. Through public education, lobbying, public policy research, and grassroots organizing, NARAL resists anti-choice violence and campaigns designed to restrict abortion rights. It promotes pregnancy prevention programs and reproductive healthcare.

National Organization for Women (NOW)
733 15th St NW, 2nd Floor,
Washington, DC 20005, U.S.A.
☎ (202) 628-8669   🖳 www.now.org

For over 30 years, NOW members have struggled for women's rights. Their campaigns include ending violence against women; supporting abortion rights; advocating for rape, harassment, and abuse survivors; ending racism, sexism, and homophobia; and electing feminist legislators at every level of government. Their tactics include massive marches, lobbying, education/conferences, litigation, organizing, and non-violent civil disobedience.

Planned Parenthood
810 Seventh Avenue,
New York, NY 10019, U.S.A.
☎ (800) 230-PLAN
💻 www.plannedparenthood.org

Planned Parenthood®
Federation of America, Inc.

Planned Parenthood is a national organization dedicated to sexual and reproductive health. Their mission is to provide comprehensive reproductive health care services, empowering sexuality education, and advocacy for public policies that ensure reproductive health, freedom, and research. Planned Parenthood provides reproductive health care to over five million women, men, and teenagers annually at over 850 health centers.

THE BEST OF THE REST

Here is a list of more incredible organizations working to build a better world on a daily basis. Be sure to contact them to find out more about each organization.

Activism

Direct Action Network
💻 www.directactionnetwork.org

Student Environmental Action Coalition
☎ (215) 222-4711
💻 www.seac.org

United Students Against Sweatshops
☎ (202) 667-9328
💻 www.usasnet.org

Ruckus Society
💻 www.ruckus.org

Animal Rights

EarthSave
☎ (800) 362-3648
💻 www.earthsave.org

Farm Animal Reform Movement
☎ (301) 530-1737
💻 www.farmusa.org

In Defense of Animals
☎ (415) 388-9641
💻 www.idausa.org

Vegetarian Resource Group
☎ (410) 366-8343
💻 www.vrg.org

Community

Center for Community Change
☎ (202) 342-0594
💻 www.communitychange.org

Institute for Community Economics
☎ (413) 746-8660
💻 www.iceclt.org

Institute for Local Self-Reliance
☎ (202) 232-4108
💻 www.ilsr.org

South West Organizing Project
☎ (505) 247-8832
💻 www.swop.net

Economic Justice

Center for Responsible Business
☎ (800) 729-4237
💻 www.cepnyc.org

Jobs with Justice
☎ (202) 737-6444
🖥 www.jwj.org

National Labor Committee
☎ (212) 242-3002
🖥 www.nlcnet.org

Environment

Community Coalition for Environmental Justice
☎ (206) 720-0285
🖥 www.ccej.org

Earth First!
☎ (541) 344-8004
🖥 www.earthfirst.org

GrassRoots Recycling Network
☎ (706) 613-7121
🖥 www.grrn.org

Indigenous Environmental Network
☎ (218) 751-4967
🖥 www.ienearth.org

National Resource Defense Council
☎ (212) 727-2700
🖥 www.nrdc.org

Sea Shepherd
☎ (360) 370-5500
🖥 www.seashepherd.org

Union of Concerned Scientists
☎ (617) 547-5552
🖥 www.ucsusa.org

The Wilderness Society
☎ (800) 843-9453
🖥 www.wilderness.org

Zero Population Growth
☎ (800) 225-5993
🖥 www.zpg.org

Gay and Lesbian

ACT UP
☎ (212) 966-4873
🖥 www.actupny.org

Gay and Lesbian Alliance against Defamation (GLAAD)
☎ (800) GAY-MEDIA
🖥 www.glaad.org

Parents and Friends of Lesbians And Gays (PFLAG)
☎ (202) 467-8180
🖥 www.pflag.org

Homelessness

National Coalition for the Homeless
☎ (202) 434-1106
🖥 www.nationalhomeless.org

Human Rights

American Civil Liberties Union
☎ (212) 549-2585
🖥 www.aclu.org

Disability Rights Education and Defense Fund
☎ (202) 986-0375
🖥 www.dredf.org

National Coalition to Abolish the Death Penalty
☎ (202) 387-3890
🖥 www.ncadp.org

Prison Activists Resource Center
☎ (510) 893-4648
🖥 www.prisonactivist.org

International

50 Years is Enough
☎ (202) 463-2265
🖥 www.50years.org

FINCA (Foundation for International Community Assistance)
☎ (202) 682-1510
🖳 www.villagebanking.org

International Development Exchange
☎ (415) 824-8384
🖳 www.idex.org

International Forum on Globalization
☎ (415) 229-9350
🖳 www.ifg.org

Jubilee +
☎ no phone number
🖳 www.jubilee2000uk.org

Voices in the Wilderness
☎ (773) 784-8065
🖳 www.nonviolence.org/vitw

Military

Center for Defense Information
☎ (202) 332-0600
🖳 www.cdi.org

Peace

Peace Brigades International
☎ (510) 663-2362
🖳 www.peacebrigades.org

School of the Americas Watch
☎ (202) 234-3440
🖳 www.soaw.org

Politics

Common Cause
☎ (202) 833-1200
🖳 www.commoncause.org

League of Women Voters
☎ (202) 429-1965
🖳 www.lwv.org

Project Vote Smart
☎ (888) VOTE-SMART
🖳 www.vote-smart.org

Public Campaign
☎ (202) 293-0222
🖳 www.publicampaign.org

Public Interest

Center for Science in the Public Interest
☎ (202) 332-9110
🖳 www.cspinet.org

Race and Ethnicity

Anti-Defamation League
🖳 www.adl.org

Center for Third World Organizing
☎ (510) 533-7583
🖳 www.ctwo.org

Cultural Survival
☎ (617) 441-5400
🖳 www.cs.org

First Nations Development Institute
☎ (540) 371-5615
🖳 www.firstnations.org

Southern Poverty Law Center
🖳 www.splcenter.org

Religious

Interfaith Alliance
☎ (202) 639-6370
🖳 www.interfaithalliance.org

Interfaith Center on Corporate Responsibility
☎ (212) 870-2295
🖳 www.iccr.org

Mennonite Central Committee
☎ (717) 859-3889
🖳 www.mcc.org

Pax Christi
☎ (814) 453-4955
🖥 www.paxchristi.net

Simplicity

Center for Commercial-Free Public Education
☎ (510) 268-1100
🖥 www.commercialfree.org

Commercial Alert
☎ (202) 296-2787
🖥 www.commercialalert.org

Northwest Earth Institute
🖥 www.nwei.org

Seeds of Simplicity
☎ (818) 247-4332
🖥 www.seedsofsimplicity.org

Women's Rights

9 to 5 National Association of Working Women (see the WORK chapter)
☎ (414) 274-0925
🖥 www.9to5.org

Feminist Majority Foundation
☎ (703) 522-2214
🖥 www.feminist.org

MADRE
☎ (212) 627-0444
🖥 www.madre.org

National Organization of Men against Sexism
☎ (303) 666-7043
🖥 www.nomas.org

IN CANADA

Activist

Web Networks Community
🖥 community.web.ca
Web links to hundreds of Canadian activist organizations

Economic

The Council of Canadians
502-151 Slater Street,
Ottawa, Ontario,
K1P 5H3 Canada
☎ (800) 387-7177
🖥 www.canadians.org

Ecumenical Coalition for Economic Justice
🖥 www.ecej.org

Halifax Initiative
☎ (613) 789-4447
🖥 www.halifaxinitiative.org

Environment

GreenOntario
🖥 www.greenontario.org

Sierra Club of Canada
🖥 www.sierraclub.ca

THE TOP TEN ACTIONS FOR A BETTER WORLD

If you've read the whole book and said "Wow! What a great book!" but haven't really taken action, you may feel overwhelmed. Here's the shortlist of the ten most powerful actions for a better world:

- Buy a low emission, fuel-efficient car (TRANSPORTATION).

- Limit your work time (WORK).

- Buy less stuff (SHOPPING).

- Buy products from environmentally and socially responsible companies (SHOPPING).

- Join an organization you care about (ORGANIZATIONS).

- Eat less meat (FOOD).

- Open an account at a socially responsible bank or credit union (MONEY).

- Conserve energy and water (HOME).

- Watch less TV (MEDIA).

- Volunteer (ORGANIZATIONS).

NOTES

THE SEVEN FOUNDATIONS
OF A BETTER WORLD

1. United Nations Development Programme, *The 1999 Human Development Report* (Oxford University Press,1999).
2. United Nations Development Programme, *The 1999 Human Development Report.*
3. Jennifer Reingold, "Executive Pay: It Continues to Explode —And Options Alone Are Creating Paper Billionaires," *Business Week*, 17 (April 2000).
4. Isaac Shapiro and Robert Greenstein, *The Widening Income Gulf* (Center on Budget and Policy Priorities, 1999).
5. Edward N. Wolff, "Recent Trends in Wealth Ownership, 1983-1998," Jerome Levy Economics Institute, April 2000.
6. Lawrence Mishel, Jared Bernstein, and John Schmitt, *State of Working America: 2000-2001* (Cornell University Press, 2001).
7. Board of Governors of the Federal Reserve System, "Recent Changes in U.S. Family Finances: Results from the 1998 Survey of Consumer Finances," *Federal Reserve Bulletin*, (January 2000), p. 15.
8. U.S. Census Bureau, *Current Population Reports, P60-206, Money Income in the United States:1999* (U.S. Government Printing Office, 2000); U.S. Census Bureau, *Poverty in the U.S.:1999* (Government Printing Office, 2000).
9. Laura Daly, "Aiding and Abetting an Epidemic," *Sojourners*, (Nov/Dec 1999).
10. Larry Rohter, "Brazil, IMF At Odds Over $22 Billion in Social Programs," *Denver Post*, (21 Feb 2000), p. A4.
11. Marie Michael, "Food or Debt: the Jubilee 2000 Movement," *Dollars and Sense*, (July/Aug 2000).
12. Megan Rowling, "Nicaragua," *Z Magazine*, (Jan 2001).
13. Jubilee 2000 Coalition [online], www.jubilee2000uk.org/faq.html, [cited 20 July 2000].
14. Dennis Greenia, et al, "On The March to End Sweatshops," *Co-op America Quarterly*, (Fall 1999).
15. National Labor Committee, "Wal-Mart's Shirts of Misery," July 1999 [online], www.nlcnet.org/WALMART/bangwalhtml, [cited 18 July 2001].
16. Charles Derber, *The Wilding of America: How Greed and Violence are Eroding Our Nation's Character* (St. Martin's Press, 1996).
17. Dennis Greenia, et al, "On The March to End Sweatshops."
18. Colin Chellman and Jerome Powell, "Research Report: Codes of Conduct for Working Conditions," Council on Economic Priorities, (Oct/Dec 1998).
19. Barry Yeoman, "Silence in the Fields," *Mother Jones*, (Jan/Feb 2001).
20. Martin Wroe, "An Irresistible Force," *Sojourners*, (May/June 2000).
21. Jubilee U.S.A. Network [online], www.J2000usa.org, [cited 15 March 2001].
22. Laura Brown, "Taking Stock Against Corporate Irresponsibility," *Co-op America Quarterly*, (Spring 2000).
23. SIF Industry Research Program, "1999 Report on Responsible Investing Trends in the United States," Social Investment Forum, 4 November 1999.
24. Jack Pippa, "Janitors OK New Contract: approval comes just hours before walkout deadline," *Denver Post*, (1 Oct 2000), p. B8.
25. ACORN'S Living Wage Resource Center [online], www.livingwagecampaign.org, [cited 15 July 2001].
26. Liza Featherstone, "The New Student Movement," *The Nation*, (15 May 2000).
27. CDFI Coalition, "Directory of Community Development Financial Institutions,"[online], www.cdfi.org, [cited 1999].
28. South Shore Bank [online], www.sbk.com, [cited 15 July 2001].
29. Rose Benz Ericson, "The Conscious Consumer," Fair Trade Federation, 1999.
30. Cindy Mitlo, "Small Loans are Creating a BIG Impact," *Co-op America Quarterly*, (Fall 1999).
31. Eric Hobsbawm, *The Age of Extremes: A History of the World 1914-1991* (Vintage Books, 1994).
32. Eric Hobsbawm, *The Age of Extremes.*
33. Howard Zinn, *The Zinn Reader 1997*, (Seven Stories Press, 1997), p. 260.
34. United Nations Development Programme, *Human Development Report: 2000* (Oxford University Press, 2000), p. 36.
35. Anthony Arnove, ed, *Iraq Under Siege: The Deadly Impact of Sanctions and War*, (South End Press, 2000).
36. Anup Shah, "The Arms Trade is Big Business," Global Issues.Org [online],www.globalissues.org/Geopolitics/ArmsTrade/BigBusiness.asp [cited 28 June 2001]; U.S. Bureau of the Census, *Statistical Abstract of the United States: 1999*, (U.S. Government Printing Office, 1999, table 582 (1996 data).
37. Christopher Hellman, "Last of the Big Time Spenders: U.S. Military Budget Still the World's Largest, and Growing," Center for Defense Information, 11 November 1999.
38. Martin Calhoun, "Military Costs: The Real Total," Center for Defense Information, 24 November 1996.

39. "America's Defense Monitor" Number 1227 [TV program], Center for Defense Information, 14 March 1999.
40. *Weekly Defense Monitor,* Vol.4 Issue 17, Center for Defense Information, 27 April 2000.
41. "The School Shootings...And Beyond: Kids and Guns in America" [online], Handgun Control, Inc., www.handguncontrol.org, [cited 15 January 2001].
42. A. Kellerman and D.T. Reay, "Protection or Peril," *New England Journal of Medicine,* 314, no. 24 (1986), pp. 1357-1359.
43. Handgun Control [online], www.handgun-control.org.
44. "The School Shootings...And Beyond.
45. "The School Shootings...And Beyond.
46. "The School Shootings...And Beyond.
47. Amnesty International, "Death Penalty Facts," May 2000 [online], www.amnestyusa.org/abolish/deterrence, [cited 15 July 2001].
48. Capital Punishment Project, "Death Row U.S.A.," NAACP Legal Defense and Education Fund, 1 January 2000.
49. Amnesty International, "Amnesty International Annual Report 2000, U.S.A.", January 2000 [online], www.amnestyusa.org/annualreport.
50. Amnesty International, "Amnesty International Annual Report 2000, U.S.A.", January 2000 [online].
51. Amnesty International, "Facts and Figures on the Death Penalty," September 2000.
52. Amnesty International, "Facts and Figures on the Death Penalty," September 2000.
53. Chicago Associated Press, "Kids' Doctors Call on TV Biz," *The Hollywood Reporter,* (9-11 June 1995).
54. Chicago Associated Press, "Kids' Doctors Call on TV Biz."
55. The American Psychological Association, "Children and Television Violence"[online], helping.apa.org/family/ kidtvviol.html, [cited 18 July 2001].
56. American Academy of Child and Adolescent Psychiatry, "Children and TV Violence," No.13, April 1999 [online], www.aacap.org/publications/factsfam/violence.htm.
57. Washington State University, "Television and Violence", *Research Review,* Issue 3 (Fall 1994).
58. B.S. Centerwall, "Exposure to Television as a Cause of Violence," in G. Comstock, ed., *Public Communication as Behavior,* (Academic Press, 1989), 2: pp.1-58.
59. David Korten, *The Post-Corporate World* (Copublished, Berrett-Koehler and Kumarian Press, 1999).
60. United Nations Development Programme, United Nations Environment Programme, World Bank, and World Resource Institute, *World Resources 2000-2001 People and*

Ecosystems: The Fraying Web of Life (World Resources Institute, 2000).
61. John C. Ryan and Alan Thein Durning, *Stuff: the secret lives of everyday things* (Northwest Environment Watch, 1997); based on M. Wackernagel and W. Rees, *Our Ecological Footprint: reducing human impact on the Earth* (New Society Publishers, 1996).
62. U.S. Bureau of the Census, *Statistical Abstract of the United State: 1999* (U.S. Government Printing Office, 1999), table 1388 (1997 preliminary data).
63. Alan Durning, "Asking How Much Is Enough," in Lester Brown et al., *State of the World 1991* (W.W. Norton, 1991).
64. John C. Ryan and Alan Thein Durning, *Stuff: the secret lives of everyday things.*
65. United Nations Environment Programme, *Global Environment Outlook-1: Global State of the Environment Report 1997* [online], www.unep.org/unep/eia/geo1/exsum/ex6.htm.
66. Harvard School of Public Health Press Release, "Air Pollution Deadlier Than Previously Thought," 2 March 2000 [online], www.harvard.edu.
67. United Nations Environment Programme. *Global Environment Outlook-1: Global State of the Environment Report 1997.*
68. David L. Levy, "Business and Climate Change," *Dollars and Sense,* (Jan/Feb 2001).
69. U.S. Bureau of the Census, *Statistical Abstract of the United State: 1999* (U.S. Government Printing Office, 1999), table 1357 [Source: Organization for Economic Cooperation and Development, Paris, France, *Toward Sustainable Development: Environmental Indicators* (July 1998) and *OECD in Figures,* annual)].
70. 20/20 Vision, "Support Cleaner Cars For Clean Air," May 2000.
71. David L. Levy, "Business and Climate Change," *Dollars and Sense* (Jan/Feb 2001); Harry Dunphy (Associated Press), "Report Finds World in Ecological Decline," *Daily Camera,* (14 Jan 2001).
72. Rainforest Action Network [online], www.ran.org, [cited 10 March 2001].
73. Edward O. Wilson, *The Diversity of Life* (Harvard University Press, 1992).
74. Greenpeace [online], www.greenpeace.org/~oceans/marinepollution, [cited 15 July 2001].
75. Douglas Frantz (*New York Times*), "Cruising Outside Pollution Laws," *Denver Post,* (3 January 1999).
76. United Nations Environment Programme, *Global Environment Outlook-1: Global State of the Environment Report 1997.*
77. U.S. Census Bureau, International Data Base [online], www.census.gov/main/www/popclock/html, [cited 15 July 2001].
78. Lester R. Brown, "Challenges of the New Century," *State of the World 2000* (W.W. Norton, 2000).

79. BTM Consult, *International Wind Energy Development: World Market Update 1997*, Ringkobing, Denmark, March 1998; Lester Brown, Michael Renner, and Brian Halweil, *Vital Signs:The Environmental Trends That Are Shaping Our Future* (W.W. Norton, 1999).

80. *Vital Signs: The Environmental Trends that are Shaping Our Future* (W.W. Norton, 1999), based on various issues of *PV News* by Paul Maycock, 1990-1998.

81. Harry Dunphy (Associated Press), "Report Finds World in Ecological Decline," *Daily Camera* (14 January 2001).

82. 20/20 Vision, "California Leads the Way to Clean Cars," *Viewpoint,* (Fall 2000).

83. 20/20 Vision, "Support Cleaner Cars For Clean Air," May 2000, [newsletter].

84. "Indicators," *YES! a journal of positive futures,* (Winter 1999/2000).

85. Brown, Lester et al, *State of the World* (W.W. Norton, 2000).

86. Jim Motavalli, "Zero Waste," *E! The Environmental Magazine,* (March/April 2001).

87. Bette K. Fishbein, John R. Ehrenfeld, and John E. Young, *Extended Producer Responsibility: a materials policy for the 21st century* (Inform, 2000), p. 244.

88. Sam Cole, "Zero Waste —on the move around the world," *Eco-Cycle Times* (Fall/Winter 2000).

89. Jennifer Bogo, "Like a Virgin: a grassroots group pressures Coke to use recycled plastic," *E! The Environmental Magazine,* (January/February 2001); City of Toronto Press Release, "Task Force 2010 seeks made-in-Toronto solutions for waste," 29 January 2001.

90. "Twelfth Annual Business Ethics Awards," *Business Ethics,* (November/December 2000).

91. USAID, "Bangladesh's Emerging Success Story In Population And Family Planning" April 1996 [online], www.usaid.gov.

92. Federal Election Commission, "National Voter Turnout in Federal Elections: 1960-1996" [online], www.fec.gov.

93. Federal Election Commission, "National Voter Turnout in Federal Elections: 1960-1996" and "Voter Registration and Turnout — 1998" [online], www.fec.gov.

94. Keith Meatto, "Donation Inflation," *Mother Jones,* (July/August 2000).

95. Public Campaign, "Why Fat Cats Are Purring about Congressional Reforms" [online], www.publicampaign.org/fatcat2.html, [cited 10 July 2000].

96. Common Cause study, 12 April 2001 [online], www.commoncause.org.

97. Ryan McPherson, Lauren Marks, Susan Anderson, Margaret Engle, and Randy Kehler, "The Color of Money: campaign contributions and race," [online], Public Campaign, 1999, < www.publicampaign.org.

98. Micah L. Sifry, "How Money in Politics Hurts You," *Dollars and Sense,* (July/August 2000).

99. Common Cause, "National Parties Raise Record $107.2 Million in Soft Money During 1999" [online], 9 February 2000; and "Reporter's Guide to Money in Politics Campaign 2000" [online], < www.commoncause.org, [cited 6 June 2001].

100. Center for Responsive Politics [online], www.opensecrets.org/parties>, based on data released by the Federal Election Commission on 1 June 2000, [cited 20 August 2000].

101. Center for Responsive Politics [online], www.opensecrets.org/parties, based on data released by the Federal Election Commission on 1 June 2000, [cited 20 August 2000].

102. Paul Taylor, "TV's Political Profits," *Mother Jones,* (May/June 2000).

103. Compiled from publicly available Federal Election Commission reports [online], www.fec.gov; "The Big Picture: The Money Behind the 1998 Elections" [online], The Center for Responsive Politics, www.opensecrets.org; and Common Cause reports [online], www.commoncause.org, [cited 20 July 2000].

104. Robert McChesney, "Oligopoly: The Big Media Game Has Fewer and Fewer Players," *The Progressive,* (November 1999).

105. Mike Budd, Steve Craig, and Clay Steinman, *Consuming Environments: Television and Commercial Culture* (Rutgers University Press, 1999).

106. Public Campaign Press Advisory [online], 12 June 2000, www.publicampaign.org; Public Campaign Press Release, "First Gubernatorial Clean Money Candidate Clears Vermont Threshold" [online], 14 June 2000, www.publicampaign.org.

107. "Hungry for Good News about the Election? Try this." *USA Today,* (6 December 2000), p. 24A.

108. Online, www.shadowconventions.com, [cited 15 January 2001].

109. Paul Rauber, "No More Spoilers," *Sierra,* (January/February 2001).

110. Marc Kaufman, "USDA Poised to Issue New Organic Food Standards; Standards for 'Organic' Food Eyed," *The Washington Post,* (3 March 2000).

111. Ben Littiston and Ronnie Cummins, "Organic vs. 'Organic'": The Corruption of a Label," *The Ecologist,* 28, no.4, (July/August 1998), pp. 195-200.

112. Tracy Rysavy, "MAI Free Zones," *YES! a journal of positive futures,* (Spring 1999).

113. Nafis Sadik and United Nations Population Fund, *The State of World Population Report 2000: Lives Together, Worlds Apart — Men and Women in a Time of Change,* (United Nations Population Fund, 2000).

114. United Nations Development Programme, *Human Development Report: 2000* (Oxford University Press, 2000), p. 4.

115. Katha Pollitt, "Underground Against the Taliban," *The Nation,* (29 May 2000).

116. Nafis Sadik and United Nations Population Fund, *The State of World Population Report 2000.*

117. International Women's Health Coalition [online], www.iwhc.org/help.html, [cited 20 May 2000].

118. Nafis Sadik and United Nations Population Fund, *The State of World Population Report 2000.*

119. United Nations Development Programme, *Human Development Report: 2000,* p. 39.

120. James Heintz, Nancy Folbre, et al, *The Ultimate Field Guide to the U.S. Economy* (New Press, 2000).

121. CNN, "Clinton Designates $6 Million to Fight Church Burnings" [online], 2 July 1996, www.cnn.com.

122. U.S. Census Bureau, *Poverty in the U.S.:1998* (U.S. Government Printing Office, 1999).

123. Edward Wolff, "Recent Trends in Wealth Ownership," Jerome Levy Economics Institute, 1998; based on Federal Reserve Survey of Consumer Finances.

124. Marc Miringoff and Marque-Luisa Miringoff, *The Social Health Of The Nation: how America is really doing* (Oxford University Press, 1999).

125. National Low Income Housing Coalition [online], www.nlihc.org, [cited 15 November 2000].

126. Jennifer Kerr, "ACLU Sues California Over Schools," *Associated Press,* (May 19, 2000).

127. Danielle Knight, "Controversy Swirls Around Mercury Shipment from U.S. to India," *InterPress Service,* (25 January 2001).

128. Robert Bryce, "Toxic Trade Imbalance," *Mother Jones,* (January/February 2001).

129. Jim Motavalli, "Toxic Targets: polluters that Dump on Communities of Color are Finally Being Brought to Justice," *E The Environmental Magazine,* (July/August 1998).

130. Human Rights Campaign, *HRC Quarterly,* (Spring 2000).

131. National Gay and Lesbian Task Force [online], www.ngltf.org, [cited 10 June 2000].

132. Laura Dely, "Aiding and Abetting an Epidemic," *Sojourners,* (November/December 1999).

133. Lester R. Brown, "Challenges of the New Century," *State of the World 2000* (W.W. Norton, 2000).

134. U.S. Census Bureau Press Release, 4 October 1999.

135. Raja Mishra, "U.S. Health Care System Ranked 37th," *The Boston Globe,* (21 June 2000).

136. "Between the Lines," *Sojourners,* (May/June 2000).

137. Jason Ziedenberg and Vincent Schiraldi, *The Punishing Decade: Prison and Jail Estimates at the Millennium* (Justice Policy Institute, May 2000).

138. Michael A. Fletcher, "Report: War on Drugs Sends Blacks to Prison At 13 Times...," *The Washington Post,* (8 June 2000).

139. Ilene R. Prusher (*Christian Science Monitor*), "Kuwati Women Seek Vote," *Colorado Daily,* (9 Aug 2000).

140. Southern Poverty Law Center 'Teaching Tolerance' campaign [online], www.splcenter.org, [cited 2 June 2001].

141. Elizabeth Martinez, "The New Youth Movement in California," *Z Magazine,* (May 2000).

142. Marc Cooper, "Measures That Mattered," *The Nation,* (27 November 2000).

143. United Nations Development Programme, *Human Development Report: 2000,* p. 9.

144. United Nations Development Programme, *The 1999 Human Development Report* (Oxford University Press,1999).

145. United Nations Development Programme, *The Human Development Report: 1998* (Oxford University Press,1998).

146. United Nations Development Programme, *The Human Development Report: 1998.*

147. Nafis Sadik and United Nations Population Fund, *The State of World Population Report 2000.*

148. Ben Schnayerson, "Bigger Is Better," *Mother Jones,* (March/April 2000).

149. Sut Jhally, *Ad and the Ego* (California Newsreel, 1996).

150. "Dealing for Dollars," *Austin American-Statesman,* (17 May 2000); American Council for an Energy-Efficient Economy, "Green Book 2000" [online], www.aceee.org.

151. Lynette Lamb, "Shielding Our Little Consumers," *The Lutheran* (May 2000).

152. Joan Lowy (Scripps Howard News Service), "Kidblitz: do advertisers rob cradle?" *The Daily Camera,* (11 December 1999).

153. Annenberg Public Policy Center, "Media In The Home 1999: The Fourth Annual Survey of Parents and Children" [online], appcpenn.org/kidstv99/survey5.htm.

154. David Leonhardt and Kathleen Kerwin, "Hey Kid, Buy This: Is Madison Avenue Taking 'Get 'em While They're Young' Too Far?," *Business Week,* (30 June 1997; Michael Jacobson and Laurie Ann Mazur, *Marketing Madness* (Westview Press, 1995).

155. Consumers Union, "Captive Kids: A Report on Commercial Pressures on Kids at School," 1995 [online], www.consumersunion.org.

156. Thom Marshall, "Gloria Shoulda Had a Coke and a Smile," *Houston Chronicle,* (29 March 1998), p. A37.

157. Tim Dickinson, "'E' is for E-Commerce," *Mother Jones,* (May/June 2000).

158. Channel One Network, *Teen Fact Book: 1997- 1998.*

159. Cara DeGette, "To Ensure Revenue, Coke Is It; Schools Urged to Boost Sales," *Denver Post,* (22 November 1998), p. B-01.

160. Mary Sutter, "Marketers Boost Pope's Visit to Mexico With Tie-ins," *Advertising Age,* (25 January 1999).

161. The Harwood Group, "Yearning for Balance: Views of Americans on Consumption, Materialism, and the Environment," Merck Family Fund, 1995.

162. Marshall Glickman, *The Mindful Money Guide* (Ballantine Wellspring), p. 188.

163. Leigh Eric Schmidt, *Consumer Rites: the buying and selling of American holidays* (Princeton University Press, 1995), p. 292.

164. Patrick Bishop, "35-Hour Work Week Proves a Winner in France," *Daily Telegraph,* (January 2001).

165. Amy Saltzman, "When Less is More," *U.S. News & World Report 1998 Career Guide,* (27 October 1997).

166. Gerald Celente, *Trends 2000: how to prepare for and profit from the changes of the 21st century* (Warner Books, 1997).

167. Juliet Schor, *The Overspent American* (HarperPerennial, 1998), p. 114.

168. Marilyn Berlin Snell, "Riders of the World, Unite," *Sierra,* (January/February 2001).

169. "Indicators," *YES! a journal of positive futures,* (Winter 1999/2000).

170. David Engwicht, *Street Reclaiming: creating livable streets and vibrant communities* (New Society Publishers, 1999).

171. Christopher Gunn and Hazel Dayton Gunn, *Reclaiming Capital: democratic initiatives and community development* (Cornell University Press, 1991), p. 28.

172. Richard Moe and Carter Wilkie, *Changing Places: rebuilding community in the age of sprawl* (Henry Holt 1997).

Money

1. Juliet Schor, *The Overspent American.*

2. U.S. Department of Commerce, *Statistical Abstract of the United States* (U.S. Government Printing Office, 1997), table 799.

3. Cecile Andrews, *The Circle of Simplicity: return to the good life* (HarperPerrenial, 1997), p. 51.

4. U.S. Department of Commerce, *Statistical Abstract of the United States* (U.S. Government Printing Office, 1996), p. 837.

5. Social Investment Forum, "1999 Report on Responsible Investing Trends in the United States" [online], 4 November 1999, www.socialinvest.org/areas/research/trends/1999-Trends.htm.

6. For an explanation of the criteria we used to construct this list, see the Shopping chapter page 83.

7. Hal Brill, Jack A. Brill, and Cliff Feigenbaum, *Investing with Your Values: Making Money and Making a Difference.* (New Society Publishers, 2000).

8. See Grameen Foundation USA, "Information on Microcredit" [online], ww.grameenfoundation.org/microcredit.html, [cited 20 May 2000].

9. "Social Investing Hits the ($170 Billion) Big Time," *BizEthics Buzz,* (January 2001).

Shopping

1. John C. Ryan and Alan Durning, *Stuff: The Secret Lives of Everyday Things,* pp. 4-5.

2. *Boycott Action News,* (Summer 1999).

3. Joel Makower, *The Green Consumer Supermarket Guide* (Penguin Books, 1991), p. 169.

Food

1. Co-op America, *National Green Pages* (Co-op America, 1999).

2. Jeremy Rifkin, *Beyond Beef: The Rise and Fall of the Cattle Culture* (Dutton, 1992), p. 267.

3. U.S. Department of Agriculture [online], www.nal.usda.gov:80/fnic/dga/dga95/grains.html; and Lee W. Wattenburg, "Inhibition of Carcinogens by Minor Dietary Constituents," *Cancer Research,* 52, no. 7, (1 April 1995).

4. Vegetarian Resource Group — Roper Poll, "How Many Vegetarians Are There?", *Vegetarian Journal,* 16, no. 5, (September/October 1997).

5. Jeremy Rifkin, *Beyond Beef.*

6. Jeremy Rifkin, *Beyond Beef,* p. 153.

7. Joanne Stepaniak and Virginia Messina, *The Vegan Sourcebook* (Lowell House, 1998).

8. H.W. Kindall and David Pimentell, "Constraints on the Expansion of the Global Food Supply," *Ambio,* 23, no. 3 (1994).

9. Norine Dworkin, "22 Reasons to Go Vegetarian Right Now," *Vegetarian Times,* (April 1999), p. 91.

10. Jeffrey Hollender, *How to Make the World a Better Place* (William Morrow, 1990), p. 122.

11. Hog Watch, "Factory Hog Farming: The Big Picture" [online], www.hogwatch.org, [cited 21 June 2000].

12. Water Education Foundation, *Water Input in California Food Production* [report], 1991.

13. Derek M. Brown, "How The Meat Industry Destroys Waterways," *Good Medicine,* 8 no. 1 (Winter 1999).

14. Tom Knudson, "Part Two: Waste on Grand Scale Loots Sea," *Sacramento Bee,* (11 December 1995).

15. Environmental Defense Fund, Annual Report, 1997.

16. Audobon Society, "Audobon's Guide to Seafood" 1999 [online], www.audobon.org, [cited 2 February 2001].

17. David Pimentel, cited in Erik Marcus, *Vegan: The new ethics of eating* (McBooks Press, 1998), p. 165.

18. United Nations Food and Agriculture Organization, *State of Food Insecurity in the World,* 1999.

19. Jeffrey Hollender and Linda Catling, *How to Make the World a Better Place.*

20. David Pimentel, "Livestock Production: Energy Inputs and the Environment," in *Canadian Society of Animal Science;* Scott and Xin Zhao, eds., proceedings of the 47th Annual Meeting, Montreal, Quebec, (July 1997) pp. 16-26.

21. Christopher D. Cook, "Hog-Tied: migrant workers find themselves trapped on the pork assembly line," *The Progressive,* (September 1999).

22. Stephen J. Hedgers, "The New Jungle" *U.S. News & World Report,* 121, no. 12, (23 September 1996).

23. Humane Farming Association, "A Look Inside the Pork Industry," 1990 [online], www.hfa.org, [cited 17 May 2000].

24. R.L. Phillips, "The Role of Lifestyle and Dietary Habits on Risk of Cancer Among Seventh Day Adventists," *Cancer Research,* 35, (1990), pp. 3513-3522.

25. John Robbins, *Diet for A New America* (Stillpoint, 1987).

26. Richard Behar and Michael Kramer, "Something Smells Foul," *Time,* (17 October 1994).

27. Erik Marcus, *Vegan: The new ethics of eating* (McBooks Press, 1998).

28. Jim Mason, "Fowling the Waters," *E Magazine,* (September/October 1995).

29. Physicians Committee for Responsible Medicine, "The Protein Myth," 1998 [online], www.pcrm.org, [cited 4 September 2000].

30. Diane MacEachern, *Save The Planet* (Dell Publishing, 1995), p. 78.

Personal

1. We owe our understanding of creativity to the incredible mentorship of Jim Downton.

2. Unicef [online], www.unicef.org/sowc98/fs01.htm, [cited 4 March 2000].

3. Barbara F. Orlans, "Data on Animal Experimentation in the United States: What They Do and Do Not Show," *Perspectives in Biology and Medicine,* 37 no. 2. (Winter 1994).

4. Arnot Ogden Medical Center [online], www.aomc.org, [cited 20 October 2000].

5. Arnot Ogden Medical Center [online].

6. National Opinion Research Center [online], www.norc.uchicago.edu, [cited 20 October 2000].

7. His Divine Grace A. C. Baktivedanta Swami Prabhupada, *Baghavad-Gita As It Is,* International Society for Krishna Consciousness,1972.

8. Stephen Mitchell, *Tao Te Ching: A New English Version* (HarperPerennial, 1988), verse 78.

9. Robert G. Hoerber, ed., *The Concordia Self-Study Bible* (Concordia Publishing House, 1990).

10. Amatal Rahman Omar, *The Holy Quaran* (Noor Foudation International, 1997).

11. Nosson Scherman, trans., *The Chumash: The Artscroll Series* (Mesorah Publications, 2000).

12. Report issued by the National Center for Health Statistics, presented by Katherine Flegal at the October 1996 meeting of the North American Association for the Study of Obesity.

13. American Medical Association [online], www.amaassn.org/insight/ gen_hlth/fitness/fitness.htm, [cited 16 May 2000].

14. Mayo Clinic [online], www.mayohealth.org/mayo/9610/htm/ sleep.htm, [cited 16 May 2000].

15. J.H. Peter, T. Penzel, T. Podszus, and P. von Wichert, eds., *Sleep and Health Risk* (Springer-Verlag, 1991), p. 555.

16. Susan M. Lark, M.D., excerpted from *The Women's Health Companion* (Celestial Arts, 1996).

17. Susan M. Lark, M.D., excerpted from *The Women's Health Companion.*

Friends and Family

1. Leo Buscaglia, *Love* (Fawcett Books, 1996).

2. Zero Population Growth Population Education Program, *Countdown to 6,000,000,000* (Zero Population Growth, 1999).

3. U.S. Bureau of the Census, *Statistical Abstract of the United State: 1999* (U.S. Government Printing Office, 1999), table 1388 (1997 preliminary data).

4. Child Welfare League of America, 440 First Street, NW Suite 310, Washington, DC 20001-2085, U.S.A.; ph: (202)638-2952. About 42% of adoptions in 1992 were by step-parents.

5. "Foster Care and Adoption Statistics," a Congressional Research Service Report for Congress, #97-111 EPW, 15 January 1997; Children's Defense Fund, "The State of America's Children," (Yearbook, 1997).

6. Jeffrey Hollender and Linda Catling, *How to Make the World a Better Place* (W. W. Norton, 1995), p. 45.

7. Jose Martinez, "Hockey dad arraigned in beating death," *The Boston Herald,* (25 July 2000), p.5.

8. Michael F. Jacobson and Lauri Ann Mazur, *Marketing Madness* (Westview Press, 1995), p. 22.

Community

1. U.S. Census Bureau, Public Information Office, 15 May 2000.

2. U.S. Census Bureau, Geographical Mobility, March 1992 to March 1993.

3. Judann Pollack, "Foods Targeting Children Aren't Just Child's Play," (*Advertising Age,* 1 March 1999).

4. Parents, Families, and Friends of Lesbians and Gays [online], www.pflag.org/schools/educators.htm, [cited 15 July 2001].

5. "Indicators," *Yes! magazine,* (Summer 1999).

6. National Low Income Housing Coalition, "Out of Reach" [annual report, 1999], www.nlihc.org.

7. Economic Policy Institute 1999.

8. Economic Policy Institute (EPI), *America's Well-Targeted Raise,* (September 1997).

9. Economic Policy Institute (EPI), *America's Well-Targeted Raise.*

10. Kathleen Haley, "Innovative Living Wage Law in San Francisco," *Business Ethics,* (September/October 2000); "Compass," *Utne Reader,* (November/December 2000).

11. ACORN'S Living Wage Resource Center [online], www.livingwagecampaign.org, [cited 15 July 2001].

Home

1. Donald Lotter, *Earthscore: A Personal Environmental Audit and Guide* (Morning Sun Press, 1993).

2. Debra Dadd-Redalia, *Sustaining the Earth* (Hearst Books, 1994), p. 257.

3. Jeffrey Hollander, *How to Make the World a Better Place,* p. 106.

4. Owen Bailey and Robert Alcock, "Home Energy Brief: #8 Home Cooling," Rocky Mountain Institute, 1997.

5. Debra Dadd-Redalia, *Sustaining the Earth,* p. 301.

6. Sue Hassol, "Home Energy Brief #4: Refrigerators and Freezers," Rocky Mountain Institute, 1994.

7. Maureen Cureton and Dave Reed, "Home Energy Brief: #6 Washers, Dryers, and Miscellaneous Appliances," Rocky Mountain Institute, 1995.

8. Diane MacEachern, *Save The Planet* (Dell Publishing, 1995), p. 48.

9. Maureen Cureton and Dave Reed, "Home Energy Brief: #6 Washers, Dryers, and Miscellaneous Appliances.

10. Maureen Cureton and Dave Reed, "Home Energy Brief: #6 Washers, Dryers, and Miscellaneous Appliances.

11. Diane MacEachern, *Save The Planet,* p. 9.

12. Diane MacEachern, *Save The Planet,* p. 23.

13. Kirk B. Smith, in "Home ECOnomics," *The Green Lifestyle Handbook,* Jeremy Rifkin,ed. (Henry Holt, 1990), p. 1.

14. Diane MacEachern, *Save The Planet,* p. 19.

15. Umoja Edwards, "The Five Bulb Challenge," *Real Money,* (Winter 2000); Michael Brower and Warren Leon, *The Consume"'s Guide to Effective Environmental Choices: Practical Advice from the Union of Concerned Scientists* (Three Rivers Press, 1999), p. 106.

16. Kirk B. Smith, in "Home ECOnomics," *The Green Lifestyle Handbook,* p. 8.

17. Sue Hassol, "Home Energy Brief: #4 Water Heating," Rocky Mountain Institute, 1994.

18. Sue Hassol, "Home Energy Brief: #4 Water Heating."

19. Bruce N. Anderson, ed., *Ecologue* (Prentice Hall Press, 1990), p. 106.

20. Jeffrey Hollander, *How to Make the World a Better Place,* p. 113.

21. U.S. Department of Commerce, *Statistical Abstract of the United States* (U.S. Government Printing Office, 1999), table 1357.

22. Zita Lynn, "Stop the Junk Mail Monster," *Eco-Cycle Times,* (Winter/Spring 1998).

23. Earthworks Group, *50 Simple Things You Can Do to Save the Planet* (Earthworks Press, 1989), p. 20.

24. Harmonious Technologies, *Backyard Composting* (Harmonious Press, 1997), p. 7.

25. Diane MacEachern, *Save The Planet* (Dell Publishing, 1995), p. 67.

26. Alan Durning, "Redesigning the Forest Economy," in *State of the World 1994,* Lester Brown, ed. (W.W.Norton, 1994).

Work

1. Phineas Baxandall and Marc Breslow, "Does Inequality Cause Overwork?" *Dollars and Sense,* 221, (January/February 1999).

2. Philip L. Rones, Randy E. Ilg, and Jennifer M. Gardner, "Trends in the hours of work since the mid-1970s" *Monthly Labor Review,* (April 1997).

3. Joel Makower, *Beyond the Bottom Line: Putting Social Responsibility to Work for Your Business and the World* (Touchstone Books 1995), p. 235.

4. Joel Makower, *Beyond the Bottom Line: Putting Social Responsibility to Work for Your Business and the World,* p. 227.

5. U.S. Department of Labor, Employment, and Earnings, 7 January 2001 [online], www.dol.gov.

Media

1. Julie Winokur, ed., *We the Media,* Introduction by Don Hazen, (New Press, 1997), p. 43.

2. Robert Mc Chesney, *Corporate Media and the Threat to Democracy* (Seven Stories Press, 1997), p. 15.

3. Robert McChesney, "Oligopoly: The Big Media Game Has Fewer and Fewer Players."

4. Nielsen Media Research, 1998 [online], www.tvturnoff.org, [cited 4 March 2000].

5. Benjamin Barber, *Harper's,* (November 1993), p. 41; Nielsen Media Research, 2000 [online], www.tvturnoff.org, [cited 4 March 2001].

6. Senate Judiciary Committee Staff Report, "Children, Violence, and the Media," 1999.

7. Nielsen Media Research, 1998.

8. Robert McChesney, *Corporate Media and the Threat to Democracy,* p. 29.

9. Michael Jacobsen and Laurie Ann Mazur, *Marketing Madness* (Westview Press, 1995).

Politics

1. 20/20 Vision [online], www.2020vision.org/admin.html, [cited 20 February 2000].
2. "Campaign Inflation," *Mother Jones,* (March/April 2001).
3. Jason Ziedenberg and Vincent Schiraldi, *The Punishing Decade: Prison and Jail Estimates at the Millennium,* Justice Policy Institute, May 2000, [analysis of U.S. Department of Justice Data].
4. Raja Mishra, "U.S. Health Care System Ranked 37th," *The Boston Globe,* (21 June 2000).
5. "World Military Expenditures," Center for Defense Information, February 2000.
6. National Gay and Lesbian Task Force [online], www.ngltf.org, [cited 22 March 2001].
7. "The End of Corporate Welfare As We Know It," *Business Week,* (10 Feb 1997).
8. Donald L. Barlett and James B. Steele, *America: Who Really Pays the Taxes* (Touchstone, 1994), p. 140.
9. Tim Dickinson, "Tax-Free, Inc.," *Mother Jones,* (March/April 2000).
10. "Estate Tax Talking Points" [online], United For a Fair Economy, www.ufenet.org, [cited 5 February 2001].

Transportation

1. U.S. Department of Transportation, "Commuting Alternatives in the U.S.: Recent Trends And A Look To The Future," 1994; U.S. Department of Transportation, *Transportation Statistics Annual Report,* 1997.
2. Pedaling into the Future," *World Watch* magazine, (July/August 1988).
3. U.S. Department of Transportation, "Commuting Alternatives in the U.S.: Recent Trends and a Look to the Future," 1994.
4. Union of Concerned Scientists [online], www.ucsusa.org/transportation/consumer.html, [cited 6 March 2000].
5. Michael Brower and The Union of Concerned Scientists, *The Consumer's Guide to Effective Environmental Choices,* Three Rivers Press, (April 1999), p. 86.
6. U.S. Department of Transportation, "Long Distance Travel and Freight," *Transportation Statistics Annual Report, 1998,* p. 107.
7. Union of Concerned Scientists [online], www.ucsusa.org/transportation/consumer.html, [cited 6 March 2000].
8. Joel Makower, *The Green Commuter* (National Press Books, 1992), p. 4.
9. Bureau of Transportation Statistics, *National Transportation Statistics 2000* (U.S. Department of Transportation, 2001), table 1-29.
10. Gary Branson, *The Complete Guide to Recycling at Home* (Betterway Publications, 1991), p.77.

11. Gary Branson, *The Complete Guide to Recycling at Home,* p.82.; Joel Makower, *The Green Commuter,* p. 64.
12. Editors of *Consumer Reports. 1999 Used Car Buying Guide* (Consumer Reports, 1999).
13. Joel Makower, *The Green Commuter,* p. 64.
14. Gary Branson, *The Complete Guide to Recycling at Home,* p.82.
15. U.S. Department of Transportation, "Commuting Alternatives in the U.S.: recent trends and a look to the future," 1994; Bureau of Transportation Statistics, *National Transportation Statistics 2000* (U.S. Department of Transportation, 2001), table 1-32.
16. U.S. Department of Transportation, "Commuting Alternatives in the U.S.: recent trends and a look to the future,"1994; Bureau of Transportation Statistics, *National Transportation Statistics 2000* (U.S. Department of Transportation, 2001), table 1-32.
17. Joel Makower, *The Green Commuter,* p. 68.
18. Editors of *Consumer Reports. 1999 Used Car Buying Guide.*
19. Michael Brower, *The Consumer's Guide to Effective Environmental Choices,* p. 90; "Support Cleaner Cars for Cleaner Air," *20/20 Vision,* (May 2000).
20. Michael Brower, *The Consumer's Guide to Effective Environmental Choices,* p. 90.
21. California Air Resources Board [online], www.arb.ca.gov, [cited 5 September 1999].
22. Jason Mark and Candace Morey, "Diesel Passenger Vehicles and the Environment," Union of Concerned Scientists, April 1999.
23. Joel Makower, *The Green Commuter,* p. 35.
24. Joel Makower, *The Green Commuter.*
25. Joel Makower, *The Green Commuter.*
26. Joel Makower, *The Green Commuter,* p. 139.
27. "Environmental Commitment" [online], www.toyota.com/ecologic, [cited 15 July 2001].
28. Jim Motavalli, "Your Next Car?" *Sierra,* (July/August 1999).
29. Jason Mark, "Zeroing Out Pollution: The Promise of Fuel Cell Cars," Union of Concerned Scientists, 1996.

Travel

1. John Naisbitt, *Global Paradox* (William Morrow,1994).

Organizations

1. A. Miranda, "Solidarity," in *Voices from the WTO: an anthology of writing by the people who shut down the World Trade Organization in Seattle 1999,* Stephanie Guilloud, ed. (Evergreen State College Bookstore, 2000), p. 73.

ACTION INDEX

❑ Give Unconditional Love And Support
❑ Forgive Others

GIVING GIFTS
❑ Give Of Yourself
❑ Donate Money For Someone
❑ Buy Socially Responsible Gifts
❑ Simplify The Holidays

CHILDREN
❑ Limit Your Number Of Children
❑ Adopt
❑ Be A Foster Parent
❑ Start A Baby-Sitting Club
❑ Spend Quality Time With Your Children
❑ Express Affection
❑ Model Peace
❑ Teach Caring And Giving
❑ Model Flexible Gender Roles
❑ Teach An Appreciation Of Diversity
❑ Teach The Difference Between Wants And Needs
❑ Choose Childcare That Supports Your Values
❑ Limit TV Watching
❑ Choose Alternatives To TV And Video Games
❑ Talk With Your Kids About TV
❑ Choose Alternatives To Violent Toys And Games

COMMUNITY

NEIGHBORHOOD
❑ Put Down Roots
❑ Get To Know Your Neighbors
❑ Help Your Neighbors And Ask For Their Help
❑ Organize A Neighborhood Event

LOCAL COMMUNITY
❑ Participate In Community Organizations
❑ Volunteer In A Soup Kitchen, Homeless Shelter, Or Food Pantry
❑ Volunteer At Your Local Animal Shelter
❑ Help Habitat For Humanity Build Homes
❑ Get Involved In Your Local Schools
❑ Decommercialize Your Schools
❑ Create Safe Schools
❑ Support Local Arts And Culture
❑ Participate In Local, County, Regional And State-Wide Community Events
❑ Set Up A Sister City Relationship

COMMUNITY ISSUES
❑ Stop Urban Sprawl
❑ Advocate For Affordable Housing
❑ Advocate For A Community Living Wage
❑ Advocate For Increased School Funding

HOME

ENERGY
❑ Contact Your Local Utility Company To Perform An Energy Audit
❑ Use Your Appliances Efficiently
❑ Weatherize Your Home
❑ Light Your Home Efficiently
❑ Choose An Environmentally Responsible Electricity Provider

WATER
❑ Install Faucet Aerators And Low-Flow Shower Heads
❑ Transform Your Toilet Into A Water Miser
❑ Use Environmentally Friendly Cleaners And Detergents

TRASH
❑ Reduce Your Junk Mail
❑ Recycle
❑ Compost Your Kitchen Scraps And Yard Waste
❑ Properly Dispose Of Household Hazardous Waste

LAWN & GARDEN
❑ Xeriscape Your Lawn And Garden
❑ Use A Manual Or Electric Lawn Mower
❑ Don't Bag Your Grass Clippings
❑ Avoid Buying Unnecessary Power Tools

YOUR HOME
❑ Live Close To Work
❑ Live In A Smaller Home
❑ Arrange Your Furniture To Encourage Conversation
❑ Grow Household Plants
❑ Use A Socially Responsible Long Distance Provider
❑ Give Away Your Clutter
❑ Consciously Choose Your Community
❑ Remodel With Green Materials

WORK
❑ Limit Your Work Time
❑ Take Your Lunch To Work

WORKPLACE RELATIONSHIPS
❑ Avoid Gossip
❑ Appreciate Everyone In Your Workplace
❑ Get To Know Your Co-Workers Outside Of Work
❑ Set Up A Workplace Carpool
❑ Make People From Diverse Background Feel Welcome
❑ Brainstorm With Co-Workers About How To Make A Better Workplace

SOCIALLY RESPONSIBLE WORKPLACE
❑ Find Out If Your Workplace Encourages Charitable Giving

ABOUT THE AUTHORS

Ellis Jones has been teaching students to make a difference in the world for the past ten years. He taught environmental education to local school children and, after receiving his Master's Degree in International Peace Studies from Notre Dame, spent two years in the Peace Corps teaching Panamanian students and teachers to care for their rainforests. A scholar of international human rights law, nonviolence, and everyday activism, Ellis focuses all of his energies on bridging the gap between academics, activists, and the average citizen.

Ross Haenfler emerged from the straight edge punk rock scene to study and participate in social movements. He teaches courses on U.S. Social Movements, Nonviolence and the Ethics of Social Action, Implementing Social Change, and Self and Consciousness. Active in the student anti-sweatshop movement and the Mennonite Church, Ross has committed civil disobedience in the movement to close the U.S. Army School of the Americas and authored a district-wide resolution condemning the school's actions.

Brett Johnson has been a dedicated member of the environmental and simple living movements for years. He coordinates his apartment complex's composting program, leads voluntary simplicity workshops, and is an eco-cycle block leader. With courses such as Self in Modern Society, and Social Conflict and Social Values, Brett enlightens students about economic and racial inequality and the increasing role of advertising in our lives. He is currently researching the voluntary simplicity movement in the U.S.

Brian Klocke is a passionate activist in the field of social justice, having taught students about corporate ethics, race relations, gender issues, and the most pressing global problems that we face at the end of the millennium. His current research focuses on how corporations shape and control our modern culture. Involved in the creation of Boulder's Cooperative Market, Brian contributed to two chapters of *The Vegan Sourcebook*.

Find out more at:
www.betterworldhandbook.com

If you have enjoyed *The Better World Handbook*,
you might also enjoy other

BOOKS TO BUILD A NEW SOCIETY

Our books provide positive solutions for people who
want to make a difference. We specialize in:

Sustainable Living • Ecological Design and Planning

Natural Building & Appropriate Technology • New Forestry

Environment and Justice • Conscientious Commerce

Progressive Leadership • Resistance and Community • Nonviolence

Educational and Parenting Resources

For a full list of NSP's titles, please call **1-800-567-6772** *or check out our web site at:*

www.newsociety.com

New Society Publishers

ENVIRONMENTAL BENEFITS STATEMENT

New Society Publishers has chosen to produce this book on New Leaf EcoBook 100,
recycled paper made with 100% post consumer waste, processed chlorine free, and
old growth free.

For every 5,000 books printed, New Society saves the following resources:[1]

28	Trees
2,527	Pounds of Solid Waste
2,781	Gallons of Water
3,627	Kilowatt Hours of Electricity
4,594	Pounds of Greenhouse Gases
20	Pounds of HAPs, VOCs, and AOX Combined
7	Cubic Yards of Landfill Space

[1]Environmental benefits are calculated based on research done by the Environmental Defense Fund and
other members of the Paper Task Force who study the environmental impacts of the paper industry.

For more information on this environmental benefits statement, or to inquire about environmentally
friendly papers, please contact New Leaf Paper – info@newleafpaper.com Tel: 888 • 989 • 5323.

NEW SOCIETY PUBLISHERS